Dynamics of New Panchayati Raj System in India

Vol. I : Select States
Vol. II : Select States
Vol. III : Select States
Vol. IV : Empowering Women
Vol. V : Panchayati Raj and Multi-level Planning
Vol. VI : Capacity Building
Vol. VII : Finance in Panchayati Raj System
Vol. VIII : Panchayati Raj and Common Property Resource Management
Vol. IX : Participatory and Direct Democracy : Gram Sabha
Vol. X : Panchayati Raj and Empowerment of Dalits
Vol. XI : State-Local Body Relationship
Vol. XII : Panchayati Raj and Socio-Political and Economic Transformation
Vol. XIII : Leadership in Panchayati Raj Institution
Vol. XIV : Thinkers Framework on Panchayati Raj
Vol. XV : Theoretical Nuances of Local Bodies

About the Editor

Prof. Ganapathi Palanithurai, Coordinator in Rajiv Gandhi Chair, Gandhigram Rural Institute is an academic activist working with the people in rural areas for building the capacity of the leaders and people to reinvent sustainable grassroots democracy. He is heading the Department of Political Science and Development Administration, in Gandhigram Rural University, Tamil Nadu. His policy advocacy role at the governmental level is increasingly felt at present in all the three levels, namely, sub-regional, regional and national as he does more fieldwork than theorisation. He has been associating himself with Centre Planning Commission, State Planning Commission of Tamil Nadu, Population Foundation of India, Ford Foundation, UNICEF, Rajiv Gandhi Foundation, CAPART, Ministry of Rural Areas and Employment and DANIDA (Danish-Indo Development Agency) in specific areas of activities in connection with empowerment of people. He is in the network of the Non-Governmental Organisations for Panchayat activities. He involves himself in capacity building exercise for local body leaders. He has to his credit twenty-nine books, seventy-five articles on three major areas, namely, Legislative Behaviour, Ethnicity and Panchayati Raj System. He was a recipient of Fellowship from Sastri Indo-Canadian Institute, New Delhi and World Academy of Art and Science, USA. He is the Chairman of the Tamil Nadu Council for Sustainable Livelihoods. He has visited the US and Canada, on academic assignments. He was a visiting fellow in the McGill University, Canada in 1989. He is a life member of Indian Institute of Public Administration, Indian Association of Public Administration, Indian Association of Political Science, Indian Association of American Studies and Indian Association of Canadian Studies. He is a member of the expert committee constituted by the Government of Tamil Nadu to monitor the training programme for local body leaders.

DYNAMICS OF NEW PANCHAYATI RAJ SYSTEM IN INDIA

VOLUME VI
Capacity Building

Edited by
G. PALANITHURAI

CONCEPT PUBLISHING COMPANY, NEW DELHI-110059

Cataloging in Publication Data—DK
Courtesy: D.K. Agencies (P) Ltd. <docinfo@dkagencies.com>

Dynamics of new panchayati raj system in India / edited by G. Palanithurai.
v. 6 cm.
Contributed articles.
Includes bibliographical references.
Includes indexes.
Contents: v. 6. Capacity building.
ISBN 8170229103 (set)
ISBN 13: 9788180695063 (v. 6)
ISBN 10: 8180695069 (v. 6)

1. Panchayat—India. 2. Local government—India. I. Palanithurai, G. (Ganapathy), 1953-

DDC 320.840 954 21

ISBN -13: 978-81-8069-506-3 (Vol. VI)
ISBN -10: 81-8069-506-9 (Vol. VI)
ISBN 81-7022-910-3 (Series)

First Published 2008

Published and Printed by

Ashok Kumar Mittal
Concept Publishing Company
A/15-16, Commercial Block, Mohan Garden
New Delhi-110059 (India)

Phones: 25351460, 25351794
Fax: 091-11-25357103
E-mail: publishing@conceptpub.com

TO

THE DIVINE MOTHER

(In India) one should begin with the old panchayat system in the villages and the work upto the top. The panchayat system and the guilds are more representative and they have a living contact with people, they are the parts of the people's ideas.

– Sri Aurobindo

The village republic will be managed by a panchayat which will be living political force and entity. Panchayats will be united in a free and voluntary association by "ever widening circle of village republics". It will not be an "apex sustained by the bottom, but an oceanic circle where centre will be the individual always ready to perish for the village, the latter ready to perish for the circle of villages and so on, sharing the majesty of the oceanic circle which they are parts".

– Mahatma Gandhi

We trust the people
We have faith in the people
It is the people who must
determine their own destinies
and the destiny of the Nation.
To the people of India, let us
ensure maximum democracy and
maximum devolution. Let the
people be empowered.

– Rajiv Gandhi

PREFACE

India is a popular and populous democracy in the world which has got its unique nature and character in terms of its functions and functional outcomes. It is always a paradox which cannot be explained through the established theories. It is unequivocally true that the efficacy and efficiency of the representative governing system primarily depend on the character, nature and awareness of the citizens and capability of the people's representatives. The fast changing society and economics need more innovations in politics, governance and administration. It is unfortunate that in Indian politics, governance and administration could not cope with the speed of change in the economy, technology, science and society. It is because in every sphere of human activity, capacity-building is being considered vital and imperative excepting in politics, governance and administration. As a result, one would find stagnation in politics, governance and administration. It is not only stagnation, but it goes beyond stagnation. To overcome the stagnation, democratic decentralization was initiated through the Constitutional Amendments. The Amendments have got full potentials to break the obstacles and barriers in governance and administration. But to realize the full potentials of the Constitutional Amendments, the stakeholders of the institutions have to build their capacity, skill, and capability. The citizens have to equip themselves and they should become well-informed citizens. To perform the above, continuous awareness creation among the citizens and continuous training of Panchayat leaders and Panchayat officials are vital, imperative and essential. This exercise requires a clear cut policy, framework, training institutions, training modules and manuals, resource-persons and resources.

In thc absence of the above, all the activities relating to capacity building is *ad hoc*, unscientific, sporadic, irregular and less efficient. Without much efforts on training, state governments allow the Panchayat leaders to perform their role and responsibilities. Yet, they produce outcome not to the level of expectation. For the past ten to twelve years, training efforts are not systematic barring in a few states. Only non-governmental organizations have evinced interest in training. As there is no policy, no budget allocation, no conviction and no political commitment, there won't be any change in training exercises. As a result, the leaders and functionaries in Panchayats have not understood the full dimensions and potentials of decentralization of powers. But, now, initiatives are being taken on the part of the Central Government to conduct capacity-building exercises for both the leaders and the officials in the Panchayati Raj System. In the meanwhile, it is felt that it is necessary to compile the existing experiences on capacity-building of local body leaders and functionaries.

The volume which is in your hand is a compilation of the experiences of different institutions in conducting capacity-building exercises in different states. The contributors mostly the resource persons involved in capacity-building and they are real scholars in local governance also.

I express my thanks to all contributors for sharing their experiences. I thank Ms. J.Vanishree, who helped me in editing the articles and I thank Mr. S.P. Ramesh for his neat compiling of the articles. I thank the three units namely my project unit, academic unit and family unit without whose support I could not have carried out my work in this regard. Hence I thank everyone in all the three units.

G. PALANITHURAI

CONTENTS

LIST OF CONTRIBUTORS

B.S.Bhargava
Senior Fellow
Institute of Social Sciences
2, 8th Main road
8th Cross, Near State Bank of Mysore
Malleswaram
Bangalore – 560 003.

Dilip Kumar Ghosh
Senior Research Officer
State Institute of Panchayats and Rural Development
Kalyani
Nadia – 741 235.

G. Palanithurai
Prof. & Head
Department of Political Science and Development Administration
Gandhigram Rural University
Gandhigram – 624 302.

G. Uma
Programme Coordinator
The Hunger Project
Gandhigram Rural University
Gandhigram – 624 302.

The Hunger Project
Shaheed Bhavan
II Floor,
18/1, Aruna Asaf Ali Marg
Qutab Institutional Area
New Delhi – 110 067.

J. Vanishree
Research Scholar
Gandhigram Rural University
Gandhigram – 624 302.

K. Subha
Regional Coordinator
Institute of Social Sciences
No.2, 8th Main Road
8th Cross, Malleswaram
Bangalore – 56003.

Mangala A. Nayak
Research Associate
Indian Institute of Management
Ahmedabad.

Mahipal
Associate Professor
Haryana Institute of Rural Development
Nilokheri.

Purvi Dass
National Resource Centre
Centre for Local Self-Governance, PRIA
42, Tughlakabad Institutional Area
New Delhi – 110 062.

Rakesh Hooja, I.A.S.,
Department of Personnel and Administrative Reforms (Training Cell)
Government of Rajasthan
Director
HCM Rajasthan State Institute of Public Administration
Centre for Management Studies and Centre for Good Governance
Jawaharlal Nehru Marg
Jaipur-302 017.

S.K. Singh
Professor & Head
Centre for Panchayati Raj
National Institute of Rural Development
Rajendra Nagar
Hyderabad – 500 030.

Y. Bhaskar Rao
Associate Professor
Centre for Panchayati Raj
National Institute of Rural Development
Rajendra Nagar
Hyderabad – 500 030.

Yatindra Singh Sisodia
Senior Fellow
Madhya Pradesh Institute of Social Science Research
19, Mahashweta Nagar
Ujjain
Madhya Pradesh.

INTRODUCTION

The 73rd and 74th Amendments to the Constitution of India are the landmark events in Indian Parliamentary Democracy which had been brought into action despite several barriers and obstacles with lot of hopes as both the amendments are stuffed with heavy potentials to transform the society from feudal to democratic mode and alter the character of our democracy from representative to participative. To realize the objectives of the Amendments, a series of activities have to be taken at different levels with the active involvement of stakeholders with a sense of commitment. Activities have to be taken not only from the top but also from the bottom. The successful functioning of the three-tier Panchayati Raj System crucially depends on the devolution of powers, resources, transfer of subjects and passing of the administrative control from the hands of bureaucracy of the district to the three-tier Panchayati Raj representatives by transferring the officials or redeploying the officials to the local bodies. The concept of establishing democratic governance down below the district at the three levels up to the Gram Panchayat needs a thorough change of the administration and change of mindset among the functionaries who are working in the line departments. Further, there is yet another factor which is crucial for the success of the local body system in building the skills, capacity and capability of the elected representatives to function as leaders to govern the institutions and administer the official machinery and development. The tasks which are to be performed by the leaders are heavy and the skills, capacity, and capability of the elected representatives are very poor as they are drawn from different socio-economic segments, and nearly half of the representatives groups are drawn from marginalized segments, namely Dalits, Adivasis and Women. They should have the capacity to manage the institutions, direct the officials, mobilizes resources, and engage the people in a democratic process. What is urgently needed is capacity building.

In the West, capacity building is an integral part of their activities and hence capacity building is made imperative for the elected representative. A large number of training institutions are created in the west to train the legislators continuously. Legislators are being trained and mandatorily the legislators have to undertake training. But in India, capacity building is considered seriously for business houses, industrial units and bureaucracy and not for the elected representatives. It has never been considered seriously for the Members of Parliament and Members of Legislative Assembly. Sporadic attempts were made in the past to train our MPs and MLAs.

No systematic efforts are on to train the Members of Parliament and Legislative Assemblies. Against this backdrop, one can imagine the capacity building for local body leaders from the perspective of stakeholders. For about ten years, the local body leaders have not been trained seriously and systematically for the whole of India. Trainings were conducted in a few states, and most of the states, it was an *ad hoc* arrangement. With the support of donor agencies and the support of the government agencies, trainings were conducted sporadically by the government training institutions and non-governmental organizations. There are a few states where the governments have committed themselves in decentralization of powers and they took the training seriously. In the whole of the country, there is no training policy at all. Some of the states have specific training policy. Nearly thirty lakh representatives have to be trained in local bodies. There is no budget allocation for local body leaders' training. In the absence of training policy and resource allocation, training is not systematic and continuous. In the absence of clear-cut direction from the governments, modules had been prepared, manuals had been compiled for training Panchayat leaders and officials. For conducting the capacity-building exercises, the institution should need clear understanding, perspectives, facilities, infrastructure, resource-persons and staff to extend-hand hold-support. In the absence of the above conditions, the capacity building exercise is half-backed which will not serve the purpose.

With the support of the Ford Foundation, Rajiv Gandhi Foundation made a systematic assessment of the training efforts undertaken by the various institutions in India. The Rajiv Gandhi Foundation has compiled a directory of Panchayati Raj Institutions in India. There are three kinds of institutions, namely central/state/semi-governmental institutions; autonomous training and research institutions and non-governmental organizations involved in the training of local body leaders in India. Nearly one hundred and thirty training institutions are involved in training of local body leaders. There were several drawbacks identified by the research team of Rajiv Gandhi Foundation in the training programmes organized by these institutions. Perspectives vary across institutions. Uniform methodology was adopted for different stakeholders by the institutions. No proper follow up action is taken up. There was no handhold support for the leaders after the training when they face the problems in the field. No systematic refresher courses were organized for the leaders. The focus was only on the implementation of the schemes and programmes. Governance and management of the institutions were not given adequate attention. Officials were left out in the whole exercise and in many places officials are treated as master-trainers. The officials who have handled the training sessions instructed the representatives that they have to follow the officials, direction as administration is a complicated matter. In many places training is considered as one-time event rather than a continuous one.

In India, there are a total of 30,99,432 elected representatives who require training and capacity building support. Of these, 3,70,550 belong to scheduled castes, 2,44,596 are tribals, 8,90,718 are women and 15,93,568 are general category of leaders in local bodies who need effective training according to their requirements. In the same way, 9,31,100 officials at central, state, district, block and village level are in need of training but nobody feels that they require training. As a result, the officials want to establish their control over the Panchayat leaders. During the Ninth Plan, we have spent Rs. 2080 crore for training the army personnels. But to train the Panchayat leaders government has allocated only Rs.17 crores during the same period.

After assuming responsibility of governance at the federal government the UPA government created a Ministry of Panchayati Raj, whereby the Central Government has given serious thought to the subject decentralization of powers. The newly created Ministry under the leadership of Mani Shankar Aiyar took initiative of organizing seven round table conferences with State Ministers of Panchayati Raj and Secretaries to push the decentralization process further. Within 150 days, 150 resolutions have been passed in all the seven round table conferences held in different places. The seventh round table was organized at Jaipur, and this round table focused its attention on capacity building. The responsibility of bringing out a stock-taking volume on capacity building was given to The Hunger Project, New Delhi.

The Hunger Project has compiled the document based on the experiences in all the states. The reports bring to the floor the dismal coverage of the functionaries and the elected leaders under training and indicated the way forward. A thorough discussion was held and formulated resolutions. They are:

1. Training and communication ought to reach all PRI functionaries and elected representatives, namely,
   (a) Gram Panchayat Members, Chairpersons and Office-bearers,
   (b) Intermediate Panchayat Members, Chairpersons and Office-bearers,
   (c) District Panchayat Members, Chairpersons and Office-bearers,
   (d) All officials concerned at National, State, District, Intermediate and Village level; and
   (e) Standing Committee members at all levels.
2. There should be special effort made towards sensitizing the media, political parties, representatives in the legislatures, civil society organizations and citizens.
3. There must be special campaigns for mobilization of Gram Sabha members.
4. There must be special training for women, SC and ST representatives as well as first time entrants into the Panchayat system within three months of their entry.
5. Training for PESA areas should be designed so as to have regard to the cultural traditions and special needs of the tribal people.
6. Training and communication should not be viewed as a single one-time intervention but should be a continuous, ongoing

process leading to enhanced sense of self-esteem and confidence. Training should cover both the "before" and "after" election periods. Initial training and communication should reach all the elected representatives within one year.

7. For those Panchayat members who need it, a functional, literacy training course should be undertaken immediately after their elections.
8. The Panchayats should be encouraged to have a sense of ownership of the training programmes and play a major role in designing content and mechanisms of training. To this end, there must be representation for Panchayat members in the governing boards of training institutions that cater to their needs.
9. Content of training should press on strategic and technical aspects and should be based on a systematic Training Needs Analysis arrived at through multi-stakeholder consultative workshops, which would precede the design of training modules and materials.
10. There should be a minimum-core curriculum that is common across the States adapting to suit local contexts. Core curriculum should include:
    (a) Vision on Purna Swaraj through Gram Swaraj;
    (b) Principles of secularism, equality and human rights emanating from the Constitution of India;
    (c) Gender equity and social justice;
    (d) Status of human development,
    (e) Poverty alleviation;
    (f) Participatory planning, implementation and monitoring;
    (g) Right to information and transparency;
    (h) Social Audit; and
    (i) Rules and regulations covering Panchayati Raj.
11. Overall perspective of training must reinforce issues of social equity, gender sensitivity and justice among all participants in the process of governance through Panchayati Raj, including all levels of the bureaucracy.

12. Thematic curriculum should include:
    (a) Human Resource Management,
    (b) Natural Resource Management,
    (c) Disaster Management,
    (d) Financial Management, including own-resource management and accounting,
    (e) Sectoral approaches in providing basic human needs.
13. Training strategy should be inclusive, participative and interactive and a composite-mix of various interventions:
    (a) Face-to-face participatory training;
    (b) Exposure visits;
    (c) Peer training/learning;
    (d) Satellite training;
    (e) Radio/cassettes/films;
    (f) Traditional means of communication;
    (g) Newsletters, digests of replies to Frequently Asked Questions and their updates; and
    (h) Resource centres and Help Desks for Panchayats.
14. Training content and processes should be relevant to the ground reality of elected representatives. It should continue to develop and evolve based on feedback and impact assessment. Training should become a two-way process so that feedback can help in reforming the content and process of training, as also result in systemic changes in Panchayat and government functioning.
15. States should move towards formation of training networks and collectivities to share experiences, learn from each other, and access material from each other. State should also institutionalize collaboration with community-based organizations at the State, District, and Block level.
16. Training should inspire elected representatives to form federations or collectivities and facilitate them to voice their demands for genuine devolution and development.
17. Trained members should be encouraged to become resource persons for further training of Panchayat representatives. Peer to peer learning, both within and outside the state through regional or national tie-ups should be encouraged and supported.

18. Training should include exposure to best practices through visits to other Panchayats.
19. All open universities may tie-up with IGNOU and build linkages with the SIRDs and other institutions engaged in training and capacity building.
20. Training programmes shall be designed especially for the secretarial and technical staff working with Panchayats through institutions such as IGNOU. Such training programmes should lead to form a certification on achieving prescribed standards of learning.
21. Education in democracy and the constitutional role of Panchayats as institutions of local self-government should be made part of school curricula.
22. It shall be the endeavour of the Central Government to provide in as short a time as possible, a Panchayat capacity-building fund through the Ministry of Panchayati Raj, which could include a certain percentage of central transfers specially earmarked for that purpose. Similarly, State Governments should also create a Panchayat Capacity Building Fund for periodic training.
23. There should be a national perspective plan on decentralized training and capacity building for all PRI functionaries with specific objectives, timeframe and resources.
24. States can benefit by the use of pedagogy and training techniques with information accessible to all. The Ministry of Panchayati Raj could develop a repository of training programmes, including training resources and manuals developed by the Commonwealth. Development of master-modules in training in issues of gender, poverty, mass communication, etc. could also be developed.
25. Independent training-impact-assessment studies should be periodically undertaken to assess the outcomes of training and inform emerging needs for follow-up.
26. States shall work towards upgradation of training centres, such as SIRDs, and extension training centres at the district, block level and below.

27. With respect to the training needs of Panchayat members from the Union Territories and States with Sixth Schedule areas, the Government of India would identify a SIRD or a group of institutions that could undertake the training.

After passing the resolutions, the Government of India under the Ministry of Panchayati Raj evolved a capability framework to train the Panchayat leaders. Based on the capability framework, the Ministry is taking steps to resource allocation for capacity building from the Planning Commission. It seems that training would be considered seriously.

S.K. Singh's article entitled "Capacity Building of Elected Panchayat functionaries: Responding to the Challenges of Tomorrow" gives an overarching bird's-eye-view of the committees on capacity building conceptually and operationally. Training objectives have been explained in this article. This article has estimated the training needs in terms of infrastructure, resources, and materials. It also suggests the training strategy and approach. It has indicated the contents for the training programme. Suggestive course modules have been explained in this article. A synoptic view of what we have to do in this context has been explained.

Yatindra Singh Sisodia in his article "Capacity Building for Panchayati Raj Functionaries" has brought to light the background with which Panchayati Raj System in India, and particularly Panchayati Raj System in Madhya Pradesh was established. He highlighted the conditions of the Panchayati Raj System in Madhya Pradesh and requirements and needs are highlighted to strengthen the system in Madhya Pradesh. He has indicated the efforts of the government institutions and non-governmental organizations in organizing training programmes for the Panchayat leaders and officials. He critically has looked into the coverage, methodology, and logistics of the training programmes organized by the training institutions. He has projected the training needs at present for the Madhya Pradesh Panchayat leaders and functionaries.

Dilip Kumar Ghosh's article "Capacity Building of Panchayat Leaders in West Bengal" explains the West Bengal devolution scenario and the training efforts on the part of the State Government.

Since the Government of West Bengal had a policy on capacity building, it was easy for the training institutions to carryout the capacity-building exercises. Major exercises have been carried out by the state training institutions in West Bengal. He has explained the type of training environment created, the methodological and nuances adopted for capacity building. He has given details of the content of the training programmes. In this article he has indicated the weaknesses in the programme. He has observed that there is no systematic evaluation of the training programme. The author further informs that no impact assessment is made either by the training institutions or by the external agencies.

G. Palanithurai's article "Capacity Building of Grassroots Leaders in Tamil Nadu" is a narration of the analysis of the capacity building exercises conducted in Gandhigram Rural University under the aegis of Rajiv Gandhi Chair for Panchayati Raj Studies with the active partnership with many government institutions and donor agencies. It is an elaborate narration of the initiatives, background, objectives, methodology, content of the training programmes conducted in Gandhigram Rural University for the Panchayat leaders. How pre-training and post-training evaluations have been attempted is explained. Gandhigram Rural University with the support of The Hunger Project has established a unit to extend handhold support to the trained leaders when they are in the field. Refreshers have been organized for the elected leaders. Since it is a nodal training institution which conducts training periodically, Panchayat leaders can make use of the centre as a helpline. It has got rich material for sharing. Proper evaluations are done both on output and outcome by the external agents.

Purvi Das's article "Capacity Building for Strengthening Local Self-Governance" is the narration of PRIA's experience in capacity building exercises conducted in different states through its partners with PRIA's perspective. She has explained the approach, perspective and methodology of PRIA in imparting training to the Panchayat leaders. In a very creative and innovative way a number of programmes have been conducted in different states. They have mobilized the Gram Sabha members and created awareness about the new Panchayati Raj System. They have done all those exercises in different phases and they have adopted different methodological nuances for different states. The impact has also been assessed. Variations of regions and human segment in terms of their needs are adequately explained.

"Training of Panchayat non-officials and officials in Rajasthan" written by **Rakesh Hooja** narrates the Rajasthan experience of capacity building. In his article, he argues from the perspective of Planning Commission that the training programmes are to be carried out in the context of the expected functions and responsibilities of the elected representatives of Local Bodies. The Tenth Five Year Plan working group documents indicated the major areas on which training has to be conducted. His focus is on the training with bias towards evolving micro plans. How to prepare a plan at the grassroots, how they have to be carried and how they have to mobilize resources have been imparted to the trainees.

G. Uma and J. Vanishree in their article "Building Women Leadership at Grassroots in Tamil Nadu" have succinctly narrated the training experiences of The Hunger Project in Tamil Nadu. The Hunger Project in Tamil Nadu has evinced keen interest in shaping the leadership of women to tackle hunger, malnutrition, anemia and HIV/AIDS. The Hunger Project has its own perspective and methodology. It is a considered opinion of The Hunger Project that many of the issues affecting the lives of the poor can be tackled very easily provided right leadership quality is developed among the leaders of Local Bodies. The Hunger Project with the collaboration of the various agencies including District Administration imparted training to the women leaders at the Gram Panchayat level. They have explained the methodology by which they have conducted the programmes. They have assessed the impact of the training through case studies. Both of them are trainers and they have been conducting training for several batches of women leaders.

"Capacity Building for Panchayati Raj functionaries in Karnataka through Satellite" by **K. Subha, B.S. Bhargava and Mangala A. Nayak** is a narration of the training programme conducted through satellite in Karnataka by the State Institute of Rural Development. They have explained the context and background of the training programme. They have brought to light the objectives of the programmes. A realistic assessment has also been made on the impact of the programme. Further, the issues and problems emerging out of the whole exercise of the training programme have been captured and explained. The innovative approach of Karnataka can be a model for other states also. The fact remains that State Institute of Rural Development, Karnataka is a good training institute and hence they are able to do so. Training institutions in other states are not in the same order of Karnataka.

Mahipal's article "Capacity Building of Zilla Parishad functionaries in Haryana" is a narration of his experiences in conducting training programmes for the Zilla Parishad members and Chairpersons. Being a Faculty in Haryana Institute of Rural Development, he has rich experience in training the functionaries and elected representatives. He has captured the experiences of conducting the same for Zilla Parishad leaders. He has explained the systematic efforts in preparing material in the form of modules and manuals for elected leaders with a focus on planning from below on social development. He has also explained the methodological nuances adopted by the institute in offering such capacity-building exercises. An assessment has been made on the programmes conducted by the institute.

R.Y. Bhaskar Rao's article on "Capacity Building in Panchayati Raj Institutions with special reference to West Bengal" has contextualized the capacity-building exercises for the grassroots leaders elected by the people for the Panchayati Raj System. He has touched upon the approaches of capacity building. He has further highlighted the PRIA's model, The Hunger Project model, the UNDP model and the NIRD model of training. Finally, he has brought to light the capacity building exercises done in West Bengal. Methodology of the training programmes has been explained. The needs of different stakeholders and how they are addressed have been assessed.

The Hunger Project initiative of organizing capacity-building exercises in different states with an objective of shaping and building the women leaders with a vision is an unique exercise and experiment with the support of Royal Norwegian Embassy. The leadership schools are in a nascent stage and yet they have recorded substantial amount of hope and with which they are proceeding. It is a collaborative exercise with various NGOs in different states. Their experiences are recorded and analysed in this article. The newly inducted leaders will be forced to reckon with the Panchayat activities in the respective areas. Moreover, they are the real change-makers and they influence the other constituencies of the Panchayati Raj.

The Ministry of Panchayati Raj, Government of India's training framework, under the caption "National Capability Building Framework for Panchayati Raj Elected Representatives and Functionaries" which is given in the appendix is a real guidepost for capacity building exercises to be conducted in India. It is a deeply and perceptively conceptualized framework which has generated a lot of discussion among different segments of the people. It is a very comprehensive, path-breaking framework evolved in the Ministry to strengthen the Panchayati Raj System. It is very realistic and doable, and hence this framework has to be pushed forward.

1

CAPACITY BUILDING OF ELECTED PANCHAYAT FUNCTIONARIES RESPONDING TO THE CHALLENGES OF TOMORROW

S.K. SINGH

Introduction

As a sequel to the Seventy Third Constitution Amendment, there are more than three million elected representatives who entered into the system for the purpose of providing better service delivery and self-governance in rural areas. Indeed the funnel of representative system has been widened and diversified: It constitutes literates, neo-literates, illiterates, women, scheduled castes, scheduled tribes and several marginalized groups. Moreover, at many places, these elected members are new entrants into the arena of panchayat system. Obviously, a large number of them will not be familiar with the art of governance. Given the situation the task before them will be complex and they have to discharge variety of functions. The convergence of such services is an essential requirement for an effective delivery mechanism. It is also widely believed that empowering Panchayati Raj Institutions (PRIs) and devolving functions as enjoined by the Constitution will be a major step forward is not only deepening the process of democracy, but also accelerating the process of empowering people and enabling them to realize their aspirations of development and growth.

The growth of panchayats in the country is varied and uneven. Some states are better placed whereas some remained static for a host of reasons. There is also cynicism among certain quarters that the panchayat system has not come up to the expected level. But the fact that they have not been properly empowered, oriented and trained is glossed over. Therefore a proper training and capacity building strategy is necessary. Thus, it should have a comprehensive approach.

In all, the PRIs have a variety of work dealing with beneficiaries and basket of services to deliver. In order to discharge their duties, the panchayats have to follow certain code of development ethics enjoined with the principles of equity, responsiveness, transparency, accountability, participation, etc. Thus, it is necessary to build their capacity so that they can play a pro-active role, gain confidence and provide leadership so that the village development takes place in the right direction.

Concept of Capacity Building

Capacity building can be defined as the development of an organisation's or individual's core knowledge, skills and capabilities in order to build and enhance the organisation's effectiveness and sustainability. It is the process of assisting an individual or group to identify and address issues and gain the insights, knowledge and experience needed to perform effectively. Capacity building can also include the creation of an enabling environment with appropriate policy and legal frameworks, institutional development and human resources development and strengthening of managerial systems.

Capacity building is facilitated through the provision of technical support activities, training, specific technical assistance and resource networking. Capacity building is recognized as being a long-term, continuing process, in which all stakeholders participate.

This Paper underlines the following basic premises that are necessary for any effective training strategy and these principles are imperative to adhere to:

- Training is not a one-time intervention, it is a continuous process and it must be periodically repeated to sustain the inputs and skills developed. The training does not only focus on sharing information, rather it is a process of exploration, discovery and growth. This process involves a common inter-learning situation for both trainers and participants.
- Training must have participatory approach thereby enhance effectiveness. Thus the training design is embedded with participation of all members to give space for thinking and doing and arouse curiosity and provoke creativity.
- The status of Panchayati Raj is at variance across the States in terms of devolution of powers, functions, finances and functionaries. Moreover, social milieu, work culture, ethos, etc. varies from State to State. Therefore, specific training need of Panchayat representatives will vary from State to State and it can be best assessed at the State level. Thus the training modules have been designed in such a way to provide cushion for incorporating state specific requirements.
- However, without sacrificing the specificity of the local requirements, there are some conceptual issues, which promote all diversities and need to be internalized by the panchayat functionaries across the State. These inputs will be common for all.

Training in Historical Perspective

The subject of Panchayati Raj has been profusely studied, examined and reviewed by various Committees constituted at the National and State level. These Committees have also given emphasis on training of Panchayati Raj Functionaries. Some observations of important committees are given below for better appreciation of the subject.

The *Balvantrai Mehta Committee (1957)* has observed that, "no efforts so far have been made either by the Government or by public or political organizations to impart any training in administrative matters to persons elected to local bodies. Such training is essential if we are to make out local bodies effective and useful. Rural administration (especially its developmental aspect) is an increasingly complex process and its machinery is also growing more complex. They have suggested various schemes for integration of the different parts of such machinery but, even so, it will continue to be complicated. It has to be handled with care, and that care can come either from a certain volume of initial knowledge or from knowledge borne out of a series of mistakes. To provide the former and avoid the latter, it is necessary that the persons elected to or aspiring to be elected to such bodies should be equipped with a certain minimum knowledge of this machinery. Organisation of 'summer schools' for this purpose will be seriously considered both by the State Governments and responsible non-official organizations like State Associations of Panchayat Samitis."

The *Ashok Mehta Committee (1978)* categorically suggested training for (a) officials, (b) elected representatives and (c) interface courses for both officials and elected representatives. On training aspect of Panchayat functionaries, the Committee has given the following suggestions:

(i) "the training programmes, covering officials as well as non-officials, would be of staggering dimension. This would require not only the activation of the existing institutions but also considerable augmentation of their numbers and resources. Suitable remedial measures should also be taken to resuscitate and revitalize the State-level training institutions."

(ii) "the National Institute of Rural Development should be the apex all-India institution for training of trainers, field studies, developing consultancy capabilities, research work and improvement in the level of training in the States. Its faculty should be strengthened and upgraded for this purpose. The Government of India has an important role to play in this regard."

(iii) "there should be an evaluation of the training programmes so that it will be possible to make necessary modulations from time to time....Importance should be attached to the programmes for adult education to develop the latent civic consciousness in all the people and thus strengthen the faith in the working of the Panchayati Raj Institutions which have a major role in organizing such programmes."

The *L.M. Singhvi Committee (1986)* recommended that every official in the administration should be made to work in the Panchayati Raj and Rural Development setting so as to sensitise our public administration to the problems of rural India. The Committee suggested that substantial training, research and public education inputs should be provided to strengthen the Panchayati Raj Institutions and the performance capabilities of those who called upon to function as voters, elected representatives, administrative officials, voluntary workers in relation to PRIs.

The views expressed by various National-level Committees clearly spells out that in order to enable the new dispensation Panchayats to discharge their responsibilities effectively, it is essential that new local leadership require skills in management of development programmes and knowledge of development strategies. This essentially calls for an appropriate training regime suitable to meet the needs and requirements so as to prepare them to take up their assignment.

Objectives

The purpose of this paper is to plan for Training and Capacity Building of PRI functionaries and elected representatives and to improve their performance. The number of persons to be trained is of the order of 3.6 million personnel. Any meaningful exercise of training and capacity building of 3.6 million persons would demand a sustained commitment of an extraordinary order, continued financial support a regular and effective monitoring of the capacity building and the final evaluation of the training being organized. Keeping this requirement in view, the paper has the following main objectives:

- To orient the Panchayati Raj Functionaries about the role, responsibilities and scope within a short span of 6 months—one year after they are elected to their respective offices;

- To enhance their skill, capacity and capability in discharging their responsibilities devolved on them;
- To sensitize and motivate the Panchayati Raj Functionaries and elected representatives to make Panchayati Raj bodies effective instruments of delivery for rural development programmes and various other services provided by the Government at the grassroots level;
- To sensitize the elected representatives and the functionaries on the problems of the poor and make PRI bodies more responsive to their needs;
- Ensure that the participatory mode of development and deepening democratic base of the country through effective functioning of the Gram Sabha;
- To develop a Corps of professional trainers, resource persons of the country for training of Panchayati Raj Functionaries and elected representatives on a continuous and sustained basis;
- To create a network of institutions for carrying on the gigantic task and identify catchments for each of the main institutions;
- To extend the reach of the training up to the GP/Group of GPs.

The detailed estimates of trainees are given below:

Table 1 : Estimates of Target Group.

Level of Functionaries	*Elected Panchayat Members*	*Panchayat Officials*	*Total*
District Level	16,834	8,025	24,859
Intermediate Level	1,57,635	60,530	2,18,165
Gram Panchayat	29,32,953	7,02,090	36,35,043
Total	**31,07,422**	**7,70,645**	**38,78,067**

(State-wise Number of Panchayats and Elected Representatives are given in Annexure-I.)

As per available estimates (subject to upgradation), the total number of elected Panchayat functionaries at all the tiers are 31,07,422. For the purpose of estimating the number of officers working at each tier of PRIs who are eligible for training, the following average number has been taken:

Zilla Parishad	:	15
Intermediate Panchayat	:	10
Gram Panchayat	:	3

Table 2 : Estimates of Officials.

Unit	*Total No. of Units*	*Average No. of Officers*	*Total*
Zilla Parishad	535	15	8,025
Intermediate Panchayat	6,053	10	60,530
Gram Panchayat	2,34,030	3	7,02,090
Total	**2,40,618**	**28**	**7,70,645**

The total number of officials to be trained is 7,70,645 at all the three tiers of PRIs. Thus, the total number of trainees both elected members and officials are 38,78,067 or 3.88 million persons.

The target group has been further classified into two broad categories:

- Firstly, the *office bearers of Panchayats* at all the three-tiers, such as, President, Vice-President and Chairpersons of Standing Committee/Subject Committee of the three-tiers of Panchayats.
- Secondly, elected members of the body at three-tiers of Panchayats.

Separate grouping is essential because the Training Module will slightly differ for each clientele group. In view of the fact that office-bearers are vested with administrative and financial powers and hence the inputs required will be more and different from the inputs required for ordinary members of the body. For office-bearers, it is necessary that their capacity be enhanced to discharge their administrative and financial functions properly. For ordinary Members, it is required to expose them about various development programmes in vogue and sensitize them to their role and responsibility in the development efforts.

Table 3 : Estimates of Office-bearers of Panchayats.

	President and Vice-President	*Chairpersons of Standing Committee*	*Total*
Per Zilla Parishad	2	7	9
Per Intermediate Panchayat	2	6	8
Per Gram Panchayat	2	5	7
Total	**6**	**18**	**24**

Table 4 : Estimates for Trainees from Office-bearers Category.

Tier	*No. of Units*	*No. of Office-bearers*	*Total*
Zilla Parishad	535	9	4815
Intermediate Panchayat	6,053	8	48,424
Gram Panchayat	2,34,030	7	16,38,210
Total	**2,40,618**	**24**	**16,91,449**

In addition to the above target group of trainees, there would be another category of persons who are to be trained as '*Trainers*'. For each district roughly 5 trainers (Resource Persons) will be identified and trained. Thus, for 535 districts at the rate of 5 trainers, the total numbers of Trainers would be 2,675.

The actual workload will vary according to the size of the State. But, on an average, each State should have at least three '*Master Trainers*' totalling approximately 100 from all over the country who will constitute the backbone of the Training Regime. The '*Master Trainers*' in turn will form teams to conduct '*Training of Trainers*'

(ToT) to produce 2,675 'Trainers' across the country with an average of 5 trainers for each district.

Table 5 : Estimates for Master Trainers and Trainers.

Master Trainers (from all over the country)	100
Trainers @ 5 for each district (535 districts)	2,675
Total	**2,775**

Table 6 : Capacity Building of Panchayat Functionaries Estimates of Office-bearers and Officials for Training.

Tier	*No. of Office-bearers*	*Officials*	*Total*
Zilla Parishad	4,815	8,025	12,840
Intermediate Panchayat	48,424	60,530	1,08,954
Gram Panchayat	16,38,210	7,02,090	23,40,300
Total	**16,91,449**	**7,70,645**	**24,62,094**

Total number of Training Programmes to be conducted at the rate of 45 persons in each programme: 54,713 or say 55,000.

Table 7 : Estimates of Elected Panchayat Members Tier-wise.

Unit	*Total Elected Members*	*Office-bearers*	*Target Group*
1	2	3	Col. 2–3
District Panchayat	16,834	4,815	12,019
Intermediate Panchayat	1,57,635	48,424	1,09,211
Gram Panchayat	29,32,953	16,38,210	12,94,743
Total	**31,07,422**	**16,91,449**	**14,15,973**

Total number of Training Programmes to be conducted at the rate of 50 persons in each programme: 28,319 or say 29,000.

Training Infrastructure

A fairly well spread network of training institutions at different levels exist in the country. There are National level, State level, Regional and District level Training Institutes available, which are giving different types of training. Besides, several NGOs, CBOs are also engaged in imparting variety of training in the country. A large number of Extension Training Centres, Panchayati Raj Training Institutes and Cooperative Training Institutes are available at district level and below. Moreover, several other departments and agencies have good training infrastructure like ATIs, Banking Training institutes, KVKs, SISIs, DIETs, etc. The help received from these training institutes could be solicited. Among the available training Institutes that includes State Institutes of Rural Development (SIRDs), which are directly funded and nurtured by the Ministry of Rural Development, and other Institutes funded by Ministry of Panchayati Raj could have a strong and natural relationship in networking. (The list of SIRDs and Training Centres is annexed). However, some of these institutes are in moribund state, which need to be revived and energized to make them operational. As the task is heavy, it requires strengthening of some of the institutions in terms of faculty, infrastructure, training equipment, etc.

These could be classified in the following broad categories:

(i) Central Government Funded Institutes e.g., NIRD, LBSNAA, IIPA, etc.
(ii) State Government Funded Institutes e.g., SIRDs, ATIs and others.
(iii) Banking Training Institutes.
(iv) Non-Government Sector Institutes e.g., IRMA, XISS, ISEC, ISS.
(v) Deemed Universities and other Technical and Academic Institutes e.g., Grandhigram Rural University, TISS, etc.
(vi) Voluntary Organisations/CBOs Training Institute e.g., PRIA, CWS, etc.

The task would be to identify good training institutes and make inventory of these institutes operating at each level. After identifying the Institutes/Organisations, it would be necessary to spell out the role, responsibilities and coordination among them. Further to say, it will require a comprehensive networking plan as it is relating to various organisations operating at various levels.

Training Strategy and Approach

In view of the size and variety of the clientele group scattered widely in small and remote villages all over the country, the training strategy has to be a multi-pronged approach to achieve the objectives. In order to organize training for such large numbers, a combination of training methods has to be adopted. Broadly, two training methodologies could be used - Institutional Training (i.e., face-to-face), and Distance Education Mode, through either satellite or video conferencing. This will improve the quality and expand the reach of training.

While distance education mode is useful to extend the reach of training to distant and remote corners in a cost effective manner, institutional training has the advantage of acquiring better understanding and exposure through exchange of opinion and experience in a close and direct interaction. It would therefore be appropriate to adopt both the approaches: institutional training for the induction or foundation courses and then switching over to distance learning mode for refresher and/or continuous education. For Distance learning mode using satellite or video-conferencing, a special strategy has to be adopted.

Since many States may not have the facility of distance learning through either satellite or video-conferencing, this means could be considered as supplementing method till all States get this facility. Nevertheless, this intervention would be useful in sensitizing the elected representatives, highlighting various development programmes and sharing best practices.

This Paper, therefore, will restrict itself to organising and imparting institutional training as a kind of induction oriented courses to all elected members and functionaries of Panchayats. However, some basic premises have been taken into account.

- The training will be in cascading mode. It will create a pool of resource persons at each level, from the National to the block level, thus a chain of trainers. The cascading training will be at four levels, i.e., the National, State, District, Block and Village Panchayat levels.
- Master Trainers and Trainers at the National level and State level may be identified by the respective State nodal institute in consultation with the State Government. The course for the Master Trainers will be conducted at the National level institute. They in turn will train trainers/resource persons for the district/block/village level. At the lower level the resource person could be a government officer (in service or retired), panchayat extension officers, NGOs and elected panchayat representatives. Selection of trainers/resource persons should be done carefully. Persons identified should have right mindset, commitment with initiative and drive. These trainers will form team to conduct training.
- The State Government will be responsible for nominating trainees for each category for each programme and ensure their participation in the programme.
- Training is not a single one-time intervention rather it should be a continuous process in order to enhance sense of self-esteem and confidence.
- Immediately after the constitution of panchayat bodies after election in any State, initial training of all elected representatives should be completed within one year.
- Apart from the training suggested, other specialized training courses may be thought of:

  (i) Financial Management,
  (ii) Special training programmes for Women, ST and ST representatives of all levels. This may be done within three months of their election,
  (iii) Training for PESA areas and Schedule VI areas,
  (iv) Interface courses for officers and elected representatives,
  (v) Disaster Management,

(vi) National Rural Employment Guarantee Scheme and Right to Information.

- Training content should provide space for incorporating state specific requirements. However, a core curriculum may be common across the States. At the end of the course, evaluation should be done and participants may be asked to suggest topics that may be dealt in the next programme. This will form the basis of Training Need Assessment for the future courses.
- In order to make Gram Sabha work, there may be special campaigns to organize the Gram Sabha to make it meaningful and purposeful. A special effort has to be initiated.

In this paper, three illustrative training modules have been designed. This can further be modified with State specific requirements.

To meet the objectives of imparting training to 3.88 million Panchayat functionaries both elected members and officials within stipulated period, this initial exercise has been formulated. While designing these modules several inputs were examined and analysed to make it comprehensive. Among them, the available training documents/literature were scanned; experiences gained by several organizations dealing with panchayat training were ascertained; training need assessment conducted by several organizations were perused and, over and above, the Resolutions of the Seventh Round Table of the Ministers, In charge of Panchayati Raj on IT enable e-governance, Capacity Building and Training conducted by the Ministry of Panchayati Raj, Government of India constituted the main inputs in it.

On this backdrop, these training modules have been designed to make it effective. For effective learning process, it is necessary to have a blend of participatory and conventional training methods. So much so, the training content and processes should be relevant and reflect the ground realities. It should have a mix of various methodologies. However, the trainers have to make a judicious choice of training methods in introducing various themes.

Training Material

Training of this magnitude will require a variety of Reading Material. Some material could be developed centrally and some by the State nodal institute. It should be in vernacular keeping in view State requirements. Print material with illustrations with pictures in simple language will be more suitable. It may be in question and answer mode to reach the participants easily. Charts, wallpapers, posters, etc. on various inputs can be prepared. Videocassettes and CDs on various critical issues may be prepared to get first hand information on the subject and best and innovative practices. A Resource Centre for Data Bank on PRIs will be useful and all stakeholders should have access to it. A separate website will be essential.

Course Design and Content

After perusing the various relevant documents, the Training of Master Trainers Course has been designed for the Resource Persons at the National and State level. Since most of the Master Trainers may not be specialists in Panchayati Raj and related issues, they can acquire sufficient knowledge with the help of manuals and course materials prepared for them. Moreover, to make the Resource Persons (Trainers) proficient in the subject-matter of the modules and gain necessary expertise in the use of participatory training methods and group felicitation, they will be given exhaustive training at the national level to maintain quality and uniformity in inputs. The Master Trainers in turn will train Trainers at the State level.

As stated above, three illustrative course designs and content that have minimum core curriculum common across the States for three categories of trainees, namely, Master Trainers, Office-bearers and Officials, and Elected Members are give below:

Training of Master Trainers

Total Number	:	100
Intake in each Programme	:	35
Duration	:	10 Days
Venue	:	National level
No. of Programmes	:	3
Time to Complete	:	One Month

Training of Trainers

Total Number	:	2,675
Intake in each Programme	:	35 - 40
Duration	:	7 Days
No. of Programmes	:	75
Venue	:	State level It will be conducted concurrently
Time to Complete	:	One month

Themes/Topics

1. Issues in Decentralization
   - Concepts, rationale and philosophy of decentralization
   - Characteristics and elements of decentralization
   - Self-governance and responsibilities
2. An Overview of Panchayati Raj
   - Evolution of Panchayats - leading to Constitutional Amendment
   - Vision on Purna Swaraj through Gram Swaraj
   - State Specific PR Act
   - Status of PR in the country and State specific position in terms of Devolution of 3Fs
   - Special features of the State PR Act
3. Role and Responsibilities of PR Functionaries
   - Enabling provision of the Act
   - Functional responsibilities assigned

4. Attitudes and Behavioural Aspects
   - Active Listening
   - Eschewing Dominance
   - Shedding Arrogance
   - Embracing Errors
   - Valuing Accountability (both performance and financial) and Transparency
   - Team Work and Team Building
   - Eliminating Biases
   - Seeking Diversity
   - Respecting Other's Views
   - Gender Sensitivity
   - Believing that people know their problems and are capable of suggesting solutions
   - Empathy
   - People's analysis, people's criteria, people's monitoring, people's evaluation; people's views and people's knowledge counts and not ours.
5. Participatory Planning, Monitoring and Evaluation
   - Planning
     — Concept of Participatory Planning and various Methods,
     — Needs/Problems identification with special reference to SC/ST/Women
     — Resource inventory and analysis
     — Prioritisation of issues, choices of solution
     — Networking with other local institutions
     — Grassroots planning from Gram Sabha
   - Monitoring
     — Monitoring and evaluation techniques
     — Indicators of Monitoring
   - Implementation and Coordination
     — Implementation processes and institutions
     — Assignment of tasks to stakeholders
     — Institutional cooperation and collaboration
6. Conduct of Business, Rules and Regulations
   - Rights and duties of the members

- Meetings
- Conduct of Gram Sabha
- Standing Committee Meetings
- Interface Meetings
- Execution of Works
- Preparing Agenda
- Review of Work and Performance

7. Poverty Alleviation Programmes
   - Various Poverty Alleviation Programmes, its Provisions and Implementation, and Targeted Results
   - Role of Panchayats in Poverty Alleviation Programmes
8. Right to Information
   - Concept and provisions of the Act
   - State specific initiations
   - Operational gaps
   - Client service
9. National Rural Employment Guarantee Act
   - Poverty and Unemployment Scenario: Past and Present Initiatives
   - Scheme Objectives, Eligibility and Statutory Bodies
   - Allocation and Release of Funds
   - Planning, Implementation, Monitoring and Evaluation
   - Nature of Works, Executing Agencies and Worksite Facilities
   - Payment of Wages, Unemployment Allowance and Dis-entitlements
   - Roles and Responsibilities of Key Agencies
   - Right to Information and Social Audit
10. Gram Sabha and Social Audit
    - Definition, purpose of Gram Sabha its powers and functions
    - Gram Sabha as a forum for deliberative democracy
    - Gram Sabha as a forum for transparency and accountability
    - Concepts and principles of social audit
    - Method of conducting social audit
    - Integrating social audit in various development programmes

11. E-Governance
    - Effort to take initiative to empower panchayats with IT capacity
    - Use of IT for convergent delivery of services
    - Means for improving internal management and efficiency
12. Gender, Equity and Social Justice
    - Concept and Strategies of Empowerment
    - Empowerment framework
    - Gender Planning: Strategic interest and practical interest
    - Gender development and governance
    - Women's component plan and Tenth Five Year Plan
    - Concept of social equity
    - Indicators of social development
    - Social Justice: Welfare Programmes
13. Management of Resources and Funds
    - Classification of resources to panchayats
    - Internal resource mobilisation
    - Flow of funds
    - Maintenance of Accounts
    - Preparation of Budget
    - Audit
    - Computer application to maintenance of accounts.
14. Training Techniques
    - Exposing to various training techniques relevant to deal with thematic issues stated above and specifically to deal with elected representatives.

Capacity Building of Panchayati Raj Functionaries
Course Module - I

Clientele Group	:	President, Vice-President Chairpersons of Subject Committees and Officials
Total Number	:	24,62,094
Intake in each Programme	:	40 - 45
Duration	:	5 Days

No. of Programmes	:	55000
Venue	:	State level and below It can be conducted concurrently
Time to Complete	:	Two Years

Themes/Topics

1. An Overview of Panchayati Raj
   - Evolution of Panchayats - leading to Constitutional Amendment
   - Vision on Purna Swaraj through Gram Swaraj
   - State specific PR Act
   - Status of PR in the country and State specific position in terms of Devolution of 3Fs
   - Special features of the State PR Act
2. Role and Responsibilities of PR Functionaries
   - Enabling provision of the Act
   - Functional responsibilities assigned
3. Participatory Planning, Monitoring and Evaluation
   - Planning
     — Participatory Planning Method, Concepts of Planning
     — Needs/Problems identification with special reference to SC/ST/Women
     — Resource inventory and analysis
     — Prioritisation of issues, choices of solution
     — Networking with other local institutions
     — Grassroots planning from Gram Sabha
   - Monitoring
     — Monitoring and evaluation techniques
     – Indicators of Monitoring
   - Implementation and Coordination
     — Implementation processes and institutions
     — Assignment of tasks to stakeholders
     — Institutional cooperation and collaboration

4. Conduct of Business, Rules and Regulations
   - Rights and duties of the members
   - Meetings
   - Conduct of Gram Sabha
   - Standing Committee Meetings
   - Interface Meetings
   - Execution of Works
   - Preparing Agenda
   - Review of Work and Performance
5. Poverty Alleviation Programmes
   - Various Poverty Alleviation Programmes, its provisions, implementation and expected results
   - Role of Panchayats in Poverty Alleviation
6. Right to Information
   - Concept and provisions of the Act
   - State specific initiations
   - Operational gaps
   - Client service
7. National Rural Employment Guarantee Programme
   - Poverty and unemployment, past and present initiatives
   - Salient features of the provisions of the NREGA
   - Planning, implementation, monitoring and evaluation of NREGA
   - Role of Panchayats in NREGA
8. Gram Sabha and Social Audit
   - Definition, purpose of Gram Sabha, its power and functions. Gram Sabha as a forum for deliberative democracy
   - Gram Sabha as a forum for transparency and accountability
   - Concepts and principles of social audit
   - Method of conducting social audit
   - Integrating social audit in various development programmes
9. E-Governance
   - Effort to take initiative to empower panchayats with IT capacity

- Use of IT for convergent delivery of services
- Means for improving internal management and efficiency

10. Gender, Equity and Social Justice
    - Concept and Strategies of Empowerment
    - Empowerment Framework
    - Gender Planning: Strategic interest and practical interest
    - Gender development and governance
    - Women's Component Plan and Tenth Five Year Plan
    - Concept of social equity
    - Indicators of social development
    - Social Justice: Welfare Programmes
11. Management of Resources and Funds
    - Classification of resources to panchayats
    - Internal resource mobilisation
    - Flow of funds
    - Maintenance of Accounts
    - Preparation of Budget
    - Audit
    - Computer application to maintenance of accounts, etc.

Course Module - II

Clientele Group	:	Elected members from Territorial constituencies of each tier
Total Number	:	14,15,973
Intake in each Programme	:	50
Duration	:	2 Days
No. of Programmes	:	29000
Venue	:	District level and below
Time to Complete	:	Two Years

Themes/Topics

1. An Overview of Panchayati Raj
    - Evolution of Panchayats - leading to Constitution Amendment

- Vision on Purna Swaraj through Gram Swaraj
- State specific PR Act
- Status of PR in the country and State specific position in terms of Devolution of 3Fs
- Special features of the State PR Act

2. Role and Responsibilities of PR Functionarics
   - Enabling provision of the Act
   - Functional responsibilities assigned
3. Poverty Alleviation Programmes
   - Various Poverty Alleviation Programmes, its provisions, implementation and expected results
   - Role of Panchayats in Poverty Alleviation
   - SGSY, PMGSY, IAY, Watershed, Drinking Water and Sanitation
4. Right to Information
   - Concept and provisions of the Act
5. National Rural Employment Guarantee Programme
   - Salient features of the provisions of the NREGA
   - Role of Panchayats in NREGA
6. Gram Sabha and Social Audit
   - Definition, purpose of Gram Sabha, its powers and functions
   - Gram Sabha as a forum for transparency and accountability
   - Social Audit by Gram Sabha
   - Integrating social audit in various development programmes
7. Delivery of basic services and panchayats
   - Orientation to various activities relating to civil functions such as, sanitations, drinking water, maintenance of street lights.

ANNEXURE-I

Statewise, Tierwise Number of Elected Panchayat Members

	Status	No. of GPs	Gram Panchayat					No. of IPs	Intermediate Panchayat					No. of ZPs	District Panchayat					Total ERS
	1		3	4	5	6		2	3	4	5	6		2	3	4	5	6		
			Gen	SC	ST	Women	Total		Gen	SC	ST	Women	Total		Gen	SC	ST	Women	Total	
1	Andhra Pradesh	21913	160386	31243	16662	68736	277027	1095	10938	2586	1093	4919	19536	22	812	196	87	364	1459	298022
2	Aruncahal Pradesh	1639	*	*	3924	2561	6485	136	–	–	1062	577	1639	14	–	–	91	45	136	8260
3	Assam	2153	14060	782	778	7851	23471	187	1236	80	86	746	2148	20	236	19	18	117	390	26009
4	Bihar	8471	96513	18650	866	40553	156582	531	9661	1859	91	4065	15676	38	966	187	9	410	1572	173830
5	Chattisgarh	9139	56481	15532	52198	41913	166124	146	1259	318	1062	906	3545	16	152	30	112	95	389	170058
6	Goa	190	982	0	0	457	1439	***	***	***	***	***		2	33	0	0	17	50	1489
7	Gujarat	13715	83951	9887	17285	41180	152303	225	2887	270	794	1312	5263	25	499	56	175	274	1004	158570
8	Haryana	5034	42800	11846	0	18356	73002	114	1879	551	0	842	3272	19	247	67	0	109	423	76697
9	Himachal Pradesh	3037	12657	4898	994	6822	25371	75	1108	437	113	562	2220	12	165	65	21	87	338	27929
10	Jharkhand	3746	*	*	*	*		211	*	*	*	*		22	*	*	*	*		0
11	Jammu & Kashmir	2683	*	*	*	*		*	*	*	*	*		*	*	*	*	*		0
12	Karnataka	5659	31051	14871	7499	35922	89343	175	1335	583	244	1375	3537	27	379	158	54	339	930	
13	Kerala	991	6802	1487	169	4801	13259	152	803	188	18	629	1638	14	165	33	4	105	307	15204
14	Madhya Pradesh	22029	119313	32585	56458	106491	314847	313	2476	682	1139	2159	6456	45	286	78	122	248	734	322037
15	Maharashtra	28553	118996	26824	31826	77548	255194	349	1902	447	528	1407	4284	33	931	225	267	658	2081	261559
16	Manipur	166	1025	38	48	611	1722	***	***	***	***	***		4	36	1	2	22	61	1783
17	Orissa	6234	49568	14930	23049	31414	118961	314	3498	1025	1704	2188	8415	30	496	139	219	296	1150	128526

Contd. ...

	Status	No. of GPs	Gram Panchayat					No. of IPs	Intermediate Panchayat					No. of ZPs	District Panchayat					Total ERS
	1		3	4	5	6		2	3	4	5	6		2	3	4	5	6		
			Gen	SC	ST	Women	Total		Gen	SC	ST	Women	Total		Gen	SC	ST	Women	Total	
18	Punjab	12445	33280	15580	0	27108	75968	140	1141	526	0	813	2480	17	130	60	0	89	279	78727
19	Rajasthan	9189	70027	24129	21126	39450	154732	237	3434	968	855	1908	7165	32	653	191	164	364	1372	163269
20	Sikkim	159	571	39	263	322	1195	***	***	***	***	***		4	50	6	36	29	121	1316
21	Tamil Nadu	12618	51155	19301	821	26181	97458	385	3384	1369	47	1770	6570	29	341	139	3	173	656	104684
22	Tripura	537	2757	876	157	1895	5685	23	100	78	15	106	299	4	28	22	4	28	82	6066
23	Uttar Pradesh	52028	293868	83443	207	230865	608383	809	25530	7743	17	18580	51870	70	1025	313	0	788	2126	662379
24	Uttaranchal	7227	237793	5378	703	18041	261915	95	1807	241	44	1133	3225	13	193	28	5	1193	45	265485
25	West Bengal	3360	22586	13645	3472	11497	51200	333	3669	2383	604	1923	8579	18	314	202	51	156	723	60502
26	Andaman & Nicabar Islands	67	498	0	0	261	759	7	42	0	0	25	67	1	20	0	0	10	30	856
27	Chandigarh	17	135	27	0	55	217	1	11	40	6	21	1	7	3	0	3	13	251	
28	D & Nagar Haveli	11	4	2	118	45	169	***	***	***	***	***	1	0	0	12	4	16	185	
29	Daman & Diu	10	33	1	12	17	63	***	***	***	***	***	1	12	0	3	10	25	88	
30	Lakshadweep	10	0	0	49	30	79	***	***	***	***	***	1	0	0	14	8	22	101	
31	Pondicherry	*	*	*	*	*	*	*	*	*	*	*	*	*	*	*	*	*		
	Total	234030	1507292	345994	238684	840983	2932953	6053	78100	22338	9516	47951	157905	535	8176	2218	1473	4967	16834	3107692

Note: Meghalaya, Mizoram & Nagaland have no panchayats
NCT of Delhi - Panchayati Raj System is yet to be revived
Source: Seventh Round Table Conference, Ministry of Panchayati Raj.

* Elections are due

*** Intermediate Panchayat does not exist (2 tier)

2

CAPACITY BUILDING FOR PANCHAYATI RAJ FUNCTIONARIES IN MADHYA PRADESH

YATINDRA SINGH SISODIA

Introduction

"My idea of village *swaraj* is that it is a complete republic, independent of its neighbours for its vital wants, and yet interdependent for many others in which dependence is a necessity. Thus the village's first concern will be to grow its own food crops and cotton for its cloth. It should have a reserve for its cattle, recreation and playground for adults and children... The village will maintain a village theatre, school and public hall. It will have its own waterworks ensuring a clean water supply. This can be done through controlled wells or tanks. Education will be compulsory up to the final basic course. As far as possible every activity will be conducted on a co-operative basis. There will be no caste, such as we have today with their graded untouchability. Non-violence with its technique of *satyagraha* and non-cooperation will be the sanction of the village community... The Panchayat of five persons annually elected by the adult villagers, male and female, possessing minimum prescribed qualifications will conduct the government of the village. These will have all the authority and jurisdiction required. Since there will be no system of punishments in the accepted sense, this Panchayat will be the legislature, judiciary, and executive combined to operate for its year in office. Any village can become such a republic without much interference."

—Gandhi in the issue of the Harijan of July 26, 1942

The views of Gandhiji expressed in 1942 are still very appropriate and timely from the point of view of village *swaraj* in India. The proposed model appears little utopian and unachievable but any step towards this direction will be a positive step to meet the destined laudable task. After independence persistent efforts have been made to make rural local self-government viable and self-sustainable on the times portrayed by Mahatma Gandhi. Unfortunately the response of the State Governments was of very different nature and as a result the pace and pattern of establishment of rural local political institutions was not very enthusiastic in the initial phase. The State Governments showed very little interest to empower these institutions and transfer of power to the representative institutions was almost negligible. However, the political leadership of some Indian States like Kerala, Karnataka, Maharashtra and West Bengal came forward to establish panchayats at local level but on the whole the pace of development was restricted that left much to be desired. Champions of local self-government debated and argued that the development planning was faulty and the results did not reach the people concerned despite plethora of schemes and massive investments in rural sector. It was also realised that the infrastructure at the local level was in a very bad state and one of the obvious reasons was poor delivery system through local bureaucracy. People's participation was rarely seen and the development model was of 'top down approach'. Accountability of the delivery mechanism was nominal as it rested with the bureaucratic hierarchy that looked at rural mass(s) as mere recipient.

Almost after forty-five years, the Central Government realised this hard truth that the delivery system was not effectively operational; it realized at last that without making people's direct and responsible participation through panchayats purposeful development in the desired manner was not possible. As a result the introduction of 73rd Constitutional Amendment Act was enacted in 1993. The execution of the Act was made mandatory for all the Indian states and panchayats have been provided a constitutional status. A special chapter has been added to the Indian Constitution on Panchayats. The 73rd Amendment has provided uniformity and formal structure to these traditional institutions of self-governance for the sake of their effective functioning. The 73rd Amendment has initiated a fundamental restructuring of governance and administrative system of the country, based on the philosophy of decentralization and power to the people. Policy planners have realised by now that the new panchayati raj institutions have the potential to usher in a new era of change and development in accordance with people's needs and priorities, and to revitalise a deeply troubled system of democracy (Behar & Kumar: 2002).

Decentralization is a much-debated issue in India and other countries with federal system of governance. Though there are various arguments for and against decentralization, arguments in favour of decentralization far outweigh those against it because of the inherent potential of democratization in the decentralized federal system through proper empowerment of people at the grassroots level. The Panchayati Raj Institutions in India have been ordained to empower the people at the three appropriate levels but the aim had remained a distant dream till the 73rd Constitutional Amendment Act came into effect in 1993 after much experimentations and churning of ideas about the advantages of the system of democratic decentralization.

A decade of panchayati raj in India has been a matter of debate and speculation about its performance and impact. All the major states have completed at least one round of panchayat elections, and in majority of cases at least two successive rounds. Almost three million people including one million women and a sizeable number of SCs/STs took part in these elections The sizeable presence of under-privileged and poor as representatives through reservations in the grassroots political institutions is a landmark development in the rural politics of the country. This significant development has special meaning because a decade earlier in most parts of rural India these groups were excluded from public life and political participation. This is also a matter of serious debate as how this excluded lot after their inclusion in active politics at grassroots would effectively tackle local power equation and set the agenda for development. Yet the fact remains that these backward and so far ignored classes have heralded their arrival on the political stage of the country in the country side.

The responses of State Governments to the implementation of Panchayati Raj varied significantly and it is very difficult to generalise about this issue on the basis of their functioning for the last one decade or so. Only a few States like Maharashtra, Gujarat, Kerala, Karnataka, West Bengal have had a track record of Panchayats since 1950s and the exemplary lead taken by the State of Madhya Pradesh after 1993 brings together a total of six states only that took steps to strengthen panchayati raj institutions. On the other hand States of Bihar and Jammu & Kashmir are considered prominent examples among states where little or no progress had taken place over the last one decade; even regular panchayat elections were inordinately delayed in these states.

A perusal of state profiles would show that Panchayati Raj reforms have certainly taken place with vigour and zeal in some western and southern parts of the country, which are relatively sound from the point of view of economy, are vibrant socially, and have active civil societies. On the contrary, the northern states with the greatest degree of poverty and inequality and deep schisms of caste and low pace of governance resulted in weak Panchayats (Robinson: 2005).

In this mixed scenario of development exemplary reforms have taken place in Kerala and Madhya Pradesh due to the strong political will of the political leadership of these states after the implementation of the 73rd Amendment Act. In Kerala, the people's planning campaign was predicted on a high level of popular mobilisation that was made possible by high level of literacy and professional support with a mass base social movement (Issac: 2000). In Madhya Pradesh, Chief Minister Digvijay Singh had introduced a series of reforms and amendments in Panchayat Raj to strengthen the grassroots institutions, specially the Gram Sabha. The example of

West Bengal is well known where the CPM government used the PRIs as a political support base in rural areas with a significant degree of success. The land reforms in West Bengal could take place due to Panchayat Raj (Webster: 1993).

After almost one decade of the implementation of the 73rd Constitution Amendment Act, it is evident from the grassroots experiences that the State Acts have been amended from time to time to make it more effective in establishing PRIs as genuine structures of grassroots democracy. Through a system of reservation, participation of the weaker sections has also been ensured in the States. The three-tiers of Panchayati Raj System have been empowered significantly to enable them to discharge their duties properly and fulfil the expectations of the people. Gram Sabhas have been bestowed with enormous power in the decision-making process. The evidences from the states suggest that the people's participation has remained low. The efforts to make the grassroots institutions viable and significant remained confined to a formality. Nevertheless a process of political socialization has begun within the society. The bureaucratic resistance is visible in many matters. The stereotype and routinised mind-set of local bureaucracy has created hurdles in the beginning but slowly and gradually the situation is changing. The bureaucracy has understood that the panchayat will remain for ever and the bureaucracy has to work within the changed scenario. The process of financial devolution from the States could not get momentum despite creation of State Finance Commission to allocate funds to panchayats. Panchayats are still dependent on State Governments for funding. The untied funds are very limited and the resource generation at local level is also not very encouraging. A perusal of a decade of functioning of Panchayati Raj put forward a mix scenario with enough evidences of positive movements and several hurdles, nevertheless a hope for the best can be expected at this juncture.

Madhya Pradesh Scenario

Madhya Pradesh was the first State in India, which had not only prepared its State legislation in accordance with 73rd Amendment Act but also conducted election in May-June 1994. Historically speaking, Madhya Pradesh Government had been doing remarkable work for the strengthening of panchayat raj system ever since its inception. The term of five years of this system was over in June 1999 and elections for the second term of the panchayats were held in January-February 2000. After completion of two terms, the elections for the third term were held in January-February 2005. The State of Madhya Pradesh has responded with innovativeness and remarkable commitment to making the system sustainable and successful. The State's effort to institutionalize the system is evident in the number of amendments that have been made to the State Panchayat Act as a dynamic response to the problems at the ground level. During the implementation of panchayati raj system, Madhya Pradesh has faced several opportunities and difficulties. The experience of the State is extremely rich and provides vital insights into the process of institutionalising panchayat raj. On the one hand, the story is of bureaucratic resistance, functional problems, political and institutional challenges, financial inadequacy and mismatch of capacities and roles. On the other hand, it involves the grassroots level in a democratic and participative governance system, and therefore potentially unleashes its considerable energy.

Why Training and Capacity Building?

For the empowerment of the people of rural region in panchayati raj functionaries, training and capacity building is a pre-condition. Efforts have been made after the enactment of 73rd Amendment to impart training at different levels. Both the Governments have provided funds to conduct training for the grassroots functionaries. But a fair review clearly brings this fact that it was a meek effort and could not make a significant effort to provide adequate training. It appears that there is a significant decline in the training initiatives. Madhya Pradesh is known for its remarkable effort to decentralise the governance and transfer of power to the panchayats. But as far training and capacity building is concerned, the commitment of government is not as desired. The reasons counted for non-training are—lack of finance, lack of infrastructural facilities, non-availability of training policy, etc. However some Organisations and Institutions

Three Tier Panchayats in Madhya Pradesh (Status as on 1st November, 2000)

Women Representation in Zilla/Janpad Panchayats as Chairpersons and Members and Gram Panchayat's Sarpanch and Panch

Sr. No.	*Panchayat*	*Designation*	*Total Seats*	*SC*	*ST*	*OBC*	*Un-reserved*	*Women*				
								Total Women	*SC*	*ST*	*OBC*	*Un-reserved*
1.	Zilla Panchayat	Chairperson	45	7	8	13	17	17	3	3	5	6
		Member	734	120	184	156	274	248	42	62	52	92
2.	Janpad Panchayat	Chairperson	313	40	115	61	97	111	13	41	24	33
		Member	6456	1006	1722	1264	2464	2159	324	583	443	809
3.	Gram Panchayat	Sarpanch	22029	3171	7343	4095	7420	7384	1053	2461	1384	2486
		Panch	314847	49448	85639	57008	122752	106491	16863	29181	19707	40740
	Grand Total		**344424**	**53792**	**95011**	**62597**	**133024**	**116410**	**18298**	**32331**	**21615**	**44166**

like—Madhya Pradesh Academy of Administration, Bhopal, Mahatma Gandhi State Institution of Rural Administration, Jabalpur, Mahatma Gandhi Gramodaya Vishvavidyalaya, Chitrakoot, Samarthan, Bhopal, Madhya Pradesh Institute of Social Sciences Research, Ujjain, Dr. Babasaheb Ambedkar National Institute of Social Sciences, Mhow, All India Institute of Local Self-Government, Bhopal, Debate, Bhopal, CASA, Indore, Eklavya, Bhopal have carried out training and capacity building on regular basis or periodic basis with the resources available and provided to them. The pedagogy, course content and methodology were also significantly different from organisation to organisation.

Planning of Training Methodology

It is known that PRIs could not work effectively due to variety of reasons. It is necessary that Panchayats should understand the whole scheme of governance including status, jurisdiction, power, responsibilities and inherent principles of governance. A demand should come from the PRRs that the legitimate powers be transferred to Panchayats. And, therefore, the need for capacity building and training comes into picture and becomes vital.

There are two options to break the culture of silence. First, the State should change the approach and attitude so that the listed items of 11th Schedule be adequately delegated and transferred to Panchayats. This is a 'top down approach' and this is like creation of Panchayats through Constitution. Second, the representatives of Panchayats should change the approach and attitude in the conduct of Panchayat affairs so that their dependence on decision-making at higher level can be minimised. This is a 'bottom up approach' and this is a better alternative because this will be based on the demands of those who are going to affect with this system. This approach will allow Panchayats to work for the maximum people who are concerned with it. And, therefore, it will lead to self-motivation resulting in the lesser dependence on politicians and bureaucracy for PRRs.

This approach can be inculcated through training and thereby the level of awareness can be increased among PRRs and personnel working in Panchayats. This approach can be instrumental in breaking the culture of silence and can be helpful in achieving the goals of economic justice, social justice and gender justice.

It is important to understand that the Panchayats are created as units of local self-governance and not as lower chains of line departments. Nevertheless, Panchayats are expected to work with politicians and bureaucracy and therefore their approach is demand oriented, hence the PRIs are expected to work with 'bottom up approach' but also keeping in mind sustainable development.

Looking Ahead

Despite the recognition of the fact that without direct and active participation of the rural people the situation of development will remain dismal, the progress made by the State for training and capacity building is not very satisfactory. Only partial willingness and commitment is shown to make the institutions of self-governance viable and functional with the required funds and functions.

If we look at the whole programme of training and capacity building over these years, the attempts made by Government and independent organisations were in isolated manner. No specific training needs assessment is done. No generic training module is developed looking into the need of the State. There is no networking of the organisations and institutions actively engaged in this task. It is realised and understood that the 'top down approach' of development is not capable enough to work and therefore the urgent need is to adopt the 'bottom up approach' (Sisodia: 2002). It is also pertinent that the delivery system has remained faulty and it could not deliver in the preceding decades and this situation has put forward strongly the need of people's direct participation in the delivery system. Another prerequisite of local governance is the accountability, which in the earlier stages of evolution of PRIs rested with upper echelons of bureaucracy, was frittered away the unhappy result was that the rural masses, for whom the panchayati raj system was inaugurated, remained far away from these institutions. The local political institutions have to be made vibrant, comprehensive and self-sustainable to work independently as units of self-governance. And therefore the training and capacity building is required urgently.

In this premise it is important to understand that decentralization provides opportunities to the people to participate in governance. The existence of grassroots political arenas makes it easier for common people to participate and exert influence in areas of self-governing institutions. When power is brought closer to the citizens, the political process becomes more tangible and transparent where more people are involved freely in the process. Decentralization paves way for an open political system as decision-making powers rest with the people. It promotes popular participation and bestows controlling function on the representative institutions. Thus the greater degree of political inclusiveness becomes helpful in resolving crises of local self-governance.

To conclude, it can be inferred that decision-makers, rooted in the locality and knowledgeable of conditions on the ground, are better placed to formulate concrete policies for that area than functionaries from outside. While professional competence may be lacking at the grassroots, such decision-makers are more able to accommodate local demands by tapping the 'silent knowledge' that exists among the local public about the problems at hand and their possible remedies. After 73rd Amendment, Madhya Pradesh has responded in a positive pace and patterns while introducing new Panchayati Raj. It is certain that this mandatory position of Panchayati Raj along with sustained efforts of State, Civil Society and rural masses will pave the way for the little republics of Gandhi's dream. It is hoped that these little republics will work for the greater equality for all to create a society of the equals in India provided the Governments make a commitment for training and capacity building. Without adequate and proper training we cannot expect grassroots panchayat functionaries to perform in the desired manner. And also the training is equally needed for local bureaucracy as well. Other than training a committed need for orientation and sensitization for all the actors involved in Panchayat affairs is needed urgently. This multi-pronged approach of training with other aspects will definitely lead to a situation where we can look for a society of equals and also a way forward to social, economic and political justice for all.

REFERENCES

Behar, Amitabh and Kumar, Yogesh (2002), 'Decentralisation in Madhya Pradesh, India: from Panchayati Raj to Gram Swaraj (1995 to 2001)', *Working Paper 170, ODI*, London, UK.

Issac, T.M. Thomas and Richard W. Franke (2000): *Local Democracy and Development: People's Campaign for Decentralised Planning in Kerala*, Leftword, New Delhi.

Robinson, Mark (2005): 'A Decade of Panchayati Raj Reforms: The Challenge of Democratic Decentralisation in India' in L.C. Jain (ed.), *Decentralisation and Local Governance*, Orient Longman, New Delhi.

Sisodia, Yatindra Singh (2002): 'Panchayati Raj System in Madhya Pradesh: An Appraisal' in G. Palanithurai (ed.), *Dynamics of New Panchayati Raj System in India*, Vol. II, Concept Publishing Company, New Delhi.

Webster, Neil (1992): 'Panchayati Raj in West Bengal: Participation for the People or the Party?', *Development and Change*, Vol. 23, No. 4.

3

CAPACITY BUILDING OF PANCHAYAT LEADERS IN WEST BENGAL

DILIP KUMAR GHOSH

With the passage of the Constitution (73rd Amendment) Act, 1992 the panchayat institutions in rural areas not only secured the constitutional legality but also got the recognition that they should be allowed to function as institutions of self-government. This Constitutional amendment created the scope (Article 243D) for the marginalised sections to enter these institutions. As a consequence, large number of women and men from scheduled castes and scheduled tribe communities became able to be the members of the panchayat structure at different levels (village, block and district). Simultaneously, by Article 243G the State Legislatures are authorised to make law for endowing the panchayats with such powers and authority as may be necessary to enable them to function as institutions of self-government and to prepare plans for economic development and social justice and to implement schemes in respect of the matters listed in the Eleventh Schedule. This Schedule contains twenty-nine items of activities for the rural areas. In this context, it is necessary that enabling environment should be created throughout the panchayat structure for fulfilling the hopes emanated from the Seventy-third Amendment. Thus, the need for capacity building of the persons coming into the panchayat bodies can be felt easily.

Capacity building is a process by which the individual members can develop their abilities to perform functions, resolve conflicts if arises and achieve the objectives set for them. In the panchayats at three tiers, namely, Gram Panchayat (at village level), Panchayat Samiti (at block level) and Zilla Parishad (at district level) persons from different categories of the society are being elected. As a result, the reality is intrinsic heterogeneity in their composition. For easy functioning of these institutions it is desirable that interventions should be there for achieving certain level of standardisation within the diversity. Training intervention is the most acceptable tool for this purpose. For this reason, the present paper only concerns with the training input provided to the panchayats.

In this study, West Bengal is considered because of its unique political characteristic. This State has the distinction of holding the panchayat general election[1] uninterruptedly since the year 1978. The present Communist led government came to the power of the State in the year 1977 and since then it maintained the continuity. Till now six panchayat general elections were held in the State with an interval of five years. From the panchayat general election held in the year 1993, the State Government made reservation of seats for the scheduled castes, scheduled tribes and women in all three tiers of the panchayat structure. This was done through an amendment of the West Bengal Panchayat Act, 1973.

With this background, the present study is being taken up with following objectives:

(i) to present different training methodology adopted by the State for the training of the panchayat members elected in 2003 panchayat general election;
(ii) to discuss the contents of training curriculum for different target groups; and
(iii) to focus the limitations of the training programmes.

The present paper is structured in following manner:

Section I presents a synoptic view of duties and responsibilities of three-tier panchayats and their composition. This section will help to understand the gamut of the huge task of providing training to

49140 Gram Panchayat members, 8500 Panchayat Samiti members and 713 Zilla Parishad members.

Section II provides a detailed discussion on methodology and contents of the training courses, duration of training courses, the participation of the members in training programmes, etc.

Section III indicates some limitations of the present training programmes. In spite of the best intention of the State Government to cover all the panchayat members, there exists scope for further improvement.

SECTION I

On the basis of the amendment in WBP Act, 1973 brought in accordance with the 73rd Amendment of the Constitution, in all three-tier seats were reserved for the scheduled castes, scheduled tribes and women. For women, one-third of the total seats in all

Table 1 : Tier-wise Members in West Bengal Panchayats.

District	*Gram Panchayat*		*Panchayat Samiti*		*Zilla Parishad*	
	Total	*Women*	*Total*	*Women*	*Total*	*Women*
Bankura	2632	855	478	164	41	14
Birbhum	2258	811	412	144	35	12
Burdwan	4346	1538	734	253	65	22
Coochbehar	1905	677	339	116	26	9
Dakshin Dinajpur	993	352	179	62	15	5
Hooghly	3440	1218	577	197	47	16
Howrah	2515	891	426	145	34	12
Jalpaiguri	2241	802	374	130	31	11
Malda	2232	795	388	135	33	11
Murshidabad	4096	1451	697	238	60	20
Nadia	3114	1128	512	174	41	16
24 Pgs. (North)	3321	1173	555	193	50	17
24 Pgs. (South)	4898	1740	845	294	66	22
Paschim Midnapore	4073	1459	733	255	62	21
Purba Midnapore	3480	1238	604	208	52	18
Purulia	2067	739	384	133	34	12
Uttar Dinajpur	1529	542	263	89	21	7
Total	**49140**	**17409**	**8500**	**2930**	**713**	**245**

Source: Administrative Report (April 2000-March 2004), West Bengal State Election Commission.

panchayat tiers are kept reserved. This enables a large number of women to come and contest for seats in the panchayats. Initially the new entrants are hesitant in handling their affairs. Training intervention can only help them to smooth out initial inertia. In Table 1, district-wise number of members in village, block and district panchayat tiers are given. This is the target population for whom capacity building exercises are launched in the State after the election in May 2003.

From Table 1 it can be seen that taking all three tiers together, the number of panchayat members to be trained is 58,353 only. The target is massive. In the State, there is only one institute in the name of State Institute of Panchayats and Rural Development (SIPRD) to cater to the needs of training. For this reason, training of all the members by this Institute is not possible. In order to overcome this constraint, the State Government adopts cascading mode of training for all the members and direct training for the members holding official positions at the block and district panchayats. Again of the panchayat members, due to reservation of seats there are representation from different social communities. Tier-wise representation is given in Table 2.

Table 2 : Category of Panchayat Members.

Tier	*Scheduled Castes*		*Scheduled Tribes*		*General*		*Total*	
	Men	*Women*	*Men*	*Women*	*Men*	*Women*	*Men*	*Women*
Gram Panchayat	8435	5276	1969	1278	21327	10855	31731	17409
Panchayat Samiti	1527	874	375	210	3668	1846	5570	2930
Zillå Parishad	126	69	33	18	309	158	468	245

Note : General category indicates non-SC/ST men and women.
Source : Administrative Report (April 2000 - March 2004), West Bengal State Election Commission.

In addition to the numbers, there are differences within the members in respect of their ages, family backgrounds, livelihood patterns, literacy rate and attainment of formal education, experiences in working with panchayats, etc. As there is no study on socio-economic profile of all the panchayat members in the State, it becomes not possible to reflect on these diversities. However, case studies[2] of a few districts conducted by SIPRD in respect of the panchayat members elected in 1998 panchayat general election can provide some clues. In general, women panchayat members in all three tiers have low educational attainment and are younger in age in comparison with the male members. Obviously, the women members are mostly new entrants to the panchayati raj system. Before 1993, there was no mechanism of reservation of seats for women. There was a system of co-opting two women only if there was no women representation in the respective bodies. Classification of the panchayat members on the basis of their occupations, broadly identifies ten types of occupations along with house-wives and unemployed youths. These are, agricultural labourers, bargadars, cultivators, rural artisans, other primary sector activities like fish catching, animal husbandry, etc., retail businesses, teacher, other services, social workers and other petty jobs. As regards the experience profile of the panchayat members, these studies show that the shares of the new entrants are heavy in gram panchayats.

With this reflection on the composition of the panchayats in three tiers, let us now have a glimpse on the responsibilities assigned to the panchayats in respective tier. In West Bengal, the panchayats function through committee system and majority decision. For the gram panchayats, five upa-samitis (sub-committees) were created by the State Government through an amendment of the earlier Section 32A of the West Bengal Panchayat Act (WBP Act). The upa-samitis are :

(i) Artha-O-Parikalpana upa-samiti (Finance and Planning Sub-committee);
(ii) Krishi-O-Pranisampad Bikash upa-samiti (Agriculture and Animal Resource Development Sub-committee);
(iii) Siksha-O-Janasasthya upa-Samiti (Education and Public Health Sub-committee);
(iv) Nari, Sishu Unnayan-O-Samaj Kalyan upa-samiti (Women, Child Development and Social Welfare Sub-committee); and
(v) Shilpa-O-Parikathama upa-samiti (Industry and Infrastructure Sub-committee).

For functioning of such upa-samiti under the general guidance and control of the gram panchayat, the WBP Act makes provision for election of one member from among the members of the upa-samiti to act as Sanchalak (Coordinator) for such upa-samiti. The Sanchalak of an upa-samiti, according to the provision of the WBP Act, "shall be responsible for convening the meetings of such upa-samiti, coordinate function of the members within such upa-samiti and prepare and place report of actions taken or proposed to be taken relating to such upa-samiti within the budgetary provision of the Gram Panchayat to the Pradhan and the Gram Panchayat from time to time." Therefore, Sanchalak is a responsible assignment in a gram panchayat. For strengthening the capacities of the Sanchalak, to discharge their functions effectively and efficiently, arrangements for training are made at district and sub-district levels. SIPRD only prepares the training booklets for each and every upa-samiti. The training booklets are prepared in vernacular and understandable language keeping in mind the low educational attainment of the gram panchayat members. 30,000 copies of each booklet are printed at a cost of around Rs. 15 lakh so that every upa-samiti member can get the respective booklet for their use. The subject-matter of each booklet is developed through a number of workshops held with the experts of different functional departments of the State Government, academicians from different fields and SIPRD faculty.

In West Bengal, the chairperson of a gram panchayat is known as Pradhan. With the increasing roles and responsibilities of the gram panchayats, particularly after the effect of 73rd Amendment to the Constitution, it is natural that the importance of this position also increases. Like reservation of seats in the gram panchayats, the office of the Pradhan in a gram panchayat also comes under reservation norm. Accordingly, in the positions of Pradhan, there come persons from scheduled castes, scheduled tribes and women. Their capacity building is a crucial task. The WBP Act makes provision for three types of duties for a gram panchayat. These are obligatory duties (Section 19), other duties (Section 20) and discretionary duties (Section 21). In the provisions containing obligatory duties, it is stated in the WBP Act that "a Gram Panchayat shall function as a unit of self-government and in order to achieve economic development and secure social justice for all, shall subject to such conditions as may be prescribed or such directions as may be given by the State Government,

(a) prepare a development plan for the five year term of the office of the members and revise and update it as and when necessary with regard to the resources available;
(b) prepare an annual plan for each year by the month of October of the preceding year for development of human resources, infrastructure and civic amenities in the area;
(c) implement schemes for economic development and social justice as may be drawn up by or entrusted upon it."

This provision itself indicates the importance of the gram panchayat tier and the office of Pradhan. In West Bengal, all programmes of the Department of Panchayats and Rural Development are implemented by the panchayats at appropriate level. Identification of beneficiaries and schemes are entrusted to the gram panchayats. Imparting training to the Pradhans and developing their managerial ability thereby are the starred items in the agenda of the State Government. SIPRD normally does not provide training to the Pradhans directly. This training is organized at the district level by the district administration. The teams of district level trainers formed by the district administration in each and every district of the State are trained at SIPRD. This training is popularly known as Training of Trainers (ToT). These district level trainers, then, provide training to the Pradhans (chairperson of gram panchayats), upa-pradhans (vice-chairperson of gram panchayats) and other members of the gram panchayats. This cascading mode of training has its own limitations. It is likely that the messages from SIPRD may be diluted in the process of transmission. In case of the block tier panchayats, SIPRD directly provide training the chairpersons. This is possible because the number of panchayat samitis in the State was 333 only. With this, let us now discuss the responsibilities of the panchayat samitis as provided in the WBP Act.

Besides having a general body, the panchayat samitis function through a set of committees known as standing committees (Sthayee Samitis). At present there are ten standing committees in each panchayat samiti and zilla parishad [Section 124 (1) for panchayat samiti and 171(1) for zilla parishad]. These standing committees cover all 29 subjects of the Eleventh Schedule. For each Sthayee Samiti, there is a chairperson known as Karmadhyaksha elected by the members of that Sthayee Samiti. Only exception is that the chairperson of the panchayat samiti (known as Sabhapati) is also the chairperson of the Artha, Sanstha, Unnayan-O-Parikalpana Sthayee Samiti (Finance, Establishment, Development and Planning Standing Committee). This Standing Committee is the most powerful among all standing committees because the chairperson of other Standing Committees are included as ex-officio members of this committee. According to the provisions of the WBP Act, the Karmadhyaksha of a Sthayee Samiti shall be responsible for the financial and executive administration in respect of the schemes and programmes under the purview and control of the concerned Sthayee Samiti within the budgetary provisions of the panchayat samiti. Standing Committee-wise coverage of the Eleventh Schedule subjects can be seen from Table 3.

Table 3 : Standing Committees and Eleventh Schedule subjects.

Name of Standing Committee	*Subject(s) covered*
(i) Artha, Sanstha, Unayan-O-Parikalpana (Finance, Establishment, Development and Planning)	Poverty alleviation programmes; market and fair; Ferries and Waterways.
(ii) Janasasthya-O-Paribesh (Public Health and Environment)	Health and Sanitation including hospitals, primary health centers and dispensaries; family welfare; drinking water.
(iii) Purta Karya-O- Paribahan (Public Works and Transport)	Rural housing; road, culverts, bridges and other means for communication; maintenance of community assets.
(iv) Krishi, Sech-O-Samabaya (Agriculture, Irrigation and Co-operation)	Agriculture including agricultural extension; land improvement, land consolidation and soil conservation; minor irrigation, water management and watershed development.

Contd. ...

Name of Standing Committee	*Subject(s) covered*
(v) Shiksha, Sanskriti, Tathya-O-Krira (Education, Culture, Information and Sports)	Education including primary and secondary schools; Adult and non-formal education; Technical Training and vocational education; cultural activities; libraries.
(vi) Sishu-O-Nari Unnayan, Jana-Kalyan-O-Tran (Women and Child Development, Social Welfare and Relief)	Women and child development; social welfare including welfare of the handicapped and mentally retarded; welfare of the weaker societies and in particular of the scheduled castes and scheduled tribes.
(vii) Bon-O-Bhumi Sanskar (Forest and Land Reform)	Social forestry and farm forestry; minor forest produce and implementation of land reforms.
(viii) Matsya-O-Prani Sampad Bikash (Pisciculture and Animal Resource Development)	Fisheries; animal husbandry, dairying and poultry.
(ix) Khadya-O-Sarbaraha (Food and Supply)	Public distribution system.
(x) Khudra Shilpa, Bidyut-O-Achiracharit Shakti (Small Industries, Power and Non-Conventional Energy)	Small scale industries; khadi, village and cottage industries; rural electrification including distribution of electricity and non-conventional energy sources.

Considering the importance of the post of Karmadhyakshas and the functioning of the Sthayee Samitis, the State Government has assigned to the SIPRD the task of imparting training to all Karmadhyakshas (both panchayat samitis and zilla parishads) of the State. It is expected that these trainings will enable them to discharge their functions properly in the interests of their respective tier. The target comprises of 3330 panchayat samiti Karmadhyakshas and 180 zilla parishad and Mahakuma parishad[3] Karmadhyakshas.

In the panchayat set up, the office of Sabhapati also has tremendous responsibility. According to the provision of the WBP Act, the Sabhapati (Chairperson of a Panchayat Samiti) shall have the general responsibility for the financial and executive administrative and control over the work of the staff of the panchayat samiti and the officers and employees whose services may be placed at the disposal of the panchayat samiti by the State Government. Need for training of the Sabhapatis has huge importance from this perspective. SIPRD directly conducts this training through its faculty and expert from different functional departments. Like gram panchayat, a panchayat samiti also functions as an unit of self-government and has to prepare a perspective development plan for five years and an annual plan for each year to achieve economic development and secure social justice for all in the jurisdiction of the panchayat samiti (Section 109 of WBP Act). Every zilla parishad also has to prepare the perspective plan for the five year term and an annual plan (Section 153 of the WBP Act). As in the case for the Sabhapatis and Karmadhyakshas of the panchayat samitis, SIPRD takes care for training of the Sabhadhipatis (Chairpersons of Zilla Parishads) and zilla parishad Karmadhyakshas.

For deepening democracy and bringing transparency in the activities of the panchayats, the State Government through a provision in the WBP Act (Section 214A) constituted a District Council for panchayats in each district. According to the underlying provisions, the leader of the recognized political party in opposition having the largest number of members directly elected with the reserved symbol of such recognized political party in the zilla parishad shall be the chairperson of the District Council. In West Bengal, the chairperson of District Council is known as Adhyaksha. For Mahakuma Parishad also similar provision has been made. The functions of the District Council include examination of the accounts of the panchayats within its territorial jurisdiction and giving necessary suggestions for improvement of the activities of the panchayats under the broad framework of the provisions of the WBP Act and the rules made thereunder. Considering the importance of the District Council, SIPRD has taken the responsibility for the training of the chairpersons and vice-chairpersons of the District Councils.

From the discussions so far made, it can be easily understood that the panchayati raj institutions in the State are entrusted with many responsibilities for the development of the rural segment. Around 72 per cent of the State's total population are in the rural areas. For ensuring effective performance of these institutions, it becomes necessary to equip the elected representatives appropriately in terms of knowledge and skills for enabling them to discharge their assigned functions. Let us now discuss in details, the nature of trainings provided to the elected panchayat representatives at different levels and with different portfolios.

SECTION II

Training of the panchayat members is essentially based on principles of adult learning. The whole process does not conform to the process of teaching or delivering instructions. The underlying assumptions in any adult learning are:

(i) Trainees see themselves not as a dependent personality, but as a self-directing human being where he or she has strong sense of personal feeling;
(ii) Trainees have a growing reservoir of experiences and always try to relate new learnings with their existing set of experiences;
(iii) Trainees are ready to learn more on the subjects which have relevance to the real life situations either in their social life or in their work places;
(iv) Trainees are more interested in solutions of the problems they face in their own situation, i.e. they prefer immediate use of learning.

In adult learning, trainees need to be treated with respect and they should be allowed to express their own feelings in the classroom situation. Efforts in this direction are always pursued at SIPRD for creating congenial atmosphere in training situation. The psychological climate that is normally created at SIPRD causes adult learners to feel accepted, respected and supported. There persists an environment of mutual respect and cooperation between the training team and the learners. As the panchayat representatives mostly are rich sources for learning about the grassroots situations, those training techniques are only adopted which can use their experiences and inherent knowledge base. In adult learning the process of planning of the training functions consists of "translating diagnosed needs into specific behavioural objectives; designing and conducting learning events to achieve these objectives; and assessing the extent to which these objectives have been achieved" (DOPT, GOI, 2000). The andragogical practice (the technical name of adult learning) emphasizes creation of such an environment where learning-teaching transaction results in mutual responsibility of learners and trainers. Contrary to the pedagogical practice, trainers here are neither teachers nor instructors. Their role is redefined as that of 'resource person' or 'procedural counsellor' (*ibid*). In fact andragogy believes that "a trainer cannot really teach in the sense of making someone learn" (*ibid*). The purpose of all these training programmes is to help and to give advice so as to enable the panchayat members to discharge their responsibilities properly. Trainers can act as the facilitators only in the functional space of the panchayats. They cannot direct or instruct keeping in the mind the principles of adult learning and the nature and characteristics of the panchayat bodies. As the panchayat representatives are coming from different strata of the rural society, they have varied social backgrounds and wider variety of experiences. The entry behaviour variations are also taken into consideration in developing learning events for them.

In systematic approach to training, performance of the learners is the central point. Otherwise, it is of no use to spend money and time on training. The first issue is to identify needs for different target group of learners. For example, at the panchayat samiti level, training design for the course of Sabhapati will differ from the course of Karmadhyakshas even if the Sabhapati is also the Karmadhyaksha of Finance, Establishment, Development and Planning Standing Committee. The process of capacity building of the panchayat members requires initial exercise of assessment of training needs for different categories of elected representatives in three tiers. In practice, this need assessment exercise is undertaken by SIPRD in collaboration with the Department of Panchayats and Rural Development. The exercise is undertaken separately (i) for the general members of three tiers; (ii) for the members holding offices like Sanchalaks of upa-samitis at gram panchayats or Karmadhyakshas of Sthayee Samitis at panchayat samitis and zilla parishads; and (iii) for the chairpersons of the gram panchayats (pradhans), panchayat samitis (sabhapati) and zilla parishads (sabhadhipatis). These exercises help in designing suitable programmes for the respective categories so as to meet their requirements and to be beneficial in augmenting their capacities. Training Need Assessment (TNA) contributes towards enhancement of the efficacy of the training programmes and helps to avoid unnecessary wastage of time and resources which may occur in the absence of TNA. Any training programme tries to bridge knowledge, skill or attitude deficiencies of the target group of learners. TNA is not an one shot operation but a continuous process like training itself because in TNA exercise both present and future needs come up. One time operation can only address the present needs.

For addressing the future needs, refresher training is helpful. In reality, however, the majority of the panchayat representatives can get a chance for one time training only in their five-year time. This is a limitation of the present strategy of capacity building of the panchayat members. The present practice of TNA exercise for designing training programmes including finalization of learning events involves both in-house deliberations with official functionaries and panchayat functionaries and field visits to the district and sub-district level office of the panchayats. This is done for capturing the grass-roots reality and making learning events need based and holistic. In the field survey, both individual performance problems and organizational problems get highlighted. It is a fact that not all performance problems can be resolved through training. Many of them like delay in decision-making over a scheme, arise not because of lack of training or inadequate training. This requires other interventions. For this reason in TNA, attempts are made to separate symptoms from causes to avoid the possibility that the training may be used to treat symptoms. Training can only help to build up knowledge and skill of members along with changes in their attitudes. The generic learning objectives of the training programmes for the panchayat members include clarity of different concepts and their respective role in the arena of panchayats and rural development. The broad objective of any training programme encompasses three objectives, viz. training objectives, performance objectives and enabling objectives. Training objectives indicate that on completion of a training course the panchayat members will achieve a satisfactory standard of performance under training conditions. This is a general expectation from any training course irrespective of the nature and status of target group learners. Performance objectives explain that after getting training for certain duration, the panchayat members on returning to their respective places (i.e. the constituencies from which they were elected) are required to perform their assigned tasks to the standards set by the WBP Act and relevant executive orders of the State Government. Enabling objectives explain the ability that individual members acquired after going through a training course. More specifically, enabling objectives of a training programme for the panchayat members in general narrate that at the end of a training course, the members will be able :

(a) to understand their respective role in their concerned tiers and in the milieu of multiparty democracy with criss-crossing of interests of various clientele groups;
(b) to carry out their defined roles with a full knowledge of their constitutional and legal authority towards betterment of the people of their respective constituency irrespective of their sex, caste, creed and political affiliations;
(c) to discharge their functions assigned for their respective offices (viz. pradhans, sabhapatis, sabhadhipatis, karmadhyakshas and the like) with the skills and knowledge delivered through the training courses; and
(d) to become more effective, in comparison with the pre-training stage, in dealing with different stakeholders of their respective areas and the government officials placed at their disposal for carrying out the functions and duties of the panchayats in appropriate tier.

Achievement of enabling objectives is reflected through the performance of the panchayats in different tiers. The investments on training that the Central and State Governments are making can only be justified in terms of real achievement of these objectives. It is expected that the objectives have to be demonstrated by way of actual improvement of functioning of the panchayat bodies at the end of completion of training programmes for different categories of representatives. Along with the knowledge of different provisions of the WBP Act, the panchayat members holding offices in their panchayats should have the skills in respect of budgeting, revenue collection, implementing schemes, formulating plans for their respective tier along with maintenance of relevant data, conducting meetings effectively and purposefully, preparation of different reports and returns, etc. Training courses are designed on the basis of the knowledge and skill requirement of the target group learners.

The panchayat members in general have the advantage of possessing ground level experiences and working with the common people. There may be differences in respect of socio-economic background and other traits like level of understanding, problem-solving ability or capacity to communicate with the cross-section of people. At the time of making arrangements for their training these possibilities are very much in the back of mind of training designers at SIPRD. Only lecture method of training is not followed. Largely, participatory approach of training has been considered in such trainings. Lecture method has inherent disadvantages in the training of adults as the learners have very little opportunity for participation in the training process. For making the sessions participatory, the widely used training methods are: brainstorming, case studies, group exercises and panel discussions. Each of these methods has their own advantages and disadvantages. For example, brainstorming method is used for problem-solving. The exercises help the learners to concretize their understanding through trial and error. Participation of learners may be with or without conscious knowledge. Those with little or no knowledge get the scope for developing themselves through conceptual clarity and participative deliberations. Still there remains the possibility that some training-participants may not participate in the process. The prominent reasons may be their shyness (this is found to be true in case of women panchayat members coming to this Institute for the first time). In such cases, the course coordinators exercise their skills to break the ice. Group exercise is a widely adopted training technique in course of training of the panchayat members. Experiential learning helps to reinforce each other in the smaller groups followed by the presentation of group exercise in the larger groups. This method is particularly pursued in case of learning sessions earmarked for skill development. It was noticed that even in the late night, the participants seemed to be grossly engaged in group exercises for finalizing their views. The groups are in general formed after observing the entry behaviour of the participants and their place of residence. Its only disadvantage is that it is very much time consuming and requires high trainers' skill for reviewing the outcome of such group exercise and transfer of learning. At the district and sub-district level trainings there remains the chances that the efficiency of this training method gets diluted. This is due to non-availability of required expertise and conducive training environment. In view of the large number of elected representatives in three tiers of the panchayat structure, it is simply impossible for this State Institute to provide training to all members within a given time frame. As such a team of trainers at the district level was formed by the district administration. The training of the district level teams is the responsibility of SIPRD.

As delineated in State Government Policy (2003) for training of newly elected panchayat members and officials of the panchayati raj institutions, sub-divisions are selected as the principal node for organizing training at the districts. This has been done in view of the large size of many districts in West Bengal. For example in Burdwan district there are 277 gram panchayats with 4346 gram panchayat members. In Table 4, district-wise number of gram panchayats and panchayat samiti (blocks) are given to have an idea on the dimension of the task of completing the first phase of training of all the panchayat members within a period of one year from the date of assuming their respective offices. It is expected that this will enable them to be acquainted 'with the perspectives and procedures relevant to their assigned tasks'.

There are 12 districts where the number of gram panchayats is more than 150. To train at least pradhan and upa-pradhan of all gram panchayats means a target of 300 persons. When sub-division-wise distribution of members would be made the task will be easy as the target group gets reduced. According to the directives of the State Government there should be a team of preferably 6 to 9

Table 4 : Number of Gram Panchayats and Panchayat Samitis in Districts: West Bengal.

District	*Number of Gram Panchayats*	*Number of Panchayat Samitis*	*Prodhan and upa-Pradhan to be trained*	*Sabhapati/ Sahakari Sabhapati to be trained*
Bankura	190	22	380	44
Birbhum	167	19	334	38
Burdwan	277	31	554	62
Cooch Behar	128	12	256	24
Dakshin Dinajpur	65	8	130	16
Hooghly	210	18	420	36
Howrah	157	14	314	28
Jalpaiguri	146	13	292	26
Malda	146	15	292	30
Murshidabad	254	26	508	52
Nadia	187	17	374	34
24 Parganas (North)	200	22	400	44
24 Parganas (South)	312	29	624	58
Paschim Midnapore	290	29	580	58
Purba Midnapore	223	25	446	50
Purulia	170	20	340	40
Uttar Dinajpur	98	9	196	18
Total	**3220**	**329**	**6440**	**658**

Source: Department of Panchayats and Rural Development, Govt. of West Bengal.
Note: The table excludes Darjeeling district. The election to the gram panchayats, panchayat samitis and Mahakuma parishad of this district was not held during the Panchayat General Election held in 2003.

resource persons for the district level trainers team. Each team will consist of 2 to 3 government officials (including retired government officers/officers of para-statal organisations), 2 to 3 ex-panchayat functionaries/total literacy campaign resource persons and 2 to 3 from non-governmental organisations working in the areas. It has been clearly specified in the instruction from the State Government that the government officers and ex-panchayat functionaries should preferably be from the sub-division itself. This condition is imposed for ensuring the availability of resource persons. However for NGOs, outsourcing is permitted provided no such person is available in the jurisdiction of the sub-division. Thus, District Level Trainers Teams (DLTT) is formed sub-divisionwise. Only for the districts with smaller sub-division, such as Cooch Behar this norm is slightly relaxed. In Cooch Behar district for five sub-divisions, three DLTTs are constituted. For training of DLTT members, 17 courses of Training of Trainers (TOT) were organised immediately after the panchayat members assumed their offices. A trainers team at the State level in the name of State Level Master Trainers' Team (SLMTT) was also formed to provide training to DLTT members. This SLMTT was composed of 63 members where at least 30 are from NGOs. The rest are from the government sector including SIPRD.

As regards the design of the training course of TOT, 6 day schedule is taken up. The design covers most of the learning events starting from training methodology to overview of different rural development programmes. A synoptic view of the training design prepared for TOT of DLTT may help to understand the coverage of subject matters.

Day	*Subject matter*	*Time allotted*
One	Participatory Training methods, use of various aids, management of training	6 hours
Two	Historical background of West Bengal panchayats West Bengal Panchayat Act and Rules; structure, functions, roles and responsibilities of panchayats	8 hours
Three	(a) Issues related to self-governance; Resource mobilisation, Budget, Audit (b) Natural resource management	6 hours 2 hours
Four	(a) Women's empowerment and role of self-help groups (b) Health, family welfare and primary education (c) Disaster management	3 hours 4 hours 1 hour
Five	(a) Overview of major rural development and social security programmes implemented by the panchayats (b) Decentralised Planning : concept, methods and implementation process	4 ½ hours 3 ½ hours
Six	(a) Practice sessions by participants (b) Training Management (c) Further review of the training design	3 hours 1 ½ hours 3 hours

For the members of the panchayats, the Department of Panchayats and Rural Development, Government of West Bengal decided to hold seven categories of training programmes to be completed within two years of assuming their offices. The categories of trainings and the location are presented below:

Particulars of Training Course	*Duration*	*Location of Training*
(i) Crash course for pradhans and upa-pradhans	2 days	Block/ sub-division
(ii) Crash course for sabhapatis and sahakari sabhapatis	2 days	District/ sub-division
(iii) Orientation course for Gram Panchayat Members	3 days	Block/ sub-division
(iv) Orientation course for Panchayat Samiti Members	3 days	District/ sub-division
(v) Orientation course for Zilla Parishad Members	3 days	SIPRD/ District
(vi) Thematic course for Karmadhyakshyas of Panchayat Samitis and Zilla Parishads	3 days	SIPRD
(vii) Refresher course for Gram Panchayat Members	3 days	Block/ sub-division

From the categorization of training programmes it can be understood that the State Government made elaborate arrangements for the training of the panchayat members in different tiers. The crash course for the gram panchayat and panchayat samiti chairpersons and vice-chairpersons are organised for making them conversant with the minimum procedures for management of their respective offices.

Orientation courses for gram panchayat, panchayat samiti and zilla parishad members are organised for enabling them to have an idea about the duties and responsibilities of the panchayat institutions. The courses are structured in such a manner that after receiving the training they would be able to identify the significance of the panchayats as an institution for good governance and social justice. The learning events of these courses can be broadly categorized into six groups. Session plan-wise allotment of time for them is given in Table 5 for understanding of the importance of these courses.

These sessions are conducted by DLTT members at district/sub-division/block venues and by the faculty of SIPRD and experts from the functional departments at SIPRD.

Table 5 : Synoptic view of learning events of the orientation courses.

Learning events category	*Gram panchayat members*	*Panchayat samiti members*	*Zilla parishad members*
(i) Office procedure	1 hr.	1 ½ hrs.	1 hr.
(ii) Structure and functions of the panchayats (respective tier)	1 hr.	2 hrs.	2 hrs.
(iii) Social issues in rural areas	3 hrs.	2 hrs.	2 hrs.
(iv) Intervention of the panchayats (respective tier)	9 hrs.	8 hrs.	7 hrs.
(v) Resource mobilisation	1 hr.	1 ½ hrs.	1 hr.
(vi) Decentralized planning	2 hrs.	2 hrs.	2 hrs.

Source : Records of SIPRD.

Note : In case of Zilla Parishad members sometimes have been kept for group exercises.

In the office procedure sessions (half hourly duration) the learning events include different provision of WBP Act in respect of the meetings of the panchayats, the systems of record keeping and documentation and rudimentary knowledge about the financial management of their respective tier. Social issues session includes interactive discussion/panel discussion on issues related to education (with focus on universalisation of primary education), health and family welfare, problems of scheduled castes and scheduled tribes, women empowerment including self help groups, infrastructure building, etc. Interventions of the panchayats in their respective jurisdictions are discussed in conformity with the provisions laid down in the WBP Act and the executive orders issued by the State Government in different times.

Thematic courses for the Karmadhyakshas of all Sthayee Samitis in panchayat samitis and zilla parishads have the main objective to build up their knowledge about the functioning of their concerned Sthayee Samitis. In these courses bulk of the sessions are devoted on the government programmes and their proper implementation by the panchayats. Before going into the role and responsibilities of the respective Sthayee Samitis, 3-hour time slot is kept for giving an idea about the structure and functions of the Sthayee Samitis, the responsibility of Karmadhyakshas and their relationship with the panchayat samiti. Artha, Sanstha, Unnayan-O-Parikalpana Sthayee Samiti (Finance, Establishment, Development and Planning Standing Committee) in fact is the apex of all the sthayee samitis. According to the provisions of the WBP Act, all Karmadhyakshas of different stahyee samitis in a panchayat samiti or in a zilla parishad are ex-officio members of Artha Sthayee Samiti. This is like a coordinating body also. The summary view of the contents of the training courses for Karmadhyakshas except Artha, Sanstha, Unnayan-O-Parikalpana are given below:

Sl. No.	*Sthayee Samiti*	*Brief contents*
(i)	Krishi, Sech-O-Samabay	Problems of agriculture development, Irrigation coverage, watershed development, cultivation of cash crops, alternative agriculture like horticulture development, programmes of cooperation department and cooperative societies [Agriculture - 15 hrs. Cooperation - 2 hrs.]
(ii)	Kshudra Silpa, Bidyut-O-Achiracharit Shakti	Role of village and small industries in rural development and employment generation, government programmes in these areas, bank loan provisions, programmes of sericulture, Khadi and Handloom Development, Rural Electrification, Programmes for development of non-conventional energy. [Village and small industry - 6 ½ hrs. Rural Electrification - 5 hrs. Non-conventional energy - 1 hr.]
(iii)	Janasasthya-O-Paribesh	Concept of Public health, Programmes of Health and Family Welfare Department, Programmes to combat Malnutrition, Sanitation, Birth and Death registration, Environment and allied issues. [Public health etc. - 9 hrs. Environment - 3 hrs.]

Contd. ...

(iv)	Siksha, Sanskriti, Tathya-O-Krira	Reflections from elementary education scenario, District Primary Education Programme, NGO involvement, Universalisation of Primary Education, Infrastructure for primary education, Sishu Siksha Karmasuchi (SSK), Rural Library, Programmes of Department of Culture and Information and Department of sports and youth affairs. [Education - 11 hrs. Others - 3 hrs.]
(v)	Shshu-O-Nari, Janakalyan-O-Tran	Status of women and children in different districts, SHG and women empowerment : concept and practice, programmes for women and child development including ICDS programme, social security concept and social welfare programmes of the State Government, Relief matters. [Women and child development - 10 hrs. Social welfare - 2 hrs. Relief - 2 hrs.]
(vi)	Matsya-O-Pranisampad Bikash	Pisciculture and Animal Husbandry development in employment generation and integrated rural development, pisciculture practice, programmes of the Department of Fisheries and Animal Husbandry and Animal Resources Development. [Fisheries - 6 hrs. Animal Resource Development etc. - 7 hrs.]
(vii)	Purta Karya-O-Paribahan	Concept of infrastructure and existing scenario, Infrastructure building for poverty alleviation and employment generation, government programmes for infrastructure building in rural areas and role of the panchayats, rudimentary technical knowledge, transport sector. [Purtakarya - 12 hrs. Transport - 2 hrs.]
(viii)	Ban-O-Bhumi Sanskar	Land Reforms and its different facets, government programmes in land reforms, forest department programmes, joint forest management and role of the panchayats. [Land Reforms - 8 hrs. Forest sector - 6 hrs.]
(ix)	Khadya-O-Sarbaraha	Concept of Food Security, Antyodaya and Annapurna Yojana, Public Distribution System and its working, Food Department's Role and function and relationship with the panchayats. [Conceptual part - 4 hrs. PDS - 4 hrs. Government Programmes - 5 hrs.]

Source: Training Modules prepared by SIPRD.

Note: Time allocation for different learning events are shown within brackets.

In case of Artha, Sanstha, Unnayan-O-Parikalpana, thrust is placed on office management, record-keeping and documentation, conflict resolution and co-ordination among sthayee samitis, budget preparation, audit, data base building for planning and plan formulation process. As the Karmadhyakshas of Artha Sthayee Samitis are also the Sabhapatis of panchayat samitis/Sabhadhipatis of zilla parishads, the training design is prepared to include all such learning events.

An important training event in the capacity building process of the panchayat members is the training for chairpersons (Adhyaksha) and vice-chairpersons (Upadhyaksha) of District Councils. The learning events include the provisions of the WBP Act in respect of structure and functions of the District Council, budget preparation at different tiers of the panchayat, major government programmes, different technicalities in the preparation of schemes for infrastructure development by different tiers of the panchayats, the conceptual underpinning of involving people in the activities of the panchayats, the methods of inspection, etc. All sessions are based on interactive discussions, experience sharing and group discussions. The use of lecture method is very limited. The duration of the course according to the design spans over three days. These participatory methods seems to be effective because majority of the participants in this course are found to be the storehouse of experiences.

This systematic approach to training of the panchayat members include development of a large number of training materials including training booklets. The outcomes of a training programme are, to a large extent, dependent on the selection and development of suitable, need-based and appropriate course materials and training aids. For the panchayat members in all three tiers, training booklets are printed and delivered to the district authorities for distribution among the members. In the training courses held at SIPRD, in addition to these booklets, copies of relevant government orders, guidelines of different programmes, brochures, etc. are also distributed. It is expected that all these become the permanent documents for the participants and can serve as reference in their work places. The booklets are prepared in Bengali for all districts except Darjeeling. For Darjeeling, Nepali version of the texts is prepared. However, the course materials/training booklets are not despatched to the participants in advance (this is true for both the SIPRD and district administration). Advance despatch has some advantages provided the participants go through them for getting an idea about the learning events before coming for the training course.

One weak spot in the whole process of providing training to the panchayat members is found to be the low attendance of Karmadhyakshas in training courses held at SIPRD. In training programmes held at districts/sub-divisions and blocks, attendance of the members is fairly good. This may be for the proximity of the training venues to their places of residence. Availability of travelling allowances and communication of training programmes well before the scheduled dates are the two important factors influencing the attendance of the members. SIPRD in general sends messages to the district authorities for onward transmission to the participants located at different parts of the districts. From district it goes to block sometimes through sub-division. The chance of transit loss cannot be ruled out in such a long route.

With the discussions on the training contents and the methodologies pursued, in the next section, some limitations of the existing system are pointed out. These limitations need to be addressed with proper care for making the capacity building exercises effective.

SECTION III

In the existing framework for training of the panchayat members, no serious attempts have been taken for evaluation of the training programmes so far completed. For increasing efficiency of the panchayat members at different tiers and holding different offices, evaluation of the training programmes is very crucial. Three things are very vital in the process of capacity building exercises. First, whether the quality of training available is satisfactory to the participants; second, does the provision of training result in their improved performance; and third, can the investment in training made by the State Government and Government of India be justified? At SIPRD, some feedback from the participants are taken after completion of a training course. This gives some clues for the first question. However, no external validation of the training programmes are conducted either by the SIPRD or by the district authorities. As a consequence, impact assessment of these training programmes cannot be made. In the cycle of systematic approach to training, if evaluations of training programmes are not made, the cycle remains incomplete. The cycle looks like this:

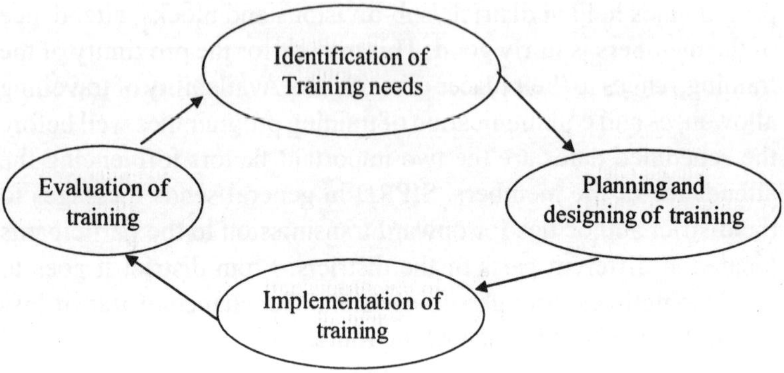

Internal validation provides feedback about the quality of training the participants received. This included content of the course, methodology pace, learning materials, resource persons, etc. But it cannot throw any light on the performance of the participants. For this purpose, evaluations of training programmes are the must. This area calls for adequate attention, because in its absence improvement in training design and identification of needs cannot be undertaken. After getting the evaluation results, the SAT cycle restarts with necessary revision of training needs. Effective system of evaluation of training of the panchayat members need to be evolved both at SIPRD and at the districts.

So far, training remains an one shot operation in case of the panchayat members. In their five-year term, generally for once they get this chance. That too within first two years of the term. Considering the huge number, SIPRD has no capacity to organize refresher courses for the Karmadhyakshas, Sabhapatis and Sabhadhipatis. For enhancing the effectiveness of the panchayat members holding offices in their respective tiers, refresher courses are essential. The interactive discussions in such courses may help them to clear doubts in many fronts of discharging responsibilities. The alternative solution is the installation of Video Conference Facility (VCF) at SIPRD to establish contact with all the gram panchayats and the panchayat samitis. This was already done in Abdul Nazir Sab State Institute for Rural Development (ANS-SIRD) in Karnataka. ANS-SIRD is ready to train 'around 80,000 elected representatives of the gram panchayats through satellite communication on sectoral issues'[4] (*The Hindu*, dated 27.2.2005). This move is expected to strengthen panchayati raj institutions and its members through capacity building. *The Hindu* news is worth quoted here :

> "Over the next two years and half years, the institute using audio and visual mode, will train over 95,000 elected representatives and well over a lakh panchayati raj functionaries. The training involves 80,000 elected members of gram panchayat and nearly 15,000 members of taluk and zilla panchayats. This satellite based training programmes, which costs around Rs. 30 crores, is the biggest exercise conducted through satellite communication in the country."[4]

In West Bengal this is not possible in near future. Till now even all blocks are not covered with computers and satellite connectivity. Majority of the gram panchayats has not even the facility of having a computer. With these initial bottlenecks, the establishment of VCF and the network is a matter of distant future. All depends on the initiatives of the State Government and availability of funds. An indication for establishing PRI-Network is made in the Annual Administrative Report (2003-04) of the Department of Panchayats and Rural Development :

> "Initiatives have been taken with the help of NIC and BSNL for effective connectivity among the different actors in Panchayat and Rural Development (P&RD) from the Panchayat Samiti and Zilla Parishads with the Department during the Tenth Five Year Plan Period."

This proposed connectivity excludes the gram panchayats which urges for better care and support. At the gram panchayat, on one hand the Pradhan acts as the Drawing and Disbursing Officer (DDO) and has to sign the cheques, and on the other hand the number of government officials having adequate knowledge and experience of working in government offices is less in comparison with the panchayat samitis and zilla parishads. Thus, the Pradhan requires huge functional support and guidance from the higher levels. At panchayat samiti and zilla parishad, the chairpersons are not required to function as DDO and have adequate staff support. For overcoming the functional disabilities of the Pradhans, it is suggested that at least three refresher courses need to be organised after the orientation course. These refresher courses may be conducted at district/sub-division level with the DLTT members. For the Pradhans of backward districts like Purulia, Bankura, Paschim Midnapore, South 24 Parganas, SIPRD may take the responsibility. The duration of a refresher course may be three days, with more time on getting their experiences and removal of the functional weaknesses through inculcation of knowledge and skill. Arrangements for exposure visits to the best practice gram panchayats and panchayat samitis may prove to be beneficial. But these are not in practice in West Bengal. As the duration of the trainings is normally short and the learning events are huge, these exposure visits may be arranged after the completion of training courses. Separate provisions for funds may be made by the State Government out of the training budget for the panchayat members. Here also SIPRD can play the role of a coordinator.

Concluding Remarks

Capacity building exercise is a continuous process. It does not end with implementation of the training programmes only. For its continuity it is suggested that the State Governments should "include training as an important activity at all levels of Panchayati Raj set up through an appropriate mechanism". (Indian Panchayati Raj Report, 2001). Strengthening and upgradation of training infrastructure in a comprehensive way can extend the scope for accommodating more training programmes. At present in West Bengal there is only one institute at the State level for the training of official functionaries engaged in rural development and the panchayat representatives. This is certainly inadequate. At a time only 130 persons can be provided with hostel facilities at SIPRD for residential training. If all functionaries in rural development sector are counted their number will be approximately 25,000. The gram panchayat functionaries for whom the State Government bears the salary etc. are normally not covered by SIRPD. In fact they have very little exposure to training. For the government officials at the panchayat samitis, it is possible to cover the Executive Officers (Block Development Officers), Joint Executive Officers (Joint Block Development Officers) and extension officers of different departments. According to the present trend, in general they also cannot get chance for training at an interval of two years. The State Government has taken the initiative to build up Extension Training Centres in five districts with 100 per cent assistance under non-recurring grant assistance from the Ministry of Rural Development, Government of India. These extension centres will meet the training requirements of the districts and function under the leadership of SIPRD. Except participation in DLTT, involvement of NGOs may be explored for this sphere as they can supplement the State efforts. The experience of working with NGOs is very positive in Total Sanitation Campaign and self-help group formation. The Tenth Five Year Plan also suggested increasing space for NGO sector and to evolve synergic relationships with the panchayats for delivery of services and augmenting own capacities. To quote:

> "The delivery of programmes would improve only if the PRIs emerge as strong players in the social and economic life of the country. NGOs and other civil society organisations can facilitate the evolution of PRIs as institutions geared to promote the well-being of the rural poor." (Volume II Chapter 3.2)

Thus, capacity building of the panchayats and their members is of great need for fulfilling the aspirations ushered in with the passage of the Constitution (Seventy Third Amendment) Act, 1992.

NOTES

1. The years of holding panchayat general elections are 1978, 1983, 1988,1993, 1998 and 2003.
2. It was possible by SIPRD to prepare study reports on socio-economic profile in respect of six districts viz. Midnapore, Bankura, South 24 Parganas, Cooch Behar, Hooghly and Howrah.
3. In West Bengal there are 18 districts with rural segment. Out of these, in each 17 districts (except Darjeeling) there is a zilla parishad. In plain area of Darjeeling district, there is a Mahakuma parishad at Siliguri sub-division. For the hill areas of the district there is no panchayat system at block and district level.
4. The proposed Extension Training Centres are in the districts of Uttar Dinajpur, Paschim Midnapore, Cooch Behar (through renovation of the existing Panchayati Raj Training Centre), North 24 Parganas and Burdwan.

REFERENCES

Department of Panchayats and Rural Development, *Annual Administrative Report, 2003-04*, Government of West Bengal: Department of Panchayats and Rural Development, 2004.

Department of Personnel and Training, *Course Materials for Design of Training Course,* Government of India: Department of Personnel and Training, 2000.

Government of West Bengal, *The West Bengal Panchayat Act, 1973*, (as modified up to the 31st January, 2004), Government of West Bengal, 2004.

National Institute of Rural Development, *India Panchayati Raj Report, Volume I,* Hyderabad: National Institute of Rural Development, 2001.

Planning Commission, *Tenth Five-Year Plan (2002-07), Volume II,* Government of India: Planning Commission, 2002.

The Hindu, Capacity Building programme for panchayat members, Karnataka (news published on 27.2.2005), 2005.

4

CAPACITY BUILDING OF GRASSROOTS LEADERS IN TAMIL NADU

G. PALANITHURAI

Capacity building is an imperative for the elected representatives of the people at all levels from Grassroots to National Parliament. Capacity building for the elected representatives is not perceived in perspective and hence it is the most neglected area in governance. For the establishment of the three-tier governance at grassroots as an institution of self-government, conscientisation and capacity building are needed exercises to be done on a war footing. It not only builds the skills and managerial capacity of the elected representatives but also builds a movement for prosperity at the grassroots as the system has been created in such a way that the performance of the Panchayats can be evaluated and monitored constantly by the people. Cleansing operations for the establishment of good governance must start from the bottom. The present article highlights the capacity building exercises conducted in Tamil Nadu against the backdrop of the prevailing negative setting and its implications. The experience brings to light the emergence of the grassroots movement to utilize power and authority to decide on issues which affect the life of the people. It also indicates what is further needed to strengthen the grassroots democracy.

Introduction

'Capacity Building' is the most urgent and imperative step in every sector to cope with the pace of development at present. In market driven development activities enhancement of capacity plays an important role in placing individuals, organizations and associations in competition. Development sectors take conscious decisions to enhance the capacity of the professionals and personnel working in organizations and institutions. New technologies and institutional mechanics require conscious steps to enhance the capability of individuals who are handling technologies and new organizational mechanisms to use the full potential of the technologies and institutional structures to bring out the maximum competence.

The 73rd Amendment to the Constitution of India has created a structure at the grassroots for governance. It has come with a set of promises and assurances to the people[1]. Compelling global, national and regional contexts make everyone look at the new system contextually. The new system has its own roles and responsibilities and, to perform the assigned roles and responsibilities, the leaders who are managing the new system should build up their skill and capacity[2]. The new system has been created to break new ground in governance and to tackle the problems and issues which are unmet and unsolved through the policy options of the governments at the state and the central level. It should be clearly noted that the new institutions have to perform a variety of activities at the grassroots for which the grassroots leaders should have a clear-cut perception of the roles and responsibilities that are to be discharged and the skills needed to manage these institutions which are under the purview of the elected Panchayat leaders[3].

It is unfortunate that, in India, capacity building is not a serious issue for the representatives of the people who determine the fate of millions of people[4]. The elected representatives of the people do not feel that it is an imperative as it is considered in other sectors. In all sectors capacity building is a much valued exercise for the enhancement of their activities in their respective domains. But in politics it is not so and, as a result, one can notice a retrograde trend in politics.

However, in the Panchayati Raj scenario, it has been felt that, to manage the Panchayats, training is essential even though there is no training policy and no conscious steps have been taken by the government to build the capacity of the elected representatives of the people in the grassroots institutions. It has been argued time and again that training is an imperative and needs to be undertaken on a war footing. Yet only a few states have taken conscious steps and in many places it is only the voluntary organizations who have imparted training to local body leaders despite several constraints, like the absence of well developed training centres, training material and well equipped trainers[5].

In Tamil Nadu it is the demand of the Panchayat leaders that training should be given to Panchayat leaders and Panchayat functionaries to manage the institutions efficiently[6]. To cater to the needs of the local body leaders, there are enough training centres in Tamil Nadu. The Government of Tamil Nadu has established Rural Extension Training Centres in different regions and, at the state level, the State Institute of Rural Development. It is unfortunate that the Government sends unwanted employees to these training centres. As a result the training centres have lost their importance and value. They are mostly defunct. Further there is no training manual to train the Panchayat leaders and functionaries[7]. Realising the problems involved in training, the Rajiv Gandhi Chair for Panchayati Raj Studies took a conscious decision that it has to train Gram Panchayat Presidents for which a training manual has to be prepared.

Training in the First Phase

When the decision was taken to train Gram Panchayat leaders, what powers were going to be devolved, how much of fiscal devolution was going to be effected and what functionaries were going to be part of the Panchayats had not been spelt out. The Government of Tamil Nadu had allowed the Panchayats to perform the old civic functions along with agency functions to carry out the schemes and programmes of the central and state governments. Based on these activities a training module was prepared and training programmes were conducted. It was just a conscientization programme to change the mindset of the leaders by indicating the spirit of the 73rd Constitutional Amendment Act and the basic details about the Panchayati Raj Act of Tamil Nadu and its implications in the socio-economic and political transformation of the rural society. Gradually the sensitization programme was extended to other tiers with the financial support of various agencies.

Table 1 : Training Programmes Organised in Gandhigram Rural Institute.

Sl. No.	*Title*	*Sponsored Agency*	*Total No. of Leaders Trained*
1.	Empowering Panchayati Raj Institutions on Issues of Population, Health and Social Development	Population Foundation of India	6834
2.	Capacity Building for Gram Panchayat Presidents	CAPART	1369
3.	Training of Presidents and Vice-Presidents in Panchayat Administration with Special Reference to Water and Sanitation	DANIDA	814
4.	Training of Women Presidents of Gram Panchayats	Social Welfare Board	825
5.	Training of Trainers in Multi Level Planning	State Planning Commission	71
6.	Capacity Building for Weaker Sections in New Panchayati Raj System	CAPART	271
7.	Capacity Building Exercise for Gram Panchayat Women Leaders	The Hunger Project	390

Source : Computed.

Capacity Building Programmes

Total number of elected local body leaders trained	:	10,584
Total number of Panchayats covered	:	4,426
Districts covered	:	11

In the whole process of training what was achieved was that the Panchayat leaders were sensitized on the issues of democratic decentralization of powers and the bases of the 73rd Amendment to the Constitution of India and the issues of social development.

In the meanwhile the First State Finance Commission submitted its recommendations and they were placed before the Legislative Assembly[8]. Subsequently the L.C. Jain Committee[9] constituted for making recommendations on entrusting responsibilities to the three tier Panchayati institutions submitted its report. Based on the report, decisions were taken and the action taken report[10] was placed before the Legislative Assembly. Political parties, Panchayat leaders, academics and NGOs criticized the Government for not devolving needed powers to the local bodies and, as a result, yet another committee was constituted, with the Local Administration Minister[11] as the Chairperson and representatives of the major political parties as members, to look into the devolution process and to make recommendations. This committee also submitted its recommendations to the Government and action has been taken on the recommendations[12]. As a result many changes have been effected in the Act and several Government Orders have been passed. Thus the first period from 1996 to 2001 marked a transition period wherein steps were taken to transfer power to the local bodies in Tamil Nadu. For the Panchayat leaders, it was a period of guessing and the officials were also in the same predicament. Virtually all the three Panchayat tiers shared the Government schemes and implemented the same and, as a result, the Panchayats became agents of the State Government. Leaders elected to Panchayats became contractors.

Initiatives of Rajiv Gandhi Chair

During this period the Rajiv Gandhi Chair for Panchayati Raj Studies took a series of steps to prepare a training manual to train the Panchayat leaders with the support of the Ford Foundation. The manual was tested and published for the benefit of the NGOs who are interested in organizing training programmes for Panchayat leaders[13]. Following the preparation of the training manual, steps were taken to collect the needed information, namely, the amendments introduced on the Act, orders passed by the Government as well as rules and schemes and programmes of the Government of India and the Government of Tamil Nadu relating to rural development. They were collected and compiled as a basic referable document and published for wider circulation and for distribution in the training programmes for Panchayat leaders[14]. Even today the government offices do not have the updated Panchayat Act. So far the Government has passed eighty-four orders for Gram Panchayat administration alone. But not even a single Government Order has been sent to the Gram Panchayats. Yet Panchayat Presidents have been taken to task by the District Collectors as they have not followed the GOs. Panchayat Presidents ask how the Panchayat can follow the GOs in the absence of the GOs. So, with the help of retired staff, all Government Orders were collected from various departments along with the updated Act and rules. It took about a year to do this.

With the training module and the information package ready, the Rajiv Gandhi Chair identified a band of retired officials at the level of Additional Director for Rural Development based on their commitment, honesty and sincerity, as resource persons to impart training along with the Rajiv Gandhi Chair team. The Rajiv Gandhi Chair team has been already oriented on social development issues besides Panchayat administration. Along with the retired officials and the Rajiv Gandhi Chair team a few resource persons were drawn from NGOs as they run organizations for specific problems in the rural society such as environment, health care of child and women, RCH, child labour, human rights and natural resources management. Thus a comprehensive team was developed.

Apart from these arrangements, a specific initiative was taken to prepare a separate module for women as they require special leadership training. The Hunger Project, New Delhi, helped the Rajiv Gandhi Chair to prepare the training module on leadership and the same was published[15].

Along with the training modules, training materials to be used in the classroom were prepared. Because the educational background of the trainees varies from illiteracy to post-graduation, training aids were prepared in the form of charts. An artist was inducted in the

Table 2 : Training Programmes Organised in Gandhigram Rural Institute.

Sl.No.	*Name of the District*	*Total No.of Presidents*			*No.of Presidents attended the training*			*Percentage of Panchayat Presidents*		
		Men	*Women*	*Total*	*Men*	*Women*	*Total*	*Men*	*Women*	*Total*
1.	Pudukkottai	326	172	498	275	140	415	84	81	83
2.	Dindigul	200	105	305	191	100	291	96	95	95
3.	Tiruchirappalli	275	132	407	255	131	386	93	99	95
4.	Sivagangai	292	153	445	242	112	354	83	73	80
5.	Ramanathapuram	282	147	429	229	116	345	81	79	80
6.	Theni	82	48	130	66	43	109	80	90	84
7.	Karur	109	49	158	91	49	140	83	100	89
8.	Virudhunagar	303	144	447	245	103	348	81	72	78
	Total	**1869**	**950**	**2819**	**1594**	**794**	**2388**	**85**	**84**	**85**

Source: Computed.

team of resource persons, as his services were needed in the vision building class. Trainees would be asked to portray the existing conditions of the villages and to project their vision of how to develop the village. The entire vision was to be brought out in a chart.

With these preparations, the Rajiv Gandhi Chair approached the CAPART (Government of India) and The Hunger Project (New Delhi) for financial support to conduct training programmes for Gram Panchayat leaders of eight districts. The two agencies extended their support to conduct the programme. With the financial support of the CAPART, men leaders were trained and with the financial support of the Hunger Project women leaders were trained.

Collaboration

Before starting the training programme, a conscious decision was taken that the training programme should be conducted in collaboration with the Government of Tamil Nadu for two reasons. Gandhigram Rural Institute should be recognized as a nodal centre for training and officials should recognize the training programme which should not be duplicated by any other agencies. Secondly, Panchayat Presidents have to be brought to the training centre by the officials. It was very difficult to bring the Panchayat Presidents to training programmes in previous exercises. Further it was decided to have at least three officials dealing with Panchayats at the Block level from every Block in the training programme. To ensure attendance in the training programme Gandhigram Rural Institute needed the support of the Government. The training had to be made official. In this regard the Government issued an order[16]. As a result it is fully a Government recognized programme.

It was a fully residential programme. The Panchayat Presidents had to stay for five days in the campus of Gandhigram Rural Institute. Of the five days, three days would be devoted to Panchayat administration and two days to social development issues. Subjects such as the bases of decentralization of powers in the context of the globalization of the economy, Panchayat administration, Panchayat finance, common property resources management, people's participation, micro level planning, economic development, accounting and auditing procedures, Gram Sabha and its implications, social justice, and the implications of reservation of seats for women and Dalits were covered in three days. Social development issues such as sanitation, water supply, gender bias, child care, pre- and post-natal care, school environment, child labour, RCH and other issues were covered in the remaining two days of the five day programme. In each one and half hour lecture, half an hour was set aside for a question and answer session. Men and women had separate training classes. Special sèssions were arranged in the night both for men and women and all their doubts were cleared. Local and specific problems of the Gram Panchayats were discussed with the resource persons individually in the Gandhigram Rural Institute Guest House. It was an advantage that the entire team of resource persons stayed in the Gandhigram Rural Institute Guest House.

A special session was devoted to eliciting the Panchayat Presidents' problems in Panchayat administration. On the last day of the training programme the trainees were taken to the field and finally, they were asked to give their feedback.

Feedback from the Training

Before starting the training programme a questionnaire was circulated among the participants. This was done with the aim of assessing their level of understanding of Panchayat administration. It was noticed that excepting the Panchayat leaders elected for a second term, all the trainees knew only that the Panchayat provides an opportunity to serve people better and deliver services and were aware of a few schemes of the State and Central Government. It was observed that the Panchayat Presidents were virtually under the control of the Panchayat clerks and lower level officials working in the Block Development Offices. After imparting training their feedback was recorded. The Panchayat leaders had now learnt the details of their powers, duties and responsibilities, sources of income to the Panchayats, Panchayat management, common property resource management, removal of encroachments and accounting and auditing procedures. They further insisted that they need periodical refresher courses at least for a day every year and that, apart from the refresher courses, they need help, information and counselling regularly for which the Rajiv Gandhi Chair has to work as a nodal centre for Panchayats[17]. From the experience of the Panchayat leaders, suggestions were made for appropriate follow-up. The following are their suggestions:

Acts which contradict the provisions of the Tamil Nadu Panchayati Raj Act of 1994 have to be identified and suitable amendments have to be made. All officials have to be trained and sensitized on the New Panchayati Raj System. Many officials at lower levels do not understand the Act and the rules and, as a result, Panchayats land themselves in trouble. For proper Panchayat administration, an administrative manual has to be prepared and published. All Government Orders pertinent to Panchayat administration have to be compiled and kept in all the Panchayat offices as it has been done in Pudukkottai District. A review has to be undertaken of the actions taken by the District Collectors on Panchayat leaders by using provision 205 of the Tamil Nadu Panchayat Act of 1994. This suggestion was made because 80 per cent of the dismissals and suspensions have been stayed by courts. It means that the officials have erred somewhere.

No proper handing over and taking over takes place in Gram Panchayat administration after the election to the Panchayats. Records created by the previous Panchayat administration are not handed over to the newly elected Presidents. A sizeable area of common properties encroached upon by influential individuals are to be recovered. It can be done by the revenue department as a special drive. Though a Government Order has been passed, no Village Administrative Officer has handed over village maps to the Gram Panchayat Presidents and the properties of the Gram Panchayats have not been shown to the Gram Panchayat Presidents. The higher officials of the Revenue Department, preferably the Secretary for Revenue, has to instruct the Village Administrative Officers through an order that all poramboke lands of the Panchayats have to be identified and shown to the Gram Panchayat Presidents and that village maps have to be given to the Panchayats. House tax collection has to be made rigorous and revision has to be enforced. In most of the places the Panchayats want a direction from the

State Government to enhance the house tax as the Panchayat is seen as leader centric. Minor minerals revenue should go to Gram Panchayats. But now it is in court. Nobody takes action in this regard. As a result minor minerals are being lifted for the advantage of the mafia. The State Government has to take the initiative to expedite the case in the court.

Drinking water supply is going to become a difficult task in the years to come in the rural areas. There is no proper water management system, no regularization of illegal tap connections. All these problems have to be solved. Water policy and water regulation rules have to be evolved. Panchayats have to take the initiative for micro level plan which would turn the activities from a supply driven mode to a demand driven one. Huge sums have been spent in the villages by different agencies but the demands of the people projected in the Gram Sabha meeting remain unmet. Departments and representatives of the people have spent the money at their disposal in the rural areas as per their wish and perception. To avoid this kind of wastage, micro planning has to be initiated and thereby planned activities have to be carried out by pooling the resources of all the Departments and representatives of the people. Panchayat leaders have to be sensitized on social development issues. Awareness has to be created among the leaders about the status of rural areas in terms of social development. Panchayats have to keep the Electricity Board cards in the Panchayat office. Panchayat leaders have to monitor the electricity consumption and meter reading. In many Panchayats, the cards are not available in the Panchayat office and the Panchayat Presidents are not aware of the expenditure on electricity, because the cards are in the EB office. Wherever the Panchayat leaders are sensitized and conscious about the expenditure, they take action to reduce electricity consumption by fitting tubelights for streetlights, removing sodium vapour lights and regulating the water supply.

It should be made mandatory that all development works, whether sponsored by sectoral departments or the Central or the State Government, should be carried out in the Panchayat area with the approval of the Gram Sabha. Panchayat Presidents are being criticized for not convening Gram Sabha meetings seriously as the

Gram Sabha attendance is poor. When the proceedings, resolutions and demands of the Gram Sabha are not seriously considered by the officials, MLAs and MPs, how can one expect people to participate in the Gram Sabha meetings? People know that the Collector is powerful, the Project Officer, DRDA, is powerful, the MLA has Rs.77 lakhs and the MP two crore rupees at his/her disposal every year and hence people meet all these representatives and the Collector. Issue of birth, death and community certificates should be entrusted to the Panchayat administration. Certificates issued by the Panchayat should be provided for public verification. Funds earmarked for Panchayat activities should be directly given to Panchayats. The District Planning Committee has to take the initiative for evolving a perspective development plan for the district. The District Planning Committee has been constituted but there is no work assignment for the committee. A District Panchayat Secretary has been appointed planning officer but no planning work has been entrusted to him. Manuals have been prepared for planning, training has been conducted for officials in multi level planning and yet there is no systematic planning at the grassroots.

Officials should not allow the husbands of the women Panchayat Presidents either to participate in the official meetings or to sign any of the papers which are to be signed by the elected women representatives. In many of the districts, lower level officials encourage the male family members of the women leaders either to attend meetings to carry out activities. If officials are very strict in this regard either genuine women will emerge as leaders or the men of the women leaders' families will change their attitude. Most of the women leaders insist that a very strict order has to be issued to the officials not to encourage the husbands of the women leaders to participate in the official meetings.

For each Panchayat an untied fund up to a maximum of Rs. 5,00,000 could be given with an instruction that the amount should be spent only for economic activities, particularly employment generation and social development, as it has been done in Kerala. For women and Dalits a special development component plan could be developed. Panchayati Raj Institutions require a State level Director to look after the functioning of Panchayati Raj Institutions as per the recommendations of the Swaminathan Committee. At present there is no State level authority to monitor the functioning of the Panchayati Raj Institutions. All officials, top to bottom, are interested in monitoring the implementation of schemes though they are not legally authorized to intervene in Panchayati Raj affairs. As a result the Panchayat administration is not properly monitored and helped. To make the Panchayati Institutions from District Panchayat to Gram Sabha institutions of self-government, their functioning has to be monitored and corrective steps have to be taken then and there, for which a State level officer has to be given charge of these institutions. Revenue from forestry has to come to Panchayats. But no effort has been made in this regard. Panchayat leaders have repeatedly pleaded in vain for the dues to Panchayats. Appropriate initiatives have to be taken by the district administration in this regard.

Village Panchayats which are very near to industrial estates can get a lot of revenue by way of house-tax, building-tax, layout approval fee and plan approval fee. But now it does not happen so in many of the cases because the Panchayat Presidents are not aware of the rules. In certain cases the rules are misused for the advantage of some leaders. In many of the cases house-tax assessment is very poor or sometimes it is wrong. Proper assessment has to be made. In many places, huge amounts of revenue are being lost due to improper assessment. This has to be rectified. Cheque transactions could be avoided and the entire amount could be sent to the bank account of the Panchayats for all activities by which corruption could be eliminated since all Panchayats maintain bank accounts. This suggestion is made because of the demands made by officials whenever they issue cheques to Panchayats. Unless the Panchayat President pays a sum, cheques will not be released. Still a major portion of the common properties are vested with traditional Panchayats. They get huge amounts of revenue from common properties but they pay very little to the Gram Panchayats. In many places auctions of commons are taken by the traditional Panchayats at a nominal rate and the same commons are reauctioned for a huge sum. The traditional Panchayats keep the lion's share after remitting the meagre dues to the Panchayats. In many places the traditional Panchayats work in tandem with formal Panchayats.

In some places they are at loggerheads. This is to be studied seriously and appropriate action has to be taken.

All sectoral departments have to inform the Panchayat Presidents about the schemes and programmes they are going to carry out in the Panchayat area. The Panchayats are given powers, not to decide about the works to be carried out but to help the sectoral departments to implement and carry out the activities. But, at present, the sectoral departments do not even consult or inform the Panchayats about the programmes being carried out in the Panchayat areas. If the annual plan preparation is done in every Panchayat, the sectoral departments' activities could be integrated with the plans of the Panchayats. Whenever a licence is issued for quarrying, a copy of the licence should be sent to the Panchayats.

Panchayat leaders at Gram Panchayat level feel that the District Collectors have to convene a meeting of Gram Panchayat leaders once in a while and help the Panchayat administration by eliminating hurdles created by lower level officials. It would help not only the Panchayat administration but also the district administration for speedy implementation of schemes and programmes. Wherever the District Collector establishes direct contact with Gram Panchayat leaders, the Panchayat administration is streamlined and strengthened and innovative practices are developed while implementing the schemes and programmes. The best innovative practices have to be documented properly and scientifically and they have to be disseminated through the media[18].

Table 3: Overall Feedback of the Participants about the Training Programme.

Sl. No.	*Training Details*	*Fully satisfied*	*To some extent*	*Not satisfied*	*Total*
1.	Materials Supplied	2124	149	115	2388
2.	Classes Handled	2218	112	58	2388
3.	Quality of Resource Persons	2220	118	50	2388
4.	Accommodation	1922	321	145	2388
5.	Food	2015	330	043	2388
6.	Classroom and Training Facilities	2119	218	051	2388
7.	Programme Coordinator's Role	2301	040	047	2388
8.	Cooperation of Officials	1880	322	186	2388
9.	Duration of Training Programme	2010	248	130	2388

Source: Computed.

At present Panchayat institutions are not functioning as a system but discretely and individually in a leader centric or officer centric manner. Both officials and leaders perceive Panchayat affairs as their affairs. Both leaders and officials are not well versed in the rules of the game. To make the Panchayat an institution of real self-government a series of steps have to be taken[19].

Integrated Analysis

Of the two-phase training, the second phase was scientific as it was conducted with the guidelines of the manual and by a good training team. The participants, namely the Panchayat Presidents, attended the programme with a volley of questions. The precise roles and responsibilities to be performed by the Panchayat leaders and the resources and grants which are due to Panchayats were clear. Information to be supplied to the leaders were compiled and distributed to them. In the training programme they were briefed about their destination and where they are now and how they have to reach their destination. In the first phase the Panchayat leaders were groping in the dark but now they were enlightened leaders with a sense of commitment. Finding the environment not positive towards devolution of powers to Panchayats, the Panchayat leaders had formed their own associations region-wise and integrated them into a federation. Women leaders had formed their own federation and Dalit Panchayat leaders had formed their own outfit[20]. These associations and federations demanded powers. Further, to clarify day to day administrative problems, Gandhigram Rural Institute with the collaboration of a popular vernacular (Tamil) daily, namely *Dinamalar* had started a weekly supplement (every Monday) under the caption 'Panchayat Malar' which carries Panchayat news and information. For the 'Panchayat Malar' the Rajiv Gandhi Chair does all the work for the entire page, recording the struggles and the successes of Panchayats, providing useful information for effective Panchayat administration, and, giving answers to the questions of the public and Panchayat leaders on the affairs of Panchayats[21]. Gandhigram Rural Institute, with the support of The Hunger Project, New Delhi, conducted a workshop for journalists and sensitized them on the issues of Panchayati Raj and development. Now the media is focusing attention on the successes and struggles of the Panchayats[22]. Gradually the grassroots movement is emerging as a popular movement, gaining momentum from the people, wherein training plays a major role.

Conclusion

Capacity building and information dissemination are the two prerequisites for the effective functioning of local bodies at present. But it is unfortunate that serious thought has not been given to training since there is no policy on training. Conducting training programmes is not easy as it requires several facilities and a well trained team of trainers. Further it requires a volley of information pertinent to Panchayati administration. By imparting training, the skills and the capacity of the Panchayat leaders have been enhanced. The existing conditions and the way in which Panchayats are being administered have been identified only through the training programmes. Steps which are to be taken to put the Panchayats on the proper track have been identified. From the experience of Gandhigram Rural Institute it is perceived that by building the capacity of the leaders of grassroots institutions, a movement can be generated with the active participation of the people for the establishment of the Panchayati System as an institution of self-government. One need not wait for the initiative of the government either for the preparation of a manual and a module for training and for conducting capacity building exercises. If a few NGOs join together the right kind of leadership can be developed at the grassroots and through them the people could be mobilized for the establishment of grassroots institutions. Through the capacity building exercise, the leaders can be sensitised as to where they are now in terms of devolution of powers and where they have to go in consonance with the spirit of the Constitutional Amendment for devolution of powers and a strong people's movement can be mobilized with the initiative of the grassroots leaders. As a result Panchayats can move to the right track to reach the destination.

NOTES

1. Rajiv Gandhi Foundation, *Charter of Panchayats*, New Delhi: Rajiv Gandhi Foundation, 1998.
2. Government of Tamil Nadu, *Democratic Decentralization: Powers Entrusted to Panchayati Raj Institutions*, Chennai: Rural Development Department, 1999.
3. D.Bandyopadhyay, Amitava Mukerjee and Mitali Sen Gavani, *Empowering Panchayats, Handbook for Master Trainers using Participatory Approach*, New Delhi: Concept Publishing Company, 2003.
4. G.Palanithurai, *Role Perceptions of Legislations: A Case Study of Tamil Nadu*, New Delhi: Konarak Publishers, 1991.
5. M.Aslam, *Directory of Panchayati Raj Training Institutions in India,* New Delhi: Rajiv Gandhi Foundation, 2001.
6. Panchayat Leaders have made such demands in their federation meetings and while submitting petitions to the Government.
7. In the month of June 2003, the Government of Tamil Nadu released the training module along with a G.O. 14440/2003 dt. 28.4.2003. It is stated in the G.O. that wherever Gandhigram Rural Institute conducts training for Local Body Leaders the Government should not conduct similar training.
8. State Finance Commission, *First State Finance Commission Report,* Chennai: State First Finance Commission, 1995.
9. State Planning Commission, *Report on Entrustment of Responsibilities to Three Tier Panchayats,* Chennai: State Planning Commission, 1997.
10. Government of Tamil Nadu, *Action Taken Report on the Entrustment of Responsibilities to Three Tier Panchayats*, Chennai: Department of Rural Development, 1998.
11. Government of Tamil Nadu, *Report on Roles, Responsibilities and Powers Devolved to Panchayats*, Chennai: Government of Tamil Nadu, 1998.
12. Government of Tamil Nadu, *Action Taken Report on the Entrustment of Responsibilities to Three Tier Panchayats*, Chennai: Government of Tamil Nadu, 1999.
13. Rajiv Gandhi Chair, *Training Module for Panchayat Training Progress,* Gandhigram: Rajiv Gandhi Chair for Panchayati Raj Studies, 2002.
14. G. Palanithurai, *Tamil Nadu Panchayati Government Act, Rules and Schemes (in Tamil),* Chennai: South Vision, 2002.
15. The Hunger Project, *Training Module for Leadership Training for Women in Panchayat,* Gandhigram: Rajiv Gandhi Chair for Panchayati Raj Studies, 2002.
16. Letter from the Director of Rural Development, Government of Tamil Nadu Rc.No.85678/2002/Training dt.17.9.2003.

17. Since the participants demanded a service and support centre to provide information to the Panchayat leaders, the Rajiv Gandhi Chair decided to launch an on line service and the Panchayat leaders have been asked to contact the phone number 0451-2451775 for any help.
18. All the points drawn from the Panchayat Presidents were submitted to the Secretary to Government, Department of Rural Development and Director of Rural Development, Government of Tamil Nadu on 30th June, 2003.
19. In the meanwhile an interface meeting between the higher officials and women representatives of Gram Panchayats was arranged and facilitated by the Rajiv Gandhi Chair on 11th July, 2003 at Chennai.
20. Gram Panchayat Presidents have formed a Federation which is called the Federation of Gram Panchayat Leaders of Tamil Nadu. Women Gram Panchayat Leaders have formed their own federation called the Tamil Nadu Federation of Women Panchayati leaders. Dalit leaders in Panchayats have for their federation. These three federations periodically meet and discuss their problems. They are drawing the support of NGOs. These federations are independent and not politically affiliated. District Panchayat leaders have their own associations but they are not effective.
21. This newspaper has a readership of 5 lakhs. The entire exercise is being done with the support of The Hunger Project.
22. The media has not developed an appropriate perspective to look at Panchayats and as a result it has only projected the official versions of the Government on local bodies. After the media workshop was conducted, the media has started covering the struggles, successes and innovations of the Panchayats and the media has started helping the Panchayats.

5

CAPACITY BUILDING FOR STRENGTHENING OF LOCAL SELF-GOVERNANCE

PURVI DASS

This publication is part of a nation-wide effort of PRIA and its partners towards Strengthening Panchayati Raj Institutions in India. This joint effort was initiated in 1995 with the following perspectives. Panchayati Raj Institutions (PRI as common term for both rural and urban) are to be viewed as institutions of local self-governance, and not as mere implementors of centrally-determined development programmes. Bottom-up comprehensive planning, based on micro-planning exercise, is to be the basis of self-governance. PRIs should not be allowed to become third tier of development administration. Emphasis must be placed on active participation in decision-making by women (and other weaker sections) with a view to enhance their role status and leadership in local self-governance. Interventions in strengthening PRI should focus on building, promoting and empowering new leadership of women, SC/ST and Dalits. PRIs should assert their access to and control over local natural and human resources, as well as other development resources being available with state and national governments. Strengthening PRIs will entail clarity of their roles, systems of governance, accountability and transparency and interlinkages. This programme is supported by a consortium of donors which include Ministry of Rural Development (MoRD), Government of India, CORDAID, Netherlands, Swedish International Development Agency (SIDA) and Swish Development Corporation (SDC).

The Context

The concept of 'Panchayati Raj' is unquestionably Indian in origin. The ancient literature, like *Rigveda, Manusamhita, Dhamashastras, Upanishads, Jatakas* etc., mentions *auto local administration* which is functioning merely by 'common consent' and with 'the real sanction of the local public opinion'. Ever successive centuries did witness adjustments and modifications almost always for better till Mughal period, but got eroded in British Raj. After about fifty years of independence it was realised that Indian States could not administer development in rural India in a desired way. In the process of identifying a suitable unit of governance to bring development in rural areas, Panchayati Raj has been thought of as vibrant and feasible unit of development administration. At present Panchayati Raj Institutions (PRIs) are suppose to carry out its functions within the framework established by the provisions of the Constitutions of India. PRIs have been proclaimed as the 'vehicle' of the socio-economic transformation in rural India.

The provisions given in the Constitution of India have some far reaching implications with respect to the governance of local areas in rural India. The comprehensive framework, if applied as envisaged, will truely transform the rural economy and give practical shape to peoples' participation in the process of economic development and social justice. It ensures full freedom to plan according to the local need and local potentials. By providing 1/3rd reservation for women and proportionate reservation for other socially excluded and deprived sections (tribals, dalits, etc.), the Constitutional framework for local bodies in India has provided opportunities for mainstreaming these sections of the society in the development.

Democratic decentralisation in India is coming after nearly 50 years of centralisation in the state machinery, public resources and bureaucratic structures. As a result, hierarchy of government departments and agencies have generated vested interests and exercise their responsibility to apply public resources in an unaccountable manner. On the other hand, nearly five decades of state led model of development delivered from the top has created a sense of passive dependence on government agencies, programmes and resources among ordinary people in rural areas.

These provisions and the field realities had given an opportunity to work on strengthening these institutions as to fulfil part of PRIA's mission. Part of PRIA's mission which could be fulfilled by strengthening Panchayati Raj Institutions are as follows:

- Work towards democratic governance in society, identify poor and the marginalised, focusing upon changing women's roles and status as agents and leaders of change.
- Economic inequity requires addressing issues of poverty and powerlessness.
- Social exclusion entails mainstreaming participation by youth, dalits, elders and focusing on the rights of the ordinary citizen.

Within the above reality, a perspective of local self-governance in rural India had been articulated from the point of view of deepening local democracy and enhancing participation of rural citizen for local development. In PRIA's approach, this perspective has been distinctly articulated.

PRIA's Perspective

- Panchayati Raj Institutions (PRIs) are to be viewed as institutions of local self-governance and not as mere implementors of centrally-determined development programmes. PRIs should not be allowed to become a third tier of development administration.
- Interventions in strengthening PRIs should focus on building, promoting and empowering new leadership of women, SC/ST and Dalits.
- Emphasis must be placed on active participation in decision-making by women (and other weaker sections) with a view

to enhance their role, status and leadership in local self-governance.

- PRIs should assert their access to and control over local natural and human resources, as well as other development resources being available with state and national governments. Bottom-up comprehensive planning based on micro-planning exercise, is to be the basis of self-governance.
- Strengthening PRIs will entail clarity of their roles, systems of governance, accountability, transparency and interlinkages between three levels.

Democratic decentralisation can truly happen when all actors performed their roles and responsibilities an envisaged in the provision in changed scenario.

Why Capacity Building?

Answer to this question is complex. Democratic decentralisation in above-mentioned scenario had led lots of uncertainty and ambiguity in functioning. The various direct actors like Government rural citizen (known as Gram Sabha members), elected members associated with the local development did not know how to work with or as an institution of local development. Not only they, even the various indirect actors like Voluntary Organisations, community based organisations etc. did not know how to intervene. The media did not know how to project this issue. Policy-makers were also grappling with the issue of matching the provisions with field realities.

Under these circumstances, the efforts to work towards realisation of the PRIA's perspective in strengthening Panchayati Raj Institutions required sustained interventions for capacity building of different developmental actors. Moreover, the complexity and diversity of the situation in India demanded various kinds of methods for capacity building.

The focus of capacity building to all actors and constituencies was to congruent in enabling effective functioning as institutions of local self-governance in the perspective elaborated above. All the capacity building interventions were interwoven, one method supplementing or complimenting others. These interventions cannot be done in isolation nor in scattered way or intermittently. Moreover mind boggling number of elected members (about 3.4 million representatives of Panchayats are at all level in which nearly 1.1 million are women. They represent more than 0.22 million Gram Panchayats, about 6000 Panchayat Samitis and about 500 zilla parishads) made the task more difficult and complex.

A network of organisations named as Regional Support Organisations in different States with same perspective for strengthening local self-governance came together and started capacity building interventions. Fig 1 shows the constituencies covered by PRIA and Network of Regional Support Organisations (popularly known as NCRSOs). Eight organisations developed

Constituencies of Capacity Building of PRIA and NCRSOs at glance

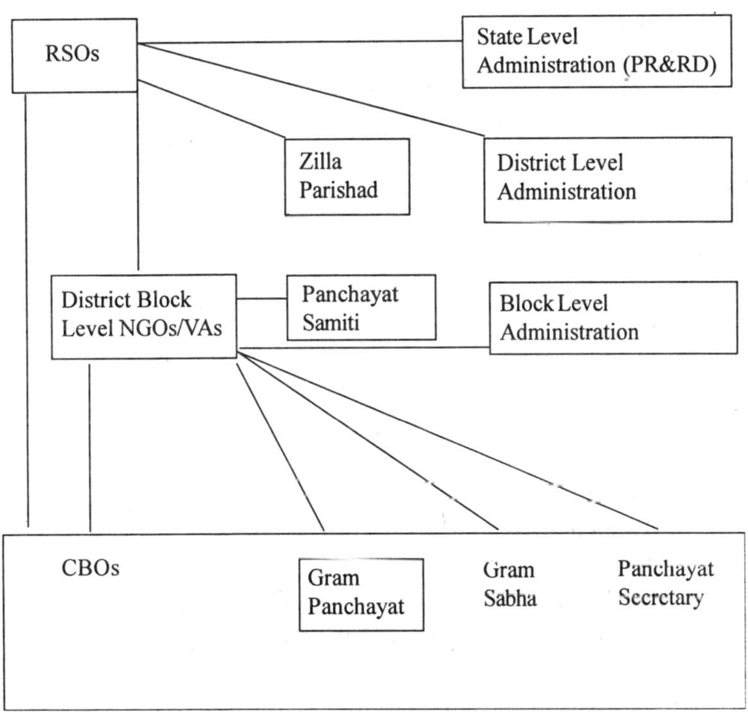

Fig. 1

strategy to work on this issue in ten States. Depending upon the capacity of RSOs it was thought of that quantitatively capacity building intervention would be spread for about 100 Panchayats in each State from September 1995. This was a small fraction of 3.4 million to made the impact visible. The map shows the area of intervention where first and second rounds (except Gujarat and Orissa—till date) of elections took place and long-term interventions were made systematically.

With the beginning of this Joint Venture, we also gave ourselves certain framework of programmatic interventions for capacity building:

Active and effective elected members

- Regular attendance in Panchayat meetings and gram sabha meeting.
- Raising questions related to Panchayat functions in these meetings.
- How many '*Prastav*' they put in meeting.
- Nature of '*Prastav*' accepted.
- Involvement in the preparation of the agenda.

Effective Gram Sabha

- Organising the regular gram sabha.
- Attendance of Dalits, OBC and Women in the Gram Sabha and participation.
- Active participation of villagers.

Developing people centred Panchayat plan

- Involvement of people and Gram Sabha in the preparation of annual plans.
- Human Resource Development as major focus of Panchayat plan (it was coined as micro-plan).
- Building linkages between different actors.

Howsoever good intention may these elected members, Gram Sabha members or Government officials have but lack of knowledge, skills of effective functioning and ability to work as team may not bring desired results.

Linkages in Dimensions of capacity building and Constituencies of strengthening Local Self-Governance

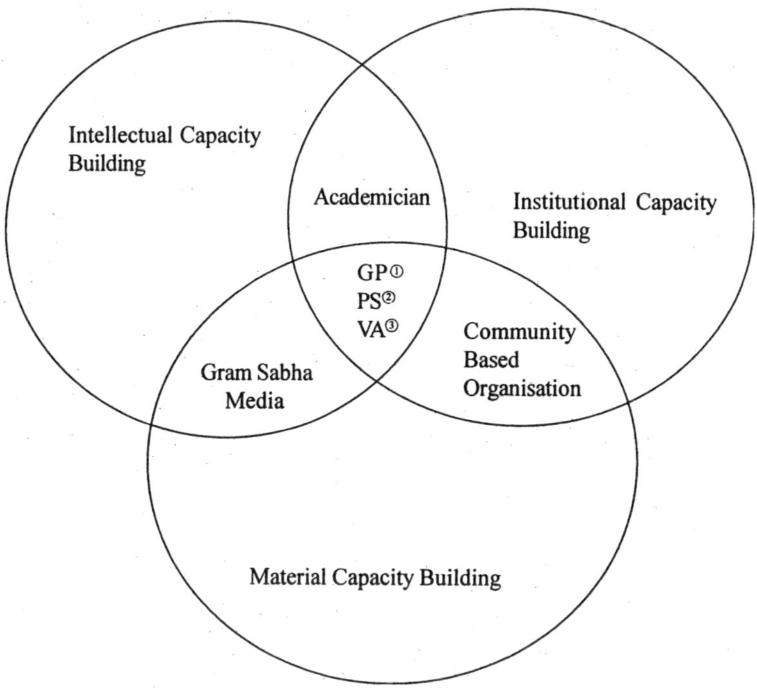

①Gram Panchayat
②Panchayat Secretary
③Voluntary Agencies

Fig. 2

In this framework, three different dimensions of capacity building that is intellectual, institutional and material interventions address the needs of different constituencies for enhancing capacity at the level of individual and organised collectives. The three dimensions of capacity building are relevant and important for effective functioning of local self-governance as individual or organised collectives. Focusing upon one or the other makes sustainability of capacity enhancement efforts doubtful.

The purpose of this paper is to make an attempt to consolidate the experiences of capacity building of four constituencies (elected Gram Panchayat members, Gram Sabha members, Government Officials and VAs) by PRIA and Network of Regional Support Organisations where systematic and sustained capacity building interventions were made. The States are Gujarat, Haryana, Himachal Pradesh, Kerala, Madhya Pradesh, Orissa, Rajasthan and Uttar Pradesh. Our capacity building interventions in future is based on this learning.

It was mid-1995. With above-mentioned perspective, PRIA and NCRSOs decided to work on this issue in ten States of India. Although as mentioned the theme of Panchayati Raj Institutions was existing since ancient time but after the conformity act it became imperative to understand the constitutional framework of democratic governance and the space it has provided. A 'five days' capacity building workshop (named as Master Training of Trainers) was organised (26th to 31st of August, 1995) with twin objectives: to build capacity of staff of PRIA and NCRSOs to understand the perspective of working on this issue and enhance knowledge on democratic governance. Four areas were identified where urgent intervention on capacity building was needed for strengthening Local Self-Governance. They were capacity building of elected members and Gram Sabha members, informative material development for them, micro plan at Panchayat level and doing research and advocacy. Total 39 participants from 10 States attended the programme. The methodologies used were participatory Training methodology besides lectures from the practitioners, group discussions and case studies were used. It was an unique experience where Head of Organisations, the experienced and inexperienced staff, the eminent practitioners were brought together and issues were thrashed out and understanding on the theme was built.

The impact:

- Since most of the staff did not have previous experience in working on this issue, the capacity of staff was enhanced.
- Eight organisations developed multipronged strategy to work in ten States*.

The capacity building of this network remained a continuous process. Specific inputs like capacity to identify research issues and develop framework for participatory research analyse and synthesise the findings and dissemination was done. It was also felt that huge data would be generated in the process and there is a need to manage this data electronically so that relevant information could be extracted. Capacity of the network to manage the data electronically was also done.

Capacity of the network to involve community in preparing the micro plan was built. With a view to deriving conceptual clarity with regard to planning with PRIs PRIA organised a five-day (25th—29th March, 1996) workshop in which 29 participants from 9 States participated. The objectives of the workshop were as follows:

- To understand and critically assess the planning process at macro and micro level.
- To develop a common understanding of a micro planning concept.
- To chart out area specific micro planning for different RSOs.

Beside these there were regular half yearly review meet to keep ourselves together on the track. These meet build the capacity of the network to reinforce the perspective, refresh the understanding, learn from others experiences, share innovative ideas, State specific field realities and difficulties faced. Attending seminar and workshop organised by others and visits to different areas have also built the capacity of the network.

---

* At present the network is working in fifteen States.

Capacity Building of different constituencies for strengthening local self-governance

As already mentioned Regional Support Organisations in selected states identified specific areas of interventions and build the capacity of various developmental actors like Gram Sabha (GS) members, Gram Panchayat members (Pradhans and Ward panches) with specific focus to women, tribals and dalits, voluntary agencies and Government Officials.

Build Capacity of Gram Sabha Members

Building capacity of elected members only may not help in realising the dream of PRIs as unit of Local Self-Governance unless the common rural citizens known as Gram Sabha members take active part in their own development. Citizens who have attained the age of 18 are Gram Sabha members. Unless they became vibrant, the elected members may not be able to develop the Panchayat in desired way or else may behave like contractors of development without having accountability and transparency to the common citizen of Panchayats. The situation is worst in remote areas, lack of awareness of GS members are common. Pradhan acts as Demi-God among the poor illiterate ward. Panches are illiterate and are not aware of the roles and responsibilities. In this situation Pradhan in these remote areas enjoy absolute authority.

In this scenario Gram Sabha members capacity needs to be built so that they can support functioning of the institutes and also keep a check on them. At present the network is working in fifteen States. They need to ask pertinent questions and suggest solutions etc. Women need to be encouraged for not only the present but also participate actively by asking questions and giving suggestions.

Given below are some of the methods where by capacity of Gram Sabha members were built.

Orientation Meetings to Build Capacity

Different States have adopted different kinds of orientation meets with GS members. The purpose of these meetings were to discuss the problems, issues and identify the needs of the people and also to link with PRIs. The major issues that evolved during the course of these meetings were:

- Infrastructure development.
- Abolition of contractors for development schemes.
- Identification of beneficiaries.
- Relationships of Gram Sabha members with government officials like Panchayat Secretary, Junior Engineer, Patwari, etc.

In *Gujarat* and *Haryana* efforts were also made to strengthen Gram Sabhas directly through intensive dialogue and orientation meetings with GS members with a special focus on women and other marginalised groups like the dalits. Meetings were held and video taped along with documentation of the same.

In *Himachal Pradesh* three meetings were held with Gram Sabha on 9th, 10th and 11th June, 1997 at Tatwani. Meharna and Lahat Panchayats in Kangra respectively. A series of meetings at gram sabha levels were done from 16th to 21st November, 1999 in the selected Panchayats of Chamba, a remote district. In these meetings suitable dates for three days workshop was also decided. First workshop at Jadeja Panchayat took place from 22nd to 24th November, 1999 and second workshop was from 25th to 27th November, 1999 at Batt Panchayat. RSO acted as facilitator besides providing learning materials. To build the linkages between other developmental actors, Zila Parishad members and local line department officials were also involved. The film 'Sanshodhan' by Govind Nihalani was also video screened. A meeting was organised at Bhaled Panchayat on 4th February, 2000 at Panchayat Ghar to sensitise the GS members about their role and responsibility. The need and importance of their participation in GS was also shared. This was attended by elected members, MM members and youth groups also.

In *Madhya Pradesh* to activate GS members on 27th November, 1999 at Madhuban, Mou, a meeting was organised with GS members by partner Organisation Amar Sahid Chetna Sansthan.

The focus of the meeting was to understand the link between GS and PRI members. The uniqueness of this meet was the cultural programme after the meet where *Bhajans* (devotional songs) on women empowerment were sung. Legal training programmes for Gram Sabha members at Sidhi were conducted to base on the demand of the field. 35 women Gram Sabha members participated in this training.

In *Rajasthan* from 1996 four strategies were developed to strengthen Gram Sabha members:

- Awaring GS members about importance of GS through panches;
- Partnership with Government in conducting GS meetings;
- Meetings with elected members and GS members' awaring them about the importance of PRI and GS;
- And through Foot trip—*Padyatra.*

In *Kerala* 130 orientation meet in 14 districts in order to strengthen Gram Sabhas were done. Altogether 8000 Gram Sabha members have participated in these programmes. The content included Panchayat Raj Act and Rules, Power and Responsibilities of Gram Sabha member, the importance of peoples' participation in various stages of planning, *Ayalkkoottom* (the neighbourhood groups) and the concept of decentralisation. Experience sharing of the participants and group discussions on field realities were common features of these meets.

The impact of these meets were as follows:

- Growing taste for capacity building.
- Demand for intensive and village level training camps.
- Widespread awareness of GS members on Panchayat related issues.
- Diminishing social ostracism against women's participants and gradual recognition of their role as elected members.

Innovative ways of meetings to upscale and stimulate gram sabha members were also done.

Innovative Ways of Orientation of Gram Sabha Members

Following paras describe innovative ways of capacity building interventions of gram sabha members in different States.

The Mahila Sammelan in Haryana

A *sammelan* took place on the 28th December of 1999 at Ratia Anaj Mandi at District Fatehabad, Harayana. 3000 women participated in the *sammelan.* Administration took special interest in the *sammelan.*

The Kavi Sammelan in Himachal Pradesh

Based on the past experiences in the state where the cultural media proved to be an effective method for awareness generation, it was decided to organise a *Kavi Sammelan.* This was held at the Senior Secondary School, Shahpur, District Kangra. It was a combined effort of RSO and VA 'Samaj Seva Parishad', in Ratia, Kangra. Eleven poets from different parts of Kangra district participated and recited their poems in *Pahadi* and Hindi on various aspects of Panchayati Raj, like role of Panchayats, importance of Gram Sabha etc. The special objectives were as follows:

- to obtain poems and songs on the issue and get it published in the form of a booklet for mass distribution.
- to provide a common platform to the poets to share their views on PRIs.

These poems have been compiled and translated into Hindi. This collection of poems Hindi and *Pahadi* have been published in the form of a booklet—"*Raj Panchayat* Da".

The Vikas Utsav (Development Fair) in Himachal Pradesh is being jointly organised by RSO and VA 'SSP' every year in April. This is second in the series. The special objective of the *Utsav* was to create awareness among people for panchayati raj; to honour two women PRI members for outstanding contribution in village development. The *utsav* was attended by women members more.

The *utsav* was addressed by VAs, Government officials, elected members and local important actors like teachers, etc. The sale-*cum*-exhibition of books and pickles were also organised.

The Padyatra in Rajasthan—Panchayti Raj Chetna Yatra was organised by Partner Organisation 'Shanti Maitri Mission', Pungal, Bikaner, Rajasthan. This *padyatra* covered thirteen villages of five panchayts (Gangajali, Mekeri, Aduru, Tharusar, Ramai) from 16th September, 1997 to 24th September, 1997. In these nine days using local resources and keeping in mind local langauge and culture importance of Gram Sabha and PRIs were discussed through drama (*Natak*), cultural programmes, exhibition, video films.

The *padyatra* started with inauguration from District Collector at Gangajali Panchayat and concluded by Minister, Rural Development and Panchayati Raj at Pungal in Bikaner. The balloons (with seeds of local trees) were aired by local school children in the inauguration programme. It served two purposes—children the future of rural India listens to the discussions of PRIs and the seeds so disbursed through balloons may grow into a tree as the season was congenial. The interesting feature of this *padyatra* is that the meetings were addressed all along by those who have understanding of PRIs. The outcome of this *padyatra* were as follows: The local Government officials, elected members, Ministers associated with Panchayats, media, local key actors, resource persons of PRIs were brought together. The GS members capacity were built to address the issues of their daily lives to the Panchayats. The message on importance of GS has subsequently yielded in active participation in GS meetings.

Pre-Gram Sabha Awareness Campaign in Haryana

A 'Gram Sabha Awareness Campaign' was organised in three phases prior to the Gram Sabha meeting scheduled for October 2, 1999 at Block Ratia in District Fatehabad.

First phase—A poster was prepared to make people aware about the Gram Sabha scheduled for October 2 in collaboration with the Directorate of Panchayat, Haryana. These posters were distributed all over Haryana in all the 5,958 panchayats of 110 blocks of 19 districts.

Second phase—Focused the intervention in two districts, i.e. Fatehabad (five blocks) and Rohtak (one block). Each panchayat was visited, the Gram Sabha members and elected members were met and issues were identified for GS meeting.

Learning from the Gram Sabha Campaign

- People in large were not aware about the Gram Sabha meeting.
- In many places even the sarpanch was not aware about the issues to be discussed during the meeting.
- The dates allocated by the State Government were not suitable to majority of people as this is the harvesting time and everybody leaves for the farms by early morning. They have to miss a day's wage to attend the GS.

Impact of the Campaign

- GS members in general and women in particular attended the meeting and raised issues of drinking water, toilets, schools, roads, etc.

Third phase—As a follow-up the issues that were discussed during the Gram Sabha meeting are being followed up with the Pradhan and Block Development Officer (BDO).

Capacity Building of Community-based Organisations

Special focus was made to strengthen community-based organisations so that as organised collectives they could support PRIs. The objective is to use these groups to sensitise other GS members to take active part in GS. The content of the meet generally focused on holistic development and strength of Gram Sabha. The physical development is only a part of the holistic development. The holistic development also includes moral development, spiritual development, economic development and social development. The strength of Gram Sabha is not known to the members of Gram Sabha, hence the quorum is never completed.

Strengthening Mahila Mandals: The orientation workshop was conducted with the association of partner VA. New Hope for two days (7th and 8th of November, 1995) for the village women (consisting of Mahila Mandal members, balwadi workers and co-operative groups) of two blocks of Kangra district at Palampur.

Strengthening Youth Groups: Involving Nehru Yuva Kendra to orient youth on Panchayati Raj was done on March 5, 1997 at Ahmedabad, Gujarat. Total 23 female and 3 male participants attended the programme.

Strengthening Youth Groups and Mahila Mandals together: In Haryana Posters on role of Gram Sabha were prepared and widely disseminated through existing village groups like Mahila Mandals, youth groups, etc.

Strengthening Neighbourhood Groups *(Ayalkkoottom)*

As already mentioned in Kerala through 130 orientation meet in 14 districts *Ayalkkoottom* (the neighbourhood groups) were specially focused to build the capacity.

Interactive Meet with Mahila Mandals and Elected Members

A meet was organised at Bangana Block on 20-2-2000 by GoHP and VA 'Energy Environment Group', Una, HP. This was attended by all the Pradhans, Upa-pradhans, Panches and members of Mahila Mandals of all Panchayats (25) of Bangana Block. The media also covered this programme.

Strengthening Village Education Committee

In *Uttar Pradesh* RSO organised joint programme with VECs and elected members in 14 Panchayats to strengthen the link between Panchayats activities and their extended roles.

Strengthening Self-Help Groups

A meeting was organised on 19th February, 2000 at SSP office for the role of SHGs in GS meeting. 47 members from Shivika, Ratia,

Anadika , Laxshmi Naushera, Chamunda and Jwala, Naushera took part in the meeting.

Strengthening Water Committee in Gujarat: Training of village water committee members of Amereli District by partner organisation CEE was done on May 1996 at Ahmedabad where 10 female and 25 male participants attended the programme.

In Process of Preparation of Micro Plan

Micro planning process requires people to interact with each other to share their concerns and ideas for planning for a sector. If the planning process has to be democratic and sustainable, then all concerned peoples (the stakeholders) feelings, ideas and plans have to be taken into consideration. Coming together on a common platform is also an empowering process for the poor and disadvantage. People get an opportunity to clarify their stands, their misconceptions. Therefore, micro planning requires:

1. All stakeholders to come together.
2. Mobilising the disadvantaged and the poor.
3. Providing them with an opportunity to interact and share.
4. Facilitate sharing of problems and developing action plans on solutions.
5. Constants follow-up on action plans made.

A micro plan may not generate all needed resources, but it can create goodwill, cooperation, and mutual support in ensuring quality of services and maintenance of community infrastructure. It creates opportunity to constructively channelise the community human power for collective development. Micro plan is an important instrument for human resources development and developing community cohesiveness. It may not be the right mechanism for infrastructure development, but in the process people can identified what kind of infrastructure are their need.

Haryana

During July 26-27, 1996 a two days meeting was organised at Khetavas GP with VA Asha Sadan. The purpose of this meeting was to explore the possibility of long-term involvement of micro plan exercise. Panchayat members from seven wards, MM members, YG members, GS members actively participated. Total 50 participants (30 women and 20 men) attended the meeting. As follow-up series of meetings with local villages and VAs were held. Micro Plan Process at Dhana panchayat, Salwan Block, District Rewari RSO undertook intensive micro planning activities with the involvement of the elected representatives and community members. Following the participatory research methodology, the entire exercise took 9 months after which people centred micro plans emerged in both the Panchayats. Through continuous interactions several issues, needs, priorities, resources, etc. were brought to the forefront. Follow-up of those plans were being carried out.

Himachal Pradesh

On experiment basis micro plan exercise was carried out at Kehar Panchayat in Mandi Sadar block of Mandi District from 1996-1998. Beside this panchayat, similar exercise has been replicated by the initiative of Pradhan of Salwan panchayat of Mandi District. A sequence of events in conducting micro plan at Kehar given below indicates active participation of Gram Sabha members. Detailed issue based on micro plan at Khanora Panchayat, Garla Panchayat, Mayna Panchayat, Maroohn Panchayat, Vyara Panchayat is given separately.

What happens when people do not involve?

Micro Plan Process at Mansimbal Panchayat, Bhawarna Block, District Kangra

Micro Plan in this Panchayat was initiated in by RSO and Block Development (BD) Office. Panchayat Secretary and Pradhan took initiative but people did not join in the process. There were no information gathering through door to door survey through which rapport is build. The meetings were called on each ward. Pradhan, Upa-Pradhan, Panch of that ward and PS member were present. However, not more than ten or twelve GS members attended those meetings. Finally, prioritisation was done by Panch and present GS members with help of Pradhan, Panchayat Secretary(PS), Upa-Pradhan. A compilation of the wards priortisations were done in Panchayat Ghar in Panchayat meeting. The report was written by PS and submitted to BD office.

Lessons Learnt: Contrary to other places Government took interest but Gram Sabha members did not find micro plan as important thing, which can solve day to day problems.

Kerala

In order to enhance the capacities of the local voluntary workers, the elected members of the Panchayats and the local leaders with skills in the use of micro-planning techniques, special workshops were conducted in the Block of Sasthamcotta, and six other Panchayats in different parts of the state with the collaboration of local voluntary groups.

From July to September 1996, orientation sessions were conducted in 3 places: West Kallada for one day, at Kasergod for 3 days and at Idukki for 3 days.

On 13th October, 1996, an orientation seminar was held at Neendakara, Alappuzha in collaboration with VA 'WIN'. It was attended by 60 of whom 20 were women. The themes of the seminar was centred around topics such as social audit by people, people centred planning, transparency in the functioning of the Panchayat, peoples participation in programme planning, implementation, monitoring and evaluation. A one-day orientation was conducted at PARAPPA, Kasergod district on 11-12-96 with VA 'Society of Love'. It was attended by 63 persons of whom 33 were women. The content of the programme included micro plan processes, and peoples participation in the developmental activities.

Madhya Pradesh

Samarthan directly intervened in the two Panchayats (Jamunia Jank and Rajpura) of the Sehore district for micro plan. After the intensive work of one year with these two Panchayats new 10 Panchayats have also been selected in the Sehore district. The process has been replicated.

> **Implementation of people plan in Jamunia Tank and Rajpura Panchayats**
> In the Jamunia Tank Panchayat, implementation of the plan prepared by the people is on going. Construction of a culvert (*pullia*) has been completed. The construction work was done by the people themselves in the *harijan* (Scheduled Caste) dominated area. In Rajpura Panchayat a drain has been constructed for which the people contributed Rs.16,000. Besides this, a road has been constructed in this Panchayat for which the Panchayat has contributed Rs. 20,000 and a similar amount has been collected from the community. RSO has contributed Rs. 11,000 for this purpose. Moreover, in Hasanpur village, Rajpura Panchayat, the community has contributed and influenced the Panchayat in the construction of a 2 kms. long road. The youth especially, took the initiative to mobilise local resources in terms of local human and materials.

Based on the experiences of micro planning in the two Panchayats mentioned above, one area where micro planning has been replicated is in Kathawn Hazi Panchayat, Gohad Block, Bhind District. This was initiated in October 1998. The planning process has been carried out in four phases. The entire planning process was completed in about six months.

In Orrisa RSO conducted successfully micro-planning exercises at the Panchayat Baligaon, Koraput district. The 'Baligaon micro-planning' process report was completed in 1999 and translated into Oriya for wider dissemination. The training programmes on micro planning for PRI members and Gram Sabha members of Atalguda, Kanguguda and Jaliaguda villages in Koraput district were also conducted. In 1999 RSO and VA 'Gopinath Yuvak Sangh' jointly initiated a micro-planning exercise in Panchayat Rajas of Khurda District. The October 1999 super cyclone, however, interrupted the process.

Rajasthan

Four Panchayats of Jawaza Block, Ajmer District (Naikalan, Durgawas, Kabra and Jawaza) has been identified for micro plan. The "Jawaza Project" (Rural University Experiment in educational innovation), VA 'MMVS' and the presence of Artisan Alliance Group (AAJ) and other local NGOs of the weavers and leather workers helped in initiating the process with the Panchayats and villagers.

Uttar Pradesh

Madhupur and Pipra were selected for micro plan. Both are headed by women Pradhan while Pradhan of Madhupur belongs to general category and a school teacher, that of Pipra is a scheduled caste house wife with hardly and exposure to public life and cannot even sign.

Information Dissemination

Information dissemination is method through which the capacity of Gram Sabha members were built. Panchayat Resource Centres at Panchayat level or Village Information Centres at Village level or of Block or District Resource Centres at Block or District level were opened as sources of information dissemination to build capacity of Gram Sabha members. There are informations which are important for Gram Sabha and elected members do not trickle down to Panchayat level. Hence these centres would fill this gap there are many schemes which needs to be implementation through Panchayats but they themselves may not be aware of it.

Panchayat and PM's Girl Child Scheme

The Union Government has decided to mobilise Panchayats and Aganwadi workers for implementation of Prime Minister's Girl Child Scheme which is intended to benefit an estimated 22 lakh families living below poverty line. The girls eligible for the grants under the scheme will be identified with the help of these two institutions for admission into schools.

> The news was spread in the region in end 1996 that the cheques issued by the Panchayats should be countersigned by BDO for any withdrawal in connivance with the Bank. VA 'Shakti' took up this issue and found that no government order had been passed. Panchayat Sarpanch were informed about it and BDO had also agreed not to harass Sarpanchs by such tactics in future.

Conducting Gram Sabha Meetings

Besides this prior to gram sabha (the dates are either announced or fixed) Gram Sabha members were motivated to attend the Gram Sabha Meetings. It is interesting to note that neither GS members are willing to attend nor the elected members are keen to let them know the actual purpose of GS and share the statement of expenditure of last six months which is mandatory under provision.

> In GS meeting of Dadamb, Kangra, HP a women member has asked Panchayat member to furnish the details of annual income-expenditure before signing their names in the attendance register. Instead pradhan asked them to sign the register first. Members insisted and Pradhan could not convince members to sign in the register and Pradhan Ms. Panana Koti left the place.

Building Capacity of the Gram Panchayats Members

As already mentioned the elected members do not know their roles and responsibilities given in the provision. They consider themselves as contractors of infrastructure contradiction. To build chair capacity to function as unit of local self-governance various methods were need. Beside structured events on site support were also provided. As already mentioned a micro-planning process which involves all stakeholders. Also build their capacity. The impact of such interventions is given at the end of this chapter. Negotiations with higher tiers and with bureaucracy were also done. Capacity building needs of elected members were assessed during the field visits and informal interaction with various stakeholders in the field or at the State level. But in some States formal interactions were organised to understand the needs of capacity building.

Workshops on assessing capacity building needs of elected members

In Himachal Pradesh, two such workshops were held in Kangra District with VA 'New HOPE and Samaj Seva Parishad'. The first one was held at Kher on 3rd May, 1996 New HOPE, while the second one was held at Ratia on 4th May, 1996 with Samaj Seva Parishad. The objectives of these two workshops were: To identify the existing problems which are hampering the effective functioning of Panchayats and also to identify possible solutions; to identify training needs of the PRI members; to build rapport with PRI members and establish a network between PRI members, PRIA and the two voluntary agencies.

In Rajasthan prior to capacity building intervention, the needs were identified. The training needs articulated by ward members, Gram Panchayat, Panchayat Samiti and Zilla Panchayat members after first election after functioning for more than two years were still on following : Panchayati Raj Act the new set up, Rural Development Scenario, Administration and Financial Management of PRIs and Behavioural skills like leadership and team building, participatory decision-making.

Beside these efforts in mid-1999 a study to understand the capacity building needs of elected women members exclusively at Sikar District was done. The major findings were as follows:

Almost all women were elected for the first time and they were illiterate. They do not take part in panchayat or Gram Sabha meetings. Instead of them their husbands go and attend the meetings. They were also not aware of their duties and responsibilities. Although training have been attended by the elected members but since they were not exclusively for women, they did not get chance to participate actively. Only lecture methods were used. Learning materials were very difficult to comprehend.

Capacity Building of Gram Panchayat Members

Different States had different approaches for structured events in capacity building interventions. One common thing which was woven all along is that simplified act was prepared by RSOs and given to the elected members.

The objectives were mainly

- To impart knowledge regarding the history of Panchayati Raj Institutions.
- To understand 73rd Amendment with the focus on development, decentralisation and local self-governance.
- To generate a simplistic understanding of the new Act and its features.
- To discuss strategies for effective implementation of the Act.
- To equip the participants with the necessary skills and capacities required to charge their role effectively.
- To focus on the role and responsibilities of the Gram Sabha and the need to activate it.

Following pages will describe various models, modules, designs, methodology and learning materials used in these events.

Several other educational materials and other important information was collected prior to these training's. Attempts were made to use several participatory methods to involve the participants and deepen their understanding of roles and responsibilities vested onto them by this Act. Role of Gram Sabha was emphasised in all the training and wherever possible local resource persons (GS, GP members) were used.

Gujarat

Training for Panchayat leaders were organised by Prayas on March 30, 1997 at Mangrole, Bharuch where 3 male and 25 female participants attended the programme. Training of selected Panchayat was conducted at Gaddu on September 18-19, 1996 where 15 males and 7 females attended the programme. Training of selected Panchayat at Poshina at Sabarkantha District was conducted at Ambaji on September 12-14, 1996 where 23 female and 7 male participants attended the programme. Similarly training of selected

Panchayats of Poshina by NPYM was done at Ambaji on February 20-22, 1997 where 16 female and 4 male participants attended the programme.

In Haryana, a series of capacity building interventions were done from 16th-18th June, 9th-11th July, 16th-18th July, 29th-30th July, 1996 with VA 'Haryana Nav Yuvak Kala Sangam' at Meham Block, District Rohtak. A sample training design is given in Annexure V.

In Himachal Pradesh RSO organised a 'one day' capacity building programme with VA 'Chinmaya Tapovan' at Sidhbari, near Dharamshala, HP. The participants were elected representatives from different Panchayats of Kangra district. In all there were 40 elected PRI members.

A workshop on 'Field Experience Sharing' was organised on 23rd May, 1999 at Himachal Panchayat Sansadhan Kendra, Maiti. 4 pradhans, 4 panches, 1 up-pradhan and 1 Panchayat Samiti member and 1 CBO member attended the workshop besides the VA.

> This training proved to be especially helpful for the ward members who had not had such an opportunity earlier.

Issue emerged

No fix time for the beginning of the monthly meetings; Absence of GP members both at monthly meetings and Gram Sabha meetings; Quorum and participation of youth and women in GS, Lack of untied funds and peoples participation in development.

In June and July 1999 training of elected members at Panchayat level was undertaken in two Districts Mandi and Kangra. This was done in collaboration with Government of Himachal Pradesh, Panchayat Training Institute at Baijnath and was sponsored by UNICEF. In Mandi, training of Pradhans and Up-Pradhans was done in all 10 blocks in two phases. A total of nearly 800 members were trained. A similar training programme was also undertaken in Kangra district, where ward members, Pradhans and Up-Pradhans of 13 blocks were trained. A total of 4000 elected representatives of Gram Panchayats and Panchayat Samitis were trained in Kangra.

A series of clustered training programme was conducted by VA in thirty Panchayats of Pachchad Block, Sirmour District. The learning materials with partial complimentary were provided on payment.

Kerala, RSO conducted a two-day intensive training for Panchayat members at Harippad, Alapuzha Districts. 35 elected representatives including Pradhans and Up-Pradhans from six Panchayats participated, of which 14 were women. The training included skills related to preparation of reports and minutes, effective communication, leadership styles and accounting procedures. Two leadership programmes were also conducted one in Parappa, Kasargod District and the other in Alapuzha.

A special management training was organised at West Kallada for three days from 17 to 19 November, 1996 focusing on leadership and communication skills. It was attended by a group of 35 persons, consisting of Panchayat members, Convenors and Resource persons from the government sponsored peoples campaign for the 9th Plan and representatives of the VAs.

Madhya Pradesh

A Training for Gram Panchayat representatives and secretary to increase awareness of the State Act has been undertaken in February 1996.

During the follow-up trainings and also informal meetings at Panchayat level majority of Sarpanch and Secretaries were asking for support in maintenance of Panchayat accounts. On an experimental basis Samarthan organised one day workshop on 16th June, 1996 for Sarpanchs and Secretaries of Village Panchayats in Janpad Panchayat building Morena. Social Characteristics of the Group was as follows: SC—52, ST—0, Others—73 (Total—125 ; 118 male and 15 Female). Level of literacy of elected Panchayat was low and the level of literacy of newly appointed Panchayat Secretaries was medium. Major objectives were primarily to sensitize and build clear understanding on the importance of effective accounting system and secondly, to provide knowledge and understanding on the standard accounting systems procedures.

Outcome

- A preliminary understanding on the major provisions of State PR Act was developed.
- Major areas of weakness were identified.
- A common understanding on the needs to strengthen capacities for accounting system was developed.

Regional workshop on Panchayati Raj Institutions and participatory development in Vindhya region for 4 days was conducted in 1998 where 40 participants attended the programme. The objective was to build the perspective on Panchayati Raj Institutions and Participatory development.

During this year a Panchayat and Health programme was conducted to orient on leprosy. This one day orientation programme was attended by 62 participants. Being leprosy prone areas this has helped them to plan strategy for health and leprosy awareness in Panchayats. One day meeting with elected Sarpanch of the villages of Morar Block was organised by VA 'Gopal Kiran Shiksha Aur Sanskriti Samiti'.

All the VAs have conducted trainings for elected members. They not only arranged local resource persons but also managed local resources for these trainings. RSO had provided a very limited financial support, in the range of Rs. 350-400 per training.

In Orissa RSO conducted orientation-*cum*-awareness programmes for people in general and Panchayat representatives in particular so that the significance of participation in Palli (Ward) Sabhas and Gram Sabhas could be recognised. The faculty and material support was provided by RSO to the VAS when they were conducting training programmes for elected members till 1998. RSO conducted eight training programmes, in which 288 PRI representatives and prospective trainers participated. It collaborated with VA 'Lok Vikash' to organise five training programmes in Jalpur district.

In *Rajasthan*, Government training institutes have organised training programmes for elected members in 1995 and 1996. It is interesting to note that one lakh twenty thousand elected members were to be trained by these institutes but neither there were co-ordination among these in States not did they involve other Non-Government training institutes. Logistical problems, inexperienced resource persons, lack of seriousness about training programmes on the part of trainers and participants had diluted the impact. The learning materials which were distributed were inadequate to address the day to day problems of conducting the affairs of PRIs. Ward members were not trained in few areas. The trainings did not give due attention to different needs of women elected members hence they did not find training very useful. Besides all learning materials were meant for only literate, whole lot of illiterate members were excluded.

In *Uttar Pradesh*, RSO organised two 'one day' training for members of Gram Panchayats and Gram Sabhas. Total 42 persons participated from 14 Gram Panchayats and the Village Education Committees. These were held in Lucknow. 'Three days' PRI training for elected Panchayat members (4-6 July, 1996) was organised by VA 'Gramonati Sansthan, Mahoba', UP. Total 45 participants attended the training. (Male—20, Female—25, ST—2, SC—35, Others—8). Block Development Officer and District Development Officer attended the meeting. Twelve VAs conducted capacity building events in its operational area. RSO provided resources as trainers and materials to conduct the programme and give effective feedback.

Micro Plan Processes

As already mentioned in chapter on capacity building of Gram Sabha members about micro plan processes in different States. Since that all stakeholders were involved in this process given below are the impact of this capacity building intervention:

- *Increase in Level of confidence of Gram Sabha and the elected members:* Regular interaction with the representatives and the community has lead to increase in the levels of confidence of the community and the representatives. The women Sarpanches and the representatives have gained confidence. The increased confidence of the representatives has helped her in establishing contacts with the local administration and the other tiers of the Panchayats. The Sarpanch now attends various state level meetings.

- *Accessibility to the Information:* The informations in their day to day life could be accessed from the sources. Some examples—
  Providing information to the community regarding various schemes.
  Encouraging discussions in Gram Sabha.
  Discussing issues in the Gram Panchayat meetings.
  Seeking clarifications with the Government Officials.
  Negotiating with the local level MP/MLA for getting benefits.
- *Increase in the awareness levels of the Gram Sabha and the elected members:* The various awareness programmes has raised the level of awareness among the community members and an understanding has been created on the powers and the functions of the Gram Sabha their understanding has helped in establishing proper coordination with Panchayats.
- *Participation of the Gram Sabha and the elected members has increased:* The GS has started coming together and analysis the situations. The community has prepared plan according to their need and they have also taken the responsibility of implementing these plans.
- *Increase in participation of the women and marginalised groups*: The women have started coming to attend meetings and they have started raising issues and discussing these issues in the Panchayats. The *dalit* ward members have started conducting meetings at their Ward to resolve their issues.
- *Regularisation of Panchayat and Gram Sabha meeting:* Meeting have been regularised. GS have started participating ward level meetings to identify and prioritise problems before gram sabha meetings. The regular attendance of women has increased in the meetings.

- *Formation of community level groups* : Various community level groups have been formed such as Mahila Mandal, Youth Mandals. These mandals have come up as pressure groups and they are intensively supporting Panchayats to carry out their functions.
- *Establishing viable linkages* : The process of bottom up planning has helped the gram sabha, Gram Panchayat to have proper coordination and also establish linkages with the other institutions and agencies etc.
- *Local Government (District and Block level) have recognised the process:* Some State Governments had accepted as an effective way of planning at the Panchayat level and utilising available resources for development.

For first time elected tribals, women/Dalit members

Exclusive events were organised for elected tribal women and Dalit members.

Environment Building: Women Pradhan and VA Heads

Before actually starting capacity building interventions, in State like *Uttar Pradesh*, environment building prior to capacity building intervention was done. Two workshops were organised. The first was a workshop for elected women Panchayat representatives held in July 1995 in Lucknow. The workshop provided an opportunity to 43 participants. Panchayat representatives to articulate their expectations from VAS. It also sharpened our own understanding of ground realities.

Training Needs

In Rajasthan, a study done in Sikar and Jhunjhunu District shows even after functioning for more than two years still women felt the training needs are attaining literacy. The articulation and assertion training to overcome psyche and political culture of oppression, exploitation and resultant deprivation. Mobilisation of support networks and pressure sub-groups to resist political of 'no-confidence motion' to oust them from power positions were the foremost needs. The legal literacy, confidence and self-esteem building, overcoming fear traditional institutions, taboos etc. were also expressed as needs.

Exclusive Women Trainings

At *Devgadh Baria* by VA conducted training for Women Panchayat leaders. 30 women attended the programme. Educational material was also provided.

In *Rajasthan, PRIA* along with the district administration, had conducted a series of training programmes in three blocks of Sikar and Jhunjhunu. A total of 500 women elected representatives as well as women Gram Sabha members were trained.

First time they got an opportunity where the voices were heard in front of the trainer. They also got an opportunity to interact with Government Officials.

> Pradhan Mau Gram Panchayat in Shrimadhopur block. She is 27-year-old married and educated upto high school. She is very dynamic women, elected for the first time as Pradhan. She claimed that she belongs to erstwhile ruling party. When the state ruling party was in power she has very effectively handled the Panchayat work and implemented all development schemes and programmes. People accepted her as a good leader. But when government of other party has acquired power in the state, the situation has changed drastically. Since last year she is facing real difficulties in the Panchayat. During Gram Panchayat meeting, drunkerd people constantly create problems and paralysing the work of Panchayat even she is not able to get the funds in spite of all the necessary formalities completed by her.

In *Orissa,* RSO along with Lok Vikas organised the, 'four days training and orientation workshops' for elected women representatives Panchayats of the Badachanda Block, Jeypore District. 37 elected representatives took part in the programme.

In *Uttar Pradesh, RSO* organised 'one day' training for women members at Auraiya. 33 women from 14 Gram Panchayats participated.

Innovative ways of Strengthening Women Leadership

Mahila Sammelan in Haryana

'Strengthening leadership of women in PRI' was the theme around which a Sammelan was organised at Rewari district, Haryana by RSO on 7th March, 1999. Over 900 women leaders participated in this state level meeting inaugurated by the State Panchayat Minister. They spoke about the issues and problems that needed to be addressed in order to strengthen their leadership. The process was initiated by sharing the findings of a study on women in PRIs carried out by RSO in that area. According to this study an increasingly large number of women elected members are effectively taking on their roles as leaders.

Mahila Sammelan in Madhya Pradesh

The story of Rummebai—a tribal women panchayat leader in Madhya Pradesh: The Chief Minister of Madhya Pradesh organised a Mahila Sammelan in Bhopal where chairs were laid out for the Ministers and mats were laid on the floor for elected women representatives. The meeting began. One of the women representatives stood up and questioned the Chief Minister, "you keep talking about women and women's equality. You talk of reservation for women and we are in politics now, the people have elected us. Is there a shortage of chairs in Bhopal?" The next day chairs were brought in and the Chief Minister thanked the women representative for having raised the issue. The women who raised this question was Rummebai Invati, a 37-year-old member of the Kurai Block Panchayat of Seoni district of Madhya Pradesh.

Tribal Panchayats

In *Madhya Pradesh,* Mohanpur Khurd in Guna district is a tribal Panchayat. This tribal Panchayat has its own tribal Panchayat *vis-à-vis* new Panchayat. This Panchayat has women Sarpanch, the wife of local money-lender, who is also a tribal and has a strong control over the community. One day meet was organised for discussing various issues related to Panchayat and their day to day issues. The elected members and senior villagers expressed need for a training to know about Panchayati Raj Act and amendments properly. VA 'Prayatan' took the responsibility of conducting the training.

In *Orissa,* a training programme for elected tribal women representatives in Boipariguda Block of Koraput District was organised.

On Site Support

Beside these structured events to elected members regular on site support was provided by VAs.

> The news was spread in Madhya Pradesh in end 1996 that the cheques issued by the Panchayats should be countersigned by BDO for any withdrawal in connivance with the Bank. Shakti took up this issue and found that no government order had been passed. Panchayat Sarpanch have been informed about it and BDO has also agreed not to harass Sarpanchs by such tactics in future.

The trained VAS personnel were to work closely with elected Panchayat representatives not merely as trainers, but also as effective Capacity builders.

Negotiating with higher levels

Capacity building of gram panchayat members with high level that is Panchayat Samiti and Zila Parishad level to develop effective linkages between three tiers was also done.

Interface between the three tiers

In Haryana

In order to strengthen the organic link between the three-tiers as envisaged in the Act, RSO and its collaborating VAs have held a series of one-day dialogues between representatives of the three-tiers at Block Jhajjar, Districts Rewari. This was the first occasion where representatives of all three-tiers came together under one roof to discuss issues related to economic development and social justice along with strategies to strengthen the organic link so that each one has an important role to play in the process. Issues of accountability and transparency leading to good governance were discussed at length by all the three-tiers. It was discovered that many of the problems could be solved at their level since they arose purely out of gaps in communication and linkage between the three-tiers. There is very little understanding of the underlying perspective of decentralisation, with this amendment was made. By and large, elected representatives of all three tiers see themselves as mere implementers of centrally determined schemes of the government. The government too promotes and reinforces this role of the representatives.

Concentrated efforts were made at block Barara, District Ambala with the VA 'Racheri Janta Vikas Gram Udyog Samiti'. In order to ensure the active participation of the block and district level government functionaries, efforts were made to involve them from the planning stage. This proved to be quite successful as they sent out invitation letters on their letterheads (in addition to RSO). 40 participants including elected representatives from the Zilla Parishad (both chairperson and members), Panchayat Samiti and Gram Panchayats along with several block level functionaries actively participated. Meaningful discussion took place on the roles and responsibilities of elected representatives at each level, the barriers to their effective functioning and need to strengthen the organic link. Spaces and mechanisms were discussed through which the three tiers could strengthen their links and functioning in the existing scenario.

Capacity Building of Panchayat Samiti Member

In *Himachal Pradesh*, Government under UNICEF project had requested RSO to conduct 'Training Programmes for Elected Panchayat Samiti Members' to build their capacity as an effective PRI functionaries. From 12th to 30th of July training programmes were organised at all thirteen block of District Kangra. The design flowed from power structure and Constitutional Amendments, new Panchayati Raj and HP Panchayati Raj, social and gender justice, constitutions of Panchayat Samiti and Standing Committees, no confidence motion against chairman and vice-chairman, powers and functions of Panchayat Samiti, control, audit and inspection, information regarding various government schemes like Jawahar Rojgar Yojna and watershed development.

The Learning

- Gram Panchayat has both administrative and financial powers in practice while Panchayat Samiti have none.
- Panchayat Samiti members four times a year. The resolutions passed are sent to ZP and concerned authority but no one takes any notice of the resolutions.
- Panchayat Samiti members are not gram Panchayat members hence are not welcomed in the panchayat meetings.
- Panchayat Samiti members suggested that this tier be abolished and lakhs of rupees can be saved as they do not add value by their presence in three tiers.
- Block Development Officer's Annual Confidential Reports are not being written by Panchayati Samiti chairman hence they no longer attend the meetings.
- Only grant Panchayat Samiti gets in JRY. They divide the fund among themselves equally.
- The standing committees have no finance hence there is no point of having audit, finance and planning committee.
- Government do not pay any attention to the social justice committee.
- Majority of Panchayat Samiti members have not seen HP acts and rules.
- Government is not ready to hand over the powers. Unless Panchayat Samiti members stand united they will not be able to get power from Government.

Training Needs of Panchayat Samiti and Zilla Parishad in Rajasthan

A study has been done in Rajasthan where training needs of the Panchayat Samiti and Zilla Parishad along with Government counterpart was done in 1997. Joint trainings at this level was advocated.

Training Needs

- Greater need for problem-solving orientation in training sessions, catering to resolve field related problems. Inputs on birth-death registration, domicile certificate, conversion of *abadi* lands, public distribution system, mobilising financial resources of Panchayats desired, as presently not being covered in detailed clarity.
- Integrating gender issues in development areas.
- Assist women Sarpanches and ward members for greater effectiveness in their role performance.
- Need for behavioural issues like motivation, coordination, conducting meetings and minutes recording, team building, community participation and communication skills, etc.

In Uttar Pradesh

A training for elected Block level members was organised by VA 'Vir Bundelkhand Samajothan Mauranipur' on 1-3 July, 1996. Total 35 participants attended the training. (Male—30, Female—5, ST—7, SC—None, Others—28). People were eager to know more about their functions and funds.

Orientation of Zilla Parishad Members

In *Orissa* RSO and All Orissa Panchayat Parishad (AOPP) jointly conducted a training programme for Zilla Parishad members.

Capacity Building of Government Functionaries

The three levels of elected members have corresponding three levels of Government functionaries to deal with as shown in the Fig. 2. Panchayat Secretaries (Panchayat Secretaries) is at Gram Panchayat level, Block Development Officials at Block level and District level administration at district level.

Capacity Building of Panchayat Secretaries

Panchayat Secretaries also known as Panchayat Karmies are only Government functionaries who have direct link with Gram Panchayats but there is an acute shortage of properly trained PS. Even senior PS are not very effective as they have also not undergone any orientation course to work in the new atmosphere ushered in by the conformity act.

In **Kerala** K. Sreedharan from Trichur, a Panchayat Secretary who has attended training programme conducted for elected members have started contributing articles in publication like "*Panchayat Raj*", published by the Directorate of Panchayat, Government of Kerala.

In **Madhya Pradesh**, orientation programmes were organised for Panchayat Karmies and Key Resource Persons (KRP). A large number of local youth have been appointed as Panchayat Karmies by the Panchayats. There was a felt need to orient them to understand the new Panchayati Raj Systems as well as their role in it. They also needed to know how to manage the registers and accounts of the Panchayats. As a result, training camps for Panchayat Karmies were organised in three clusters in Sehore district by Samarthan. About 45 Panchayat Karmies were oriented on the following issues:

- Their roles and responsibilities.
- Relationship building skills with the Sarpanch, Gram Sabha and Government officials.
- Accounts and book-keeping.
- Sensitization on gender issues to promote women's participation.

- Importance of the Gram Sabha and ways of promoting information sharing with Gram Sabhas.

After these orientation and training campus, the Panchayat Karmies identified around 18 people from the Panchayats who were later oriented at the Panchayat to support the activities of the Gram Panchayats.

In *Rajasthan*, the original two-year training programme for Panchayat Secretaries had been reduced to a 45 days training programmes in 1995-96 leading to training gaps.

The Government Training Institutes

The Government training institutes has the responsibility of building the capacity of the elected members. But these institutes has certain strengths and limitations in strengthening these institutions. Ideally every divisional HQ should have a regional training centre for panchayat level training.

Physical Infrastructure

All the Government run training institutes in all the States have sufficient physical infrastructure available. But most of the training institutes lack basic training materials like projector, flip charts and markers.

Rajasthan Government Training Institutes have sufficient infrastructure like training halls, rooms, spacious land, staff quarters etc. But even after spending Rs. 35 lakhs on construction works in 1995 and 1996 in Dungarpur centre the basic training materials like projector flip charts and markers were not available. Three Training Institutes at Ajmer, Jodhpur and Dungarpur in Rajasthan are sharing a workload of 10-11 Districts. There is a mismatch between establishment costs and training programme costs.

Learning Materials

Even the learning materials are outdated. Difficult to read as because of poor quality of photocopy. The language is mostly official. Even if it is in local language it is generally very difficult to comprehend, as simple language is not used.

Human Resources

To run training institutes the trainers are pooled from different Government departments mostly on deputation. They may not have competencies as trainers besides having knowledge base for Panchayati Raj Institutions. Even the staffs are not generally orientated to the new role. They lack understanding of Participatory Training Methodology. More so with general feeling that training institute is a punishment posting not much pride is associated to the work.

RSO in different states are trying to use the available sources of Government training institutions to felt gap of resource.

Capacity Building of Voluntary Agencies

Each State level RSO build the capacity of VA staff for strengthening Local Self-governance. The VAs, who have grassroots presence and would work with elected members direct, were identified and selected by RSOs with mutual consent. The strengths of these organisations were the good rapport and ability to work with the community. They were aware of the local language, culture, difficulties faced by the community and their needs.

For Capacity building of the VAs two approaches were made depending upon their link with the field:

- The intervening areas which were new for the RSOs the strategy was to after selecting VAs, a Head of Organisations orientation meet was organised. This helped in two ways, firstly, perspective on working on this thematic area was developed; secondly, the training needs and ground realities were understood.
- Where the RSO had been working for long like in Gujarat, the State Level Training of Trainers programme was organised where capacity of both the Head of Organisations and staff was built to work on this thematic area.

Building Capacity of Head of Organisation

Head of Organisations meet was organised in some States with following objectives:

- To identify the need of training and acquaint them with the future strategy.
- Also to sensitize the heads so that they consider the programme their own.

In *Haryana* on 19th and 20th December, 1995 a workshop was held in PRIA. Total 18 participants from 16 organisations attended the workshop.

> The foremost suggestion that emerged was to hold a state training of trainers at Haryana in order to equip their staff with the details of the act enhance their training capacities.

Kerala

From 14th to 15th October, 1996 Sahayi conducted a two-day State Level Consultation of members of voluntary organisations in Kerala on the role of the voluntary groups in strengthening the PRI. It was attended by participants from 38 organisations from 12 districts of the State.

Himachal Pradesh

The training was held on 22nd and 23rd of January, 1996. A total of 25 participants from 18 organisations attended this meeting. They were mostly from 5 districts, namely Chamba, Kangra, Mandi, Una and Hamirpur.

Uttar Pradesh

On 19-20 October, 1995 a meet was organised where total 38 participants attended the programme. (Male—28, Female—10, SC—7, ST—7, Others—24). On 15-17th November, 1998 to upscale the intervention another Heads of Organisations meeting was done at Banda where more VAs capacity was built to work on this issue. A two-day meeting was organised at Jhansi from 5th to 6th July, 1999 in order to obtain the profiles of Jhansi based voluntary organisations and to develop working relationships and develop a rapport with them.

Impact—A network of VAs was floated who were willing to work on this issue on long-term basis.

Capacity Building of Staff of Voluntary Organisations

Based on the training needs all participating regional support organisations State Training of Trainers (STOT) Programme were conducted. The main objectives of STOT were as follows:

- To develop an understanding of local self-governance and the new Panchayati Raj Act.
- To understand the concept of participatory training and the role of trainer.
- To develop a different strategy towards the development of elected women Panchayat representatives.
- To formulate future strategy for Panchayati Raj intervention by individual organisation.

Although in the beginning intensive capacity building intervention like STOT was done but after this on the site and structured capacity building of staff were done continuously and regularly.

Gujarat

In Gujarat, STOT was organised during January 10-13, 1996, for the staff of voluntary agencies. In this training programme, thirty-two functionaries (15 females and 17 males) from 13 VAs were participated. On November 20, 1996 a one-day training programme on budget preparation was organised. With VA 'ASAG' and VA 'SARATHI' staff orientation programme was conducted and facilitated on April 13, 1996 at Godhar. Thirty participants 25 male and 5 female attended the programme.

> The unique feature of Gujarat intervention was two-phased STOT. This has given more space to understand some concepts of strengthening PRIs and then practice this in the field. The second phase had helped in refining the old concepts and bring in new ones.

Another advanced State level training programme was held during January 29-31, 1997 in which 42 functionaries from 22 organisations participated.

Staff of VA 'Rajpipla Social Service Society' underwent a three-day training on Tribal Self Rule.

Haryana

A 'seven-days' STOT was organised at Rai in Haryana. Twenty-eight representatives from eleven organisations participated in this training. During October 14-16, 1996 PRIA organised a two-day meet for voluntary organisations of Haryana at PRIA. The aim was to share the experiences of one year work on PRI, evolving a common goal/perspective and determining the future. Fifteen participants from ten organisations attended the programme. The outcome was that the network of VAS strengthened, common perspective developed, clarity on PRI and future plan made.

Himachal Pradesh

During 23rd to 27th February, 1996, a 'five days' STOT was organised at the Regional Mountaineering Centre, Mcleodganj, District Kangra. There were representatives from 12 organisations. Uniqueness of this STOT is this that elected panchayat members also attended the programme. An orientation-cum-capacity building workshop on strengthening Panchayati Raj Institutions was conducted at Shimla from 28th to 30th Oct. 1999. The participants were representatives of NGOs, elected members, Mahila Mandals and Youth Groups. The workshop was attended by fourteen VAs, two CBOs, two elected members. Total twenty-three participants attended this programme. Participants shared their future action plan also. A 'two days' workshop was organised on 3rd and 4th of February 2000 at Municipal Conference Hall at Nahan, Sirmaur with VA 'YUMDHA'. The workshop was attended by VA members, elected members, intellectuals, Mahila Mandal and Youth group members. The highlight of this workshop was that the Zilla Parishad Chairman was supposed to inaugurate the programme and leave but when experiences was shared he took special interest and had attended all the sessions. Total thirty-seven participants attended the programme.

Kerala

The 'seven days' STOT was conducted from 17th to 23rd January, 1996 at the West Kallada Social Welfare Society in the Sasthamcotta block in which 37 delegates from 25 organisations, from 9 districts of Kerala participated. A State level orientation on micro-planning was organised at the community Panchayat Hall of Ahirappally Panchayat in Trichur district from 13th to 16th December, 1996. The main aim of the programme was to train a core team of facilitators from 18 collaborating VO groups in relation to micro-plan work. A one day micro-planning orientation was conducted at Santhigram in the Trivandrum district on 9th December 1996. It was attended by 39 VAs.

Madhya Pradesh

The STOT was organised in January 1996 in Bhopal. 13 Participants from 9 organisations (from Bundelkhand, Malwa and Chhattisgarh regions) attended the training workshop. The attendance in this workshop was low because of heavy rains in many of the regions which hampered the travel of a large number of participants. Another training was also held in July 1996 for staff of VA to increase and systematise their accounting procedures. As a follow-up measure of the trainings, all the said organisations have agreed to conduct accounts training for their respective Panchayats. 55 Mahila Samakhya (A grassroots programme for women) Sahyogini (staff) training was done for 2 days in 1998 to orient the Sahyogini and the Panchayat representatives.

Orissa STOT was organised between 17-23rd May, 1999, in which 25-community organiser and field coordinators of different NGOs working in seven districts of Orissa took part.

Uttar Pradesh

Owing to territorial constraints coupled with geographical pattern of the networking, two separate STOTs were organised: One at Lucknow for VAS of eastern UP and the other at Chitrakoot for the VAS of Bundelkhand.

Eastern Uttar Pradesh

On 15-21 November, 1995 STOT was organised where total 30 participants attended the programme (M—15, F—15, SC—5, ST—13, Others—12). In this training as many as 16 resource persons gave their views and ideas in strengthening Local Self-Governance. This has also helped in building link with local key organisations like UNICEF, Panchayati Raj Department, CAPART, SIRD etc.

Bundelkhand Region: A training of Trainers programme was organised from 27th November - 3rd December, 1995 at Banda where total 22 participants attended (M—14, F—8, SC—5, ST—10, Others—8). The objectives, methodology, contents remained the same.

VA 'Disha Samajik Sansthan', Saharanpur. A training programme was organised by RSO for staff. Another training programme for "Panchayati Activists" was organised from 20-23rd September, 1999 for another VA 'Pratinidhi Sansthan', Barhaz, Balia. A two-day orientation training was provided to VA 'Mahila Evam Bal Kalyan Utthan Samiti', Para Chaura Bagh, Ghazipur from the 26th-27th September, 1999, on social work, group formation, their responsibilities.

There were hurdles in understanding the concept, preparation and implementation of micro plans. A 'Micro Plan Refresher Training Workshop' was organised for thirty VAS in March 1998 by RSO to identify the hurdles and overcome it collectively.

Conclusions

The complex regional variance in India has arrays of constituencies at different levels of understanding who are critical direct or indirect actors of Panchayati Raj Institutions. This has made us realised that capacity building interventions is the need of the hour. It should be need based and situation specific. The concrete evidences of working on this issue for last 6-7 years has reinforced our faith in capacity building interventions to yield results.

Significance of Capacity Building

Capacity building interventions has made the constituencies realised the need of appropriate and timely informations. This has created a demand for the information and access to informations on a regular basis. Hitherto the informations has been treated as property of few privileged class. This has been demystified. Capacity to process the information and shared among others has had a cascading effect on elected members. The ability to question Government functionaries who holds all the powers of development of the Panchayats had been in increase. Although with those who has the power for so long the magic wand approach may not work immediately, however, questioning collectively is a significant step towards development of panchayats. More and more capacity building interventions have been demanded by the elected Gram Sabha members.

There is a significant increase in level of awareness of Gram Sabha members and elected members. This has helped in understanding different processes of functioning of these institutions. The underlining stake of various stakeholders has been more clear and the need for functioning as individuals and collectives have been understood.

These interventions have also developed skills of different constituencies to conduct meetings, provide leadership, timely decision making, communicate effectively and managing the resources in an appropriate manner.

Capacity Building for Empowerment

These capacity building interventions when focused specially to hither to excluded class like—the women, dalits and tribals—had more impact. Since these classes has different framework for learning hence these interventions have made them realised their own potential. These opportunities has brought the changes in the behavioural pattern. The behavioural changes are otherwise dormant life pattern of first time elected members has helped in mobilising human, material and natural resources. Capacity building interventions address the role as decision-making body. These has helped in playing their role more effectively and with confidence. The realisation to the importance of the information and access to resources have come through these interventions and helped them to be empowered.

Our experiences show that in spite of having certain disadvantages the women elected members after capacity building interventions could address issues like land grabbing, selling of illicit liquor etc. is indeed an empowering process. Sometimes even male elected members would not like to raise tricky issues like these in their own Panchayats fearing bad reputation.

The tribals whose rights of livelihood through forests were snatched for the name of protecting the flora and fauna are now collectively coming together for their rights to protect the forest within the jurisdiction of their Panchayats. There are instances where connecting roads through the forests were not being built for so long under the pretext that the trees cannot be fell. After the capacity building interventions and access to informations the connecting road could be built by the Panchayats. And it was an all women tribal Panchayat.

So far dalits in a village have been doing certain specific activities through generation which were thought of suitable to them. They were neither allowed to sit in *Chaupal* (the concrete structure in centre place of a Panchayat generally under a huge shaded tree) nor allowed to speak. But after the events they themselves took initiatives to go to *Chaupal*. Now they have been not only allowed to sit and attend the meetings but also air their views. There are examples where the dalit ward member who since generations is ferrying goods through the mule in hills have not attended any Panchayat meeting after being elected. After capacity building interventions he has realised the importance of the meeting and started attending the meeting and could articulate his view on the matter concerned.

Methods in Capacity Building

The previous sections describe our experiences of using various methods of capacity building interventions for varied constituencies. Though there are State specific variations however some common methods which weave all along are found very effective.

Educational Materials

The materials prepared by the RSOs and the partners were innovative, region and language specific. Special framework was thought of prior to developing materials. Almost all the RSOs have simplified the State Panchayat Act in a simple State language. This has helped the literate constituency to understand the premises in which they are intervening. In structured events simplified materials were disseminated for future references. Various forms of learning materials were prepared. They were in shape of posters, pamphlets, fliers, handbills, newsletter, etc.

Since in India after every 50 kms. even the colloquial language changes, special emphasis was given on languages. Bright primary colours have been used for more impact. There were simple sketches which could be understood by everyone.

The oral traditional methods of *Nukkad Natak* (Plays at Street corners), folk songs were also used for both literate and illiterate groups. Interactive games and flip charts were prepared and found very useful in capacity building interventions. All events were documented and disseminated for others' references. This has helped in organisational/institutional learning too.

Workshops

The workshops are found to be very effective where participants could bring their own experiences and field realities and work together to formulate common understanding and strategies. The workshops take care the learnings of the participants from one stage to another. Group discussions were found to be especially useful. The unique features in these workshops were the future action plans whereby participants own agenda in terms of actions could be incorporated. These were found more effective with Government functionaries and staff of VAS.

Camps

One day or half day camps has enabled us to reach quantitatively to GS members or elected members in their own context with minimum resources. Although this has limitation of taking up one or two issues in each camp depending upon the duration but the positive side of it is that keeping in mind the number of GS members and elected members in India this is very effective method. Our recent experiences of *Campaign mode of capacity building* coined as PRAJA has helped us reach to Gram Panchayat members after second round of election to about 0.66 per cent of blocks (As mentioned total number of blocks are around 6000, 39 blocks have been intervened in last three months) in four States (Haryana, Himachal, Rajasthan and Uttar Pradesh). This has proved to be low cost intensive method whereby we can reach to elected members soon after they have been elected and orient them to the new roles and responsibilities. Moreover the elected members felt that their identity have been honoured by at least calling them to a capacity building intervention. They were happy to be able to express their views and develop a link among themselves. Similarly in one State (Madhya Pradesh) clustered approach of campaign mode has helped us to reach out to the Panchayats. This method is very effective with elected and Gram Sabha members. The challenge is to made these campaign self-sustainable without the use of imported intervention outside the context and how to keep this alive and regular.

Trainings

Trainings had been always participatory with focus of learnings to 'KAS' that is Knowledge, Attitude and Skills. The exchange of knowledge, behavioural changes and skill building by practically doing are the foremost areas addressed in the trainings. Large and Small Group Discussions, Role plays, case studies (oral and written), exercises, simulations etc. and learning materials were used to substantiate the learning. The outcome is very impressive but cost in terms of time and resources are quite high and this may not help to reach to all elected members soon after the elections. Once the training is delayed there are likelihood that the elected members may not understand the true role as envisaged in the provisions and may fall back to the prey of powerful stakeholders and act as the third tier of implementer. This method is found to be useful with VA staff.

Field Visits

The base of field visits are 'the learning by seeing'. Field visits have been found very useful whereby the elected members and VA members could see the successful (or not so successful) models. The focus is that how it has been done elsewhere and how it could be replicated in their own context. Though this method needs coordination time and bit expensive but the impact is always more. Our experiences of visits made by elected members specially women or dalit members to another Panchayat where the Panchayat is being (For woman or dalit visitor to woman or dalit headed) developed in similar context helps. This brings enthusiasm and more concrete action taken by VAS and elected members after the visit.

Projects

Different other developmental actors work on various developmental projects in the Panchayats. These need to be integrated with Panchayats. Hence the capacity building interventions if integrates with ongoing projects or schemes has more impact. The watershed development projects, total eradication of leprosy or blindness projects etc. in the Panchayat needs to be integrated with the panchayat activities rather than as a stand alone interventions. This will strengthen Panchayats rather than promote parallel bodies who may hinder the functioning of constitutionally framed bodies. Projects could be more effective and enlarged.

Linkages

The capacity building interventions provide a platform for the participants to come together. This creates lateral as well as horizontal linkages. Among themselves they can develop horizontal linkages and may act as peer pressure group. Lateral linkages between three tiers help them understand each other functions and role better and jointly may bring desired changes fast. The administrative linkages developed are also useful for day to day work of panchayats. The challenges are how to make self-sustainable linkages without being externally pushed. These linkages could be of different levels like lateral network of all Gram Panchayats members, network of all Panchayat Samiti members, network of all Zilla Parishad members, network of all Local CBOs or horizontal network at block or Zilla level. Experience shows that cluster network can be sustained with less effort.

Enabling Environment for Capacity Building

The enabling environment for capacity building is as important as the interventions. This is more true for those who have not been brought to main stream of development and provisions have given them an opportunity. Prior to women capacity building interventions if the environment is built by visiting the families or briefing the family members about the objectives and expectations, the impact is more. Sometimes even after doing this due to social system a woman member may not be allowed to come to the event alone hence for effective learning another family member could be invited. In India Government servants are accepted as the most powerful persons. Hence BDOs or District administration needs to be put in picture before any capacity building interventions. This helps in rapport building beside the proper environment is built. The experience of strengthening of these institutions in the past 6-7 years makes it clear that effective local self-governance is still a distant dream and requires enormous capacity building interventions to realise its potential.

6

TRAINING OF PANCHAYAT NON-OFFICIALS AND OFFICIALS IN RAJASTHAN

RAKESH HOOJA

Introduction

The Planning Commission Working Group on Decentralized Planning and Panchayati Raj Institutions for the Tenth Five Year Plan (2002-2007) has suggested that the scope of training for Panchayati Raj functionaries (both elected representatives or "non-officials" and the officials attached to Panchayati Raj Institutions or PRIs) should include training about the following:

1. Duties and responsibilities and power and authority of PRIs.
2. Financial management—resource mobilization, accounting, auditing, etc.
3. Social issues—reproductive health, child development, environmental issues, human rights, etc.
4. Constitutional provisions, concerned acts, rules and regulations, development schemes etc.
5. Training content should also include how to work in a group, building espirit-de-corps, developing leadership skills, decision-making acumen, motivation and morale building, etc.

6. Self-governance, social justice and ethics in public affairs.
7. Training can be organized under the following heads for Panchayats and municipalities:
   (a) Participatory Poverty Assessment,
   (b) Participatory Vulnerability Mapping,
   (c) Participatory Resource Planning,
   (d) Participatory assessment and action related to education, health and infrastructure,
   (e) Participatory Heritage Mapping,
8. Training content should aim at linking training interventions to development programmes.
9. Emerging areas like Natural Disaster Management, micro level planning, etc. should also be included in training programmes.

Gender Sensitization

The Working Group also suggests that training programmes for panchayati raj related functionaries should concentrate on providing basic skills of planning to the rural population and that the training must focus on the significance of preparing people for proper planning for socio-economic development in the light of the area in which they live. Further, it has been suggested that the training approach should keep in mind the impact of specific customs, traditions and conventions of the people whom it is intended to train. The Working Group also asserts that such training for panchayat functionaries cannot be a one time effort, but has to be a continuous process.

Later in this paper it is intended to examine to what extent the training documents of Indira Gandhi Panchayati Raj Evam Gramin Vikas Sansthan (IGPRS which is the recognized State Institute for Rural Development in Rajasthan) document Panchayati Raj Prashikshan Sandarbh Samgree (Panchayati Raj Training Reference Material) prepared for the Panchayati Raj Capacity Development Campaign 2005 of Rajasthan corresponds to the above-mentioned recommendations of the Planning Commission Working Group.

However before that, it is intended to take a look at the need for the large scale and modified Panchayat training that has become necessary after the 73rd Constitutional Amendment in the light of the expectations from decentralization through PRIs. In fact since the scope and nature of training would depend upon the expectations that society has from the panchayati raj system as a whole, after indicating some impacts of the Constitutional amendment upon training, this paper shall go into a brief discussion about the various views about the multifarious objectives of panchayati raj, i.e. what people expect can be achieved (or not achieved) through panchayati raj including some expectations that may prove to be utopian. The paper shall accordingly try to analyze the desired content of training programmes for the elected representatives as well as panchayat officials, as also the means to impart such training in a manner that is easily comprehensible to the trainees who come from rural backgrounds and many of whom may even be illiterate.

Training Impact of 73rd Constitutional Amendment

Following the 73rd Constitutional Amendment, the Government of India has been sponsoring a large number of orientation training courses for the elected representatives of panchayati raj as also for functionaries of the PR institutions. The number of persons requiring training has also gone up. For example, in Rajasthan before the amendment about 50,000-60,000 panches (or members of gram, panchayat) used to be elected and they chose their sarpanch who automatically became member of the panchayat samiti. The pradhan elected by the sarpanch-*cum*-member-panchayat samiti automatically became a member of the zilla parishad for electing the zilla pramukh. If we add coopted members, members of gram sahakari samiti who automatically used to become members of gram panchayat and MLAs and MPs who were also members of panchayat bodies then also the total of non-officials in panchayat bodies did not go up significantly. After the amendment the members of zilla parishad (997 in 1995 which went up to 1008 in 2000) are separate from the pradhans of the panchayat samiti (237), the members of panchayat samiti (5257) are different from Sarpanches (9085 in 1995 which went up to 9186 in 2000) and the number of ward panches has gone up to over 1,00,000. The total number of elected PR representatives in Rajasthan is thus almost 1,20,000. Thus, a large number of first time electees has gone up because in addition to the earlier reservation for the scheduled castes (SCs) and scheduled tribes (STs), reservation has been added for women and for other backward classes and the reserved constituencies change from one election to another. In fact 33,566 women were elected out of a total of 1,19,419 total elected non-officials in Rajasthan's 1995 PR elections which went up to 40,543 women out of 120,555 by the time of the 2000 PR elections in the state.

The larger number of persons elected to panchayat bodies for the first time automatically means that their training requirements are different from, and greater than for those who have earlier held elected office in the panchayati raj bodies. This is because their knowledge and earlier experiences, as well as current expectations from panchayati raj would be different. The large total numbers as well as greater first time electees also increase the likely number of illiterate elected non-officials requiring training. Further, the reserved seats changes after the term of those elected ends—a women's seat may become a seat for an ST or an SC seat may become a general seat, and so on. Thus, the system would ensure that many persons presently elected would be ineligible to seek re-election from the same seat once their term ends. Accordingly, each election will now automatically throw up a batch consisting of a large proportion of newly elected representatives. Thus, large scale training (including training for the large number of people elected for the first time) would have to become a regular feature between each election. In Rajasthan during 2003-04 out of 18,372 elected Sarpanches and appointed Gram Sevaks approximately 17,000 Sarpanches and Gram Sevaks underwent one week residential training by December 2003 and about 63,000 ward panches out of 1,05,000 ward panches underwent one day orientation camp training. While arrangements had been made for cent per cent training, about 5 per cent absentees occurred in the case of Sarpanches and Gram Sevaks and 40 per cent absentees in the case of ward panches. In addition Gram Sevaks were provided refresher training and in two rounds of centralized training 38,000 and then 30,000 elected women representatives were trained in the same period. In addition courses for Zilla Pramukhs, Chief Executive Officers Zilla Parishad,

Panchayat Samiti Pradhan's and Vikas Adhikaris (Block Development Officers) were also organised.

The fact that at each level, the PR body would be much larger than in the pre-amendment era, as also the breaking of the earlier organic link between each level of PR (though each state can, and many states like Rajasthan have made the gram panchayat's sarpanch and panchayat samiti's pradhan, respectively, a member of the next higher body) has changed the internal dynamics of the functioning of the panchayat body at each level. The debating aspect in each body may now far outweigh the executive tasks which would shift much more to standing committees of the particular panchayat body. This also has an effect on the type of training required by the elected representatives as well as by other functionaries who have to work in these changed circumstances.

Expectations from Panchayati Raj and Decentralization

Decentralization through PR institutions can, according to Amitav Mukherjee (1991), be seen as a means to increase popular participation, to improve development efforts (improved management of programmes), and as a means to means to bring about a dimunation of secessionist tendencies. Das (1974) has suggested the enabling of (i) strengthening autonomous local self-government institutions; (ii) each local village cluster to meet their own perceptions of needs through locally optimal arrangements rather than through some minimum standard of meeting needs to be uniformly applied; and (iii) greater adaptability, as objectives of such decentralization. For V.M. Rao (1989) the expectation is that such decentralization would enable (a) bringing the peripheral groups of the poor and disadvantaged within the mainstream of economic processes, (b) the stable and dependable provision on an adequate scale of relief and supply of minimum needs to the poor and disadvantaged, (c) planning to effectively cover resources of local level significance and the specially dispersed economic activities carried out on a small scale at the household and village level, (d) the promotion among the people of a feeling of motivation, self-help, local level leadership an active role in strategic and planning decisions. ESCAP/APDI expert group (quoted in FAO 1985) saw it as a means to a close partnership between government and the rural population, on organizing and coordinating the higher echelons of administration, paying special attention to programmes aimed at the rural poor, and to decentralizing the process of development. The advantages of decentralization can be summarized as follows:

(a) Increased people's participation;
(b) Improved quality of development efforts and improved management of programmes;
(c) Provision of resources and programmes for each area and for different groups inhabiting the area on the basis of an assessment of the specific area's problems, resources and potentialities;
(d) Spatial planning (including considering the need for relaxation of uniform norms related to distance or population thresholds) for provision of service and facilities in specific areas;
(e) Use of locational theory and rural growth centre or central place planning and centrality scoring techniques;
(f) Greater feeling of involvement in the planning effort on the part both of lower level functionaries and the local people;
(g) Strengthening of local government bodies;
(h) Locally optimal arrangement for each cluster of villages, or people within a village, to meet their own perceptions of their needs rather than through uniform standards prescribed in a uniform manner for the entire country, or state, as a whole;
(i) Better consideration of available local level resources or of the lack of and need for the same, and of local problems, than would be possible through planning at higher levels;
(j) Greater mobilization of resources at the local level;
(k) Evolution of participatory mechanisms to promote local level leadership, habits of self-help, motivation and willingness to undertake local plan formulation and implementation.
(I) Creating a psychology for development and change at local levels;

(m) Reduction in regional disparities;
(n) Meeting of basic needs of the people in a better manner which could help to bring into the mainstream peripheral groups and the poor and deprived;
(o) Better partnership may be achieved between the people and development agencies;
(p) Small mini-projects may be individually planned for using project approach based analysis at the local or district level which may not be possible at higher levels where only generalized guidelines can be framed for particular types of small schemes;
(q) Successful marriage of project planning and participatory planning may prove easier at levels closer to the grassroots;
(r) Local social or physical barriers not always apparent on maps can only be considered while planning locally and not during state or higher level plan exercises;
(s) Integrated and comprehensive multi-sector planning may prove easier at lower levels, while at higher levels mono-sector planning or sectorally segmented planning subsequently compiled, as is being done at present, may have to be resorted to.

International development experts and aid donors appear to have some additional expectations from decentralization. However, following a cross-country study, Crook and Manor (1994) have indicated that many of these expectations are misplaced and unlikely to be achieved. They indicate that not much can be expected in terms of planning from below through elected local councils like panchayats because of (a) lack of administrative capacity and of trained manpower, (b) lack of information base (no inventory of capital resources, no assessment of local economy, inadequate statistical base), (c) a short-term outlook and the liking of local politicians for keeping their list of projects open-ended and flexible at all times leading to *ad hoc* decisions and processes being followed, (d) grants from higher authorities are heavily earmarked, (e) decentralized planners have no control over resources, (f) higher authorities have little interest in decentralized planning. Similarly not much local mobilization of resources is likely because (a) in impoverished areas the amount of mobilizable resources may be limited, (b) elected councillors hesitate to impose taxes—local elites are reluctant to tax themselves, (c) local people are cynical about what local councils may do with locally raised resources and the existence of under-resourced local authorities may deepen the popular cynicism, (d) locally raised resources are inadequate for any project but the most modest development or service provision. Hence unless major Central/State Government financial support flows in on a continuous basis, local persons may not be inclined to add their meager locally raised resources to the available pool. Decentralization is unlikely to reduce Central/State Government expenditure because (i) decentralization is bound to entail significant starting up costs, (ii) decentralization by definition involves larger number of staff and more costs on travel and honoraria etc., (iii) decentralized bodies need to be provided with large amounts of resources to take up activities which would win them the confidence of the people, (iv) to monitor adequately a decentralized system requires a large monitoring bureaucracy.

Further, Crook and Manor suggest that tasks which Central/State Government try to get rid of by devolving responsibility for them upon local councils are not likely to be performed adequately because of (a) insufficient resources, (b) incapacity of the local bureaucracy, (c) disinclination of elected local bodies to tackle any of the tasks particularly if they do not entail construction of physical assets. Decentralization will do little or nothing directly to benefit vulnerable groups or to alleviate poverty because (i) decentralization empowers local and intermediate areas in which parochially minded local elites exercise dominance, or national level elites build local power bases, (ii) the personalization of power relations is more intense at intermediate or local levels. Accordingly, governments may be well advised to insulate programmes aimed at aiding the vulnerable or at alleviating poverty from decentralized planning and implementation. Democratic decentralization is not likely to help. much in terms of community participation because (a) the local councils are supra-local in character and have different interests from those of village communities and attempts at mobilization may cause these differing interests to come into conflict, (b) elections to local bodies tend to create divisions within or between local communities, (c) local socio-economic structures permit inequalities which allow elites to dominate and this weighs against community participation, (d) it is extremely difficult to combine the roles of community delegate/development animator with that of district level politician and manager of district resources. Decentralization cannot be expected to reduce absenteeism among public employees or to increase their work rate when they are on the job. Crook and Manor also indicate that decentralization inflates popular expectations much beyond what can be satisfied by local councils; that people fail to understand the limitation of what decentralized or local bodies, or even local government can achieve; and that greater transparency made possible by decentralization makes corruption more visible (and there may also occur decentralization of corruption)—leading to a mood of popular exasperation even when corruption may actually have declined.

Despite highlighting many problem areas regarding decentralization Crook and Manor feel that decentralization has, especially in their Indian case study area (the State of Karnataka), positively influenced the way that state and society interact and the popular perception of this—mainly for the better-in several ways. A similar situation has also been experienced in the state of Rajasthan, i.e. despite the likely problems of the sort indicated by Crook and Manor, the possible expected advantages of decentralization are likely to be achieved through PR to a significant extent within a multi-level framework.

We may add that the World Bank's World Development Report 1997 on the State in a changing world feels that one of the factors that can help raise state capability by reinvigorating public institutions is making the state more responsive to people's needs and bringing government closer to the people through broader participation and decentralization and an increased voice for the citizens. However, this report warns us that, while decentralizing, countries should watch out for possible pitfalls, i.e. rising inequality, micro-economic instability and the possibility of the Centre having to bail our regional and local authorities; and the risk of the capture of local governments by vested interests.

Case for Training of Elected Representatives

We have been looking at the expectations from PR and apprehensions of failure or problems of PR from the point of view of working out what sort of skills and knowledge should be emphasized in training for panchayat officials and non-officials. As regards training to reorient the thinking of elected PR leaders to empathise more with the poor and deprived, or for example to forego secessionist thinking where it already exists, or for attitudes like those which emphasize self-help—this may have to be attempted carefully because changing of attitudes is not easy and also because state sponsored training may not be capable of bringing about such attitudinal change. Also such training may run the danger of becoming a part of party based or ideological indoctrination, which perhaps should not be encouraged.

What may be more relevant and more likely to meet with success is to impart skills related to planning and implementation with perhaps some psychological orientation about team work, group decision-making, developing better leadership qualities, and interactions within meetings of large groups, etc. As regards planning, unlike the elected non-officials' expectations which seen to be concentrated only upon use of and sanctioning powers for government funds and what may more correctly be called governmental development budgeting rather than planning, comprehensive planning for the entire local area (district, panchayat samiti, or village) including all governmental and private activities had been advocated since long. This is similar to the views of Gadgil and V.K.R.V. Rao and the Constitutional Amendment which calls for preparation of plans for economic development and social justice.

Knowledge and Skills, Required for Decentralized Planning

Accordingly, the skills and knowledge that are likely to prove relevant for decentralized planning and should be imparted to those who have to operate panchayati raj are:

(a) Knowledge of the area's needs potentials, resources and resource gaps,

(b) Knowledge of state and national goals, plans, schemes and resource flows,
(c) Responsiveness to people's needs and knowledge of their aspirations,
(d) Knowledge of participatory planning and local mobilization techniques,
(e) Knowledge of how the government administrative system and the existing market system works in the region/area,
(f) Planning and project-planning expertise,
(g) Area and spatial planning knowledge and concepts,
(h) Some knowledge of various disciplines and technical subjects having a bearing on development (i.e. basic knowledge regarding agriculture, animal husbandry, civil engineering, rural industries, health and education management, and similar subjects,
(i) Ability to combine the above and prepare integrated and comprehensive plans based on a broad vision, and
(j) Knowledge of successes and failures of decentralized planning and implementation elsewhere.

Such knowledge would not be available with anyone single individual even at the highest policy level in the country. However, teams of local administrators, people's representatives, etc. could be built up gradually to develop a feel and understanding for each of the above points. For that at least initially attempts should be made to impart training not only to district and block level planners but also to relevant state level planners in:

1. Identifying locally felt-needs (as well as aspirations, which may match neither the needs nor the available resources) and mobilizing the local people to ensure people's participation and participatory planning.
2. Project/Scheme identification.
3. The project approach and basics of project planning.
4. Area planning and concepts like growth centre planning.
5. Integrating and compiling different aspects of plan proposals and proposals regarding various schemes/projects into a coherent district or local area plan.

6. Interacting with State Government planning cells and various State Government planning departments and their district level staff.
7. Interacting with the large sized panchayat bodies that shall come into existence as a result of the recent constitutional amendments.
8. National and state level planning goals.
9. Sources of and ways to gain access to, data available at national, and state levels which could prove useful for decentralized planning.
10. Now-a-days some knowledge in the use of computers could also be imparted as their use could make planning exercise much easier.

For identification of the local needs and aspirations the techniques like problem-tree analysis, or problem-matrix analysis on the one hand and rapid rural appraisal (RRA) and participatory rural appraisal (PRA) on the other need to be taught. Of course, as regards motivation of the populace there is no simple formula or technique that could be taught.

Project Identification and Local Planning

As regards project identification it could be suggested to the potential decentralized planners that project/scheme ideas can come to them from either analytical or non-analytical resources like the following:

Analytical sources	*Non-analytical sources*
1. Resource analysis of areas and households.	1. Political directions.
2. Needs analysis.	2. Political pressures.
3. Demand analysis	3. Declared government policies and objectives.
4. Market analysis.	4. Formal (and even informal) interaction amongst officers or between officials and non-officials.
5. Rapid Rural Appraisal.	5. Guidelines of Aid Giving Agencies/ National Programmes etc.

Contd...

Analytical sources	*Non-analytical sources*
6. Social mapping/ cultural inventories.	6. Replication of existing project ideas.
7. Diagnostic and strategy exercises.	7. Feedback from failed projects.
8. Brainstorming.	8. Touring in the area.
9. Survey of literature.	9. Common administrative or political experience.
10. Project/ identification missions or groups.	10. Bargaining between sanctioning and implementing agencies/ departments.
11. The population, agriculture, animal husbandry, industry, etc. census conducted at regular intervals.	11. Casual reading of newspapers, magazines, books.
	12. Meetings of villagers and panchayats bodies.
	13. Citizens petitions and applications.

Curtis and Watson have suggested that analytical sources of project ideas can be further divided into the sub-categories of administrative search and intellectual search. Some possible methods of the two types of search are given below:

Administrative Search	*Intellectual (Academic) Search*
Consult population (Surveys, local committees, discussions villagers meetings)	Analyse Economy
Consult local leaders and other key informants formally/informally (even in a seminar)	Analyse Society
Consult Government Departments through routine meetings and special working groups	Special problem-oriented analytical studies
Consult research organizations/ consultants through planning studies.	Diagnostic and strategy exercises

Roberts Chambers has indicated the following criteria for simple project selection: Cost effectiveness, decision matrices, priority ranking, check listing, preparation of lists of costs and benefits.

Just as for purposes of decentralized planning the project identification needs to be kept simple, similarly project planning also need not entail full and detailed project analysis with Net Present Value (NPV). Internal Rate of Return (IRR) and cost benefit (B/C) ratios in detail not being required for each and every project appraisal.

In fact for many small projects even rough use of the project approach with a rough comparison of costs and benefits prove adequate and would also be an improvement over the scheme budget exercise presently most often done in government. Not every project needs to have exact values assigned to the costs, benefits and rates of returns and in some cases mere qualification, and in others even identification, may be enough.

Of course, the project approach needs to be properly understood at the district and lower levels, both among administrators and amongst panchayat leaders, not only for project formulation purposes, but also for project implementation since it would help avoidance of blind application of norms worked out by some other agency without trying to see if any special local conditions exist that would lead to unintended latent impacts of implementation which had not been anticipated by the project formulator.

Similarly, if the project approach is understood at the local planning level, then better sensitively analysis is possible since, instead of abstract generalized eventualities like percentage cost or time overrun being considered at state or regional level, at the local level locally specific likely eventualities can be better identified and quantified for sensitivity analysis with respect to each such specific eventuality.

Local planners mistakenly think of project life as only covering the period up to benefit delivery or completion of construction, and have to be reminded that the period in which the impact of a project is being felt has to be considered part of project life for pre-project appraisal purposes and that intangible benefits and costs both have to be considered as have possible negative impacts of projects.

It also needs to be explained to local planners as to how project analysis needs to include technical appraisal, financial appraisal, economic appraisal, sustainability appraisal (with its sub-categories of social appraisal and environmental appraisal) and what can be referred to as acceptability appraisal (involving acceptability on the part of the beneficiaries, the non-beneficiaries in the area, and the lower, middle and senior level implementators, as well as concerned officials and non-officials since in case acceptability is not forthcoming then either the project objectives may need to be modified or special acceptability, including mechanisms, may need to be built into the project at a cost). The second best may at times be better than the optimal or the best. Only after the above have been considered can decide about accepting rejecting projects, or regarding ranking of projects be undertaken.

Area and District Planning

Most district and block-level functionaries have never really thought in terms of locational and area planning or of growth centre concepts. However, once exposed to basic area based concepts, most are quick to understand issues of both geographic and social distance and of physical and social barriers as also how to fit their projects/ schemes into a framework of spatial planning that would prove most beneficial for the area they are to plan for and implement in. They also start appreciating how sectoral plans and growth/service centre plans can each lead to modifications in each other, so that an integrated area development plan catering to both sectoral needs and central place based planning can evolve. Use of methodological devices like Gutmans Scalogram for growth centres and for facilities provided at such centres are also easily understood by them. Experiences of the Government of India-Ford Foundation Pilot Project on Rural Growth Centres may, however, caution planners that the growth centre approach has to be integrated with other approaches and cannot be the sole criteria for preparing plans.

As regards preparing holistic district plans, many writers have set forth their views over the last few decades and numerous model district plans (e.g. Mushari, Rayalseema, Dharmpur, Wardha-NIRD plans) have also been prepared. However it is felt that, if Gadgil's views from the 1960s, V.K.R.V. Rao's from the 1970s and those of the Hanumantha Rao (Working Group Report of 1984) are put across in a simplified manner to potential planners at the district or block levels, then many of the issues that run through most writings on district planning would get properly discussed.

How to Tap Funds

The training should also emphasize that a lot of sources for funds and projects may be available outside government (from banks, various trusts and autonomous bodies, etc.) or if within government then not through routine State Government budgets which are partly devolved upon panchayats, but are available upon special application being made for them. Thus panchayat bodies need to know about sources of such funds, guidelines for applying for them and ways in which to prepare implementable and sanctionable projects for such sanctioning. In todays era of economic liberalization and with the post-Fifth Pay Commission scenario, normal flow of Government funds to PR may not be large and may in fact, reduce. Hence such tapping of other sources by panchayati bodies, as also tapping of user charges, may have to be learnt by PR officials and non-officials.

Modes of Training

Both for training regarding planning and for training for actually doing things (implementing) it is case studies, examples, demonstrations, films and audio-visual aids as well as discussions rather than lectures, which should be used for both the lower level functionaries and elected persons in panchayats. Concepts need to be simplified with use of examples that are meaningful in the rural milieu.

Rajasthan's Panchayati Raj Training Document

Having, in the Preceding sections of this paper, set forth some ideas on the training content and methodologies that this author considers appropriate for panchayat personnel, and having summarized the Planning Commission Working Group's views on the matter in the introductory section of this paper, it is now appropriate to turn to the Panchayati Raj Training Reference Material document of IGPRS Jaipur.

This is the third edition of this Hindi volume of training material which was officially brought out for Rajasthan's Panchayati Raj Capacity Development Campaign 2005. It comprises brief write-ups, containing subject-matter considered relevant for Panchayat functionaries, as well as a section on training methodologies, exercises and games meant to be used by resource persons in panchayati raj capacity development workshops, and another on motivational songs in Hindi and Rajasthani.

The subjects covered in this volume are:

1. Expectations from PRIs
   (a) Eleventh Schedule of Constitution.
   (b) Participation based economic development and human development.
   (c) The concept of social justice, secularism, equality and human rights as inspired by the Constitution of India: Fundamental Rights, Directive Principles of State Policy, Fundamental Duties.
   (d) The Constitutional role of PRIs.
2. Main features of 73rd Constitutional Amendment and Structure of Panchayati Raj:
   (a) From Gram Swarajya to Poorna Swarajya
   (b) Main components of 73rd Amendment
   (c) Structures of Panchayati Raj.
3. Role of PRIs in Development Administration
   (a) Functions of Zilla Parishad
   (b) Functions of Panchayat Samiti
   (c) Functions of Gram Panchayat
4. Responsive and Compassionate Administration.
5. Right to Information and Social Audit.
6. Financial Management, Taxation and Audit in PRIs.
7. Objectives and Challenges of Rural Development
   (a) Millennium Development Goals of the United Nations
   (b) Status of Human Development—Gender equality.
8. Mutual Relations Between Peoples Representatives and Public Servants
   (a) Do's to cultivate team spirit
   (b) Don'ts to avoid lack of coordination.
9. Rights and Powers transferred to PRIs.
10. Main Developmental plans/programmes implemented relating to

(a) Poverty Alleviation
(b) Rural Development
(c) Rural Housing by PRIs
(d) Watershed Development (Haryali Guidelines of Government of India)
(e) Social Security Schemes.

11. Schemes Programmes related to Health and Education
(a) Health related Schemes
(b) Education related Schemes.

12. District Planning Committee, District Planning and Standing Committees
(a) District Planning Committee
(b) District Planning
(c) Standing Committees.

13. Role of PRIs on Disaster Management, Famine Relief and Food Security
(a) Famine/Drought Relief
(b) Disaster Management
(c) Food Security.

14. Role of Panchayat Samitis in Drinking Water and Sanitation Schemes.
15. Empowerment of Women.
16. Panchayats and land revenue related rules.
17. Financial Resources of Panchayats.
18. Meetings and Records of Panchayats
(a) Fortnightly meeting
(b) Ward Sabha—its functions and meetings
(c) Gram Sabha—its functions and meetings
(d) Gram Panchayat Registers.

19. How to compile 16-point Human Development progress card 2005 for each Panchayat.
20. Panchayat level targets -related to Millennium Development Goals and related Oaths to be taken by Panchayat representatives and workers.

Various methodologies to be employed for Panchayat training described in the IGPRs document include group exercises, group discussions, participants expression of opinions, lectures delivered by faculty, case studies, PLA (participatory learning and action) including participatory mapping, village tours, seasonal reporting, metric ranking, 'chapatti' diagramming, participatory group discussion), role play, 'rajma dana' trading game, tower construction game, web - of relations weaving game, box of questions game, use of case films and audio-visual games, interactive sessions, problem solving circles, preparation of work plans, etc.

As indicated above, the IGPR document is the third edition of the same and thus the choice of topics covered and material included must have benefited from feedback received on the use of the first two editions. A comparison of the contents of Panchayati Raj Prashikshan Sandarbh 'Sam agree' with the training contents suggested by the Planning Commission Working Group and summarized in the introductory section of this paper indicates that by end large the scope of training indicated by the Working Group has been covered by the IGPRS document.

The one point from the Working Group suggestions that has not received due attention in the Rajasthan training document is the inculcation of planning skills—and that is precisely what this, author has advocated and spelt out in detail in this paper as a major component of the knowledge and skills required by panchayat personnel so that they can undertake decentralized planning which is a major expectation from Panchayati Raj. In fact this element, along of course with the other aspects like those described in detail in the IGPRS document, used to be included in one week and other short training programmes for Panchayat representatives (non-officials) as also for Panchayat officials conducted at HCM Rajasthan State Institute of Public Administration (HCM RIPA) in the decade of the 1990s and this author recalls having been called from time to time as a guest faculty for such training programmes (he also went, though much less frequently, as a guest lecturer for IGPRS training courses). Over the years HCM RIPA has cut down on the proportion of such panchayat specific courses, and IGPRS has apparently found it appropriate to concentrate more on aspects related to the functioning of PRIs and the development schemes and programmes being implemented through the PRIS and the constitutional and statutory provisions, etc., rather than on also imparting planning skills. A reason for this could be that as much literature on the functioning of panchayati raj in 'Rajasthan reveals, district and decentralized planning has not yet really taken off in right earnest in the state. Another factor could be that the orientation of IGPRS and its faculty is more towards participation as it deals exclusively with PRIs, while HCM RIPA, being more interdisciplinary arid dealing with a variety of agency's, has faculty specializing in both participatory aspects, as also in technical planning methodologies as well as other multi-disciplinary knowledge.

Possible Achievements from Panchayat Training

However despite all the above-mentioned training and capacity building attempts, it is only the more mundane expectations from panchayati raj related to the panchayats role as an agency for development, or its internal working, that training may directly influence at least in the immediate short run. Means for panchayati raj to move towards a third tier of governance, or to increase the states capability to perform better, or for the citizens' and local communities' voice to be heard better, or the creation of a psychology for self-help, or reduction of social barriers to increase peoples participation, or the reduction of corruption, or the uplift of vulnerable groups and the poor, and similar objectives of PRIs are only marginally going to be affected by the training discussed above. Though perhaps repeated and sustained training may gradually start impacting in these spheres too.

In addition, many of the PR officials and non-officials who would be the trainees may have their own private agendas which may be at variance, with societal expectations from panchayati raj as discussed above. They may be more interested in personal prestige and position or in capturing panchayati raj bodies for their individual or group's personal benefit, or in recouping funds spent on elections through the diversion of funds or on obtaining a particular posting for their men, or even if having good intentions they may be too involved in their local problems to be able to appreciate the macro issues, or techniques, or examples of successes and failures of panchayat bodies elsewhere which are discussed during the training. They may even have come to the training institute not to learn but merely to visit the particular city and fulfil other personal or family objectives during the visit. Hence their expectations both from PR and from the training are different. Thus the impact of training would naturally be slow. However, the sustained effort based on societies' perceptions about the objectives of panchayati raj and its expectations would need to be continued. Only then would local politicians become good managers of local resources and develop constructive leadership qualities. Only then would local functionaries interact positively with panchayat leaders along with having developed their own administrative (planning, supervising and implementing) capacities. The large number of persons being trained on a sustained basis would also help gradually build up a body of locally available knowledge (even if some of the trainees would eventually cease to be members or functionaries of the panchayats). Hopefully a system of continuous and repeated training with a wide coverage of topics and themes as indicated in this the paper would make both the officials and non-officials better community animators and better agents of development, change and the fulfilling of the communities' needs (as also capable of converting Panchayati raj into a genuine third tier of India's federal governance) and thus be a means to influence elected panchayat leaders and PR officials to build up locally available pools of knowledge which would help in achieving the objectives of, and expectations from, panchayat raj.

REFERENCES

Arora, R. and R. Hooja, 1994, *Administration of Rural Development,* Arihant, Jaipur.

Chambers, R. 1978, "Project Selection for Poverty Focused Rural Development", *World Development Quarterly.* Vol. 6.

Crook, R. and J. Manor, 1994, *Enhancing Participation and Institutional Performance Democratic Decentralization in South Asia and West Africa,* ODA Report, Delhi, November 1994.

Curtis, D. and J.R. Watson, 1987, "Planning the Nonplanners Can Do", *Journal of Rural Development.*

Das, A. 1978, "Decentralization of Development Planning Implementation" *Indian Journal of Public Administration.*

FAG, 1985, *Towards Improved Multi Level Planning for Agriculture and Rural Development*, FAO Economic and Social Development, Paper 52.

Gadgil, D.R. 1996, *District Development Planning,* Gokhale Institute of Politics and Economics, Poona.

Hooja Rakesh 1986, *District Planning: Concept. Setting and State Level Applications,* Aalekh, Jaipur.

Hooja, Rakesh 1987, *Administrative Interventions in Rural Development,* Rawat, Jaipur.

Hooja, Rakesh, 1994. "Issues in Preparing Manpower for Effective Decentralized Planning", *Political Economy Journal of India,* Vol. 3 No.2.

Hooja, Rakesh, 1995, *Bibliography on Multi-level and District level and District Planning,* Madhya Pradesh Institute of Social Science Research, Ujjain.

Hooja, Rakesh, 1997, "Training of Panchayati Raj Functionaries. Some Basic Issues" in *Journal of Rural Development* Vol.-16, No.4.

Hooja, Rakesh 2005, "Training for, and Expectations from, District Planners" in *ASTI Journal of Training and Development* (forthcoming) July-December 2005.

Hooja, R. and Meenakshi Hooja 2005 *Panchayati Raj in Rajasthan: Continuity and Change*, HCM RIPA, Jaipur.

Hooja, Rakesh and P.C. Mathur (ed), *District and Decentralized Planning,* Rawat, Jaipur.

Hooja, R. and B. Yerram Raju (ed), 1993 *Decentralized Planning in Multi-Level Framework,* Rawat, Jaipur.

Indira Gandhi Panchayati Raj Evam Gramin Vikas Sansthan 2005, *Panchayati Raj Prashikshan Sandarbh Samagree,* IGP.

Mathew, George (ed), 1994 (a) *The Status of Panchayati Raj in the States of India,* Concept, New Delhi. Subsequent rewritten volume released 2000 under title *The Status of Panchayati Raj in the States and Union Territories of India 2000,* Concept, New Delhi.

Mathew, George, 1994 (b), *Panchayati Raj from Legislation to Movement,* Concept, New Delhi.

Mathur Kuldeep (ed), 1996. *Development Policy and Administration,* Sage, New Delhi.

Mathur, P.C. and Rakesh Hooja, 1996, *Projects Planning and Development Administration.*

Mishra, Shweta, 1994, *Democratic Decentralization in India*, Mittal, New Delhi.

Mukarji, Nirmal, 1989, "Decentralization Below the State Level: Need for a New System of Governance", *Economic and Political Weekly,* Vol. 214 No.9.

Mukherjee, Amitabh, 1991, "Decentralization: Some Conceptual Issues" in B.N. Yugandhar and A. Mukherjee (ed), *Readings in Decentralized Planning*, Concept, New Delhi.

Planning Commission, GOI, 1984, *Report of Working Group on District Level Planning* (Chairman C.H. Hanumantha Rao).

Prasad, Kamta, 1984, *Planning and its Implementation*, I.I.P.A., New Delhi.

Rao, V.K.R.V. 1973, "District Planning Concept" in V.S. Prakasa Rao *et al. Working Paper on District Planning Officers*, Institute of Social and Economic Change, Bangalore.

Rao, V.M. 1989, "Decentralized Planning Priority Issues": *Economic and Political Weekly*.

7

BUILDING WOMEN LEADERSHIP AT GRASSROOTS IN TAMIL NADU

G. UMA AND J. VANISHREE

Introduction

The enactment of the 73rd Constitutional Amendment Act in India has created a significant change in the political life of rural women. 33.3 per cent reservation of seats in the rural local bodies for women has provided opportunity for women to exercise the political power for the socio-economic development of their area. This critical mass of women is expected to perform a critical function, and thereby, the process of development would take a new turn and women's participation in governance would produce far-reaching implications in the lives of the people. The decentralization process has opened up opportunities for women and other marginalized groups to influence the process of governance. This is the greatest experiment in the contemporary situation by transferring decision-making power to one million elected women local-government representatives. The new dispensation has opened an opportunity for many women with different socio-economic background to climb up the ladder of power with different set of limitations and disabilities. However, there are a variety of barriers to women hailing from marginalized sections exercising their powers.[1] Really, it is a challenge to work for the social, economic and political empowerment of women, particularly those from marginalized sections. No doubt, it is necessary to work for the goal of empowering women for which the oppressive power of the existing gender relations is to be exposed and challenged[2]. Further, the gender relations have to be reshaped[3]. The critical mass will be able to perform the critical function only if they are oriented, conscientised and trained in the methodology of deconstruction and reconstruction of gender relations. Since most of the women representatives have been first timers in occupying political spaces, it is imperative that they be given opportunities for training and capacity building that informs them, strengthens and recontextualises their skills and capacities, and empowers them to become effective leaders. Given the fact that the Panchayat reforms were the product of government fiat, the extent of which women benefited from these reforms depended upon their prior history of activism[4]. Since most of the women are new to political space, a range of factors hinder women's participation in politics including inexperience in politics and lack of exposure to it, illiteracy, family responsibilities and objections from family members, restrictive social norms, lack of enabling environment for women and lack of confidence for interacting with the public. Therefore, in order to ensure women's performance better in the governance, capacity building measures and support systems for women should be made available. It is unfortunate that, in India, capacity building is not a serious issue for the representatives of the people who determine the fate of millions of people. However, in the Panchayati Raj scenario, it has been felt that, to manage the panchayats, training is essential even though there is no training policy and no conscious steps have been taken by the government to build the capacity of the elected representatives of the people in the grassroots institutions[5]. In this situation, the Rajiv Gandhi Chair for Panchayati Raj studies at Gandhigram Rural Institute took a series of steps to prepare a training manual to train the Panchayat leaders. The Hunger Project, which has a mission to empower grassroots women leaders collaborated with Rajiv Gandhi Chair for Panchayati Raj Studies and initiated the capacity building exercise in Tamil Nadu. The following is an analysis of the efforts taken by The Hunger Project in collaboration with

Gandhigram Rural Institute in building the capacity of Elected Women Representatives in Tamil Nadu.

The Hunger Project

The Hunger Project (THP) is a strategic organisation committed to end hunger. THP believes that a world "Free from Hunger" will come to fruition only when every women, men and children has equal opportunity to health, education, nutrition, livelihood and a voice in the decisions that affect their lives. THP is committed to address the social conditions that hold hunger in place such as caste, patriarchy, subjugation of women, exploitation of tribals, lack of access and control over productive assets, and domination of decision-making by a few.[6]

The Hunger Project-India has chosen as its pathway, the strengthening of women's leadership in panchayats. Their experience indicates that when women leaders at the grassroots are empowered, they take on leadership that is capable of transforming not just their lives, but those of the communities around them. They are able to address issues of basic needs, of social justice, of equity and peace for all. In order to achieve this state, in their agenda of action, The Hunger Project stressed the need for capacity building exercise. All Panchayat members must gain access to the training they need to carryout their responsibilities in all the key areas, including Panchayat finance, nutrition and health, family planning, sanitation, education and economic development. Leadership training and on-going support must be available for the development of the leadership skills women need and want—the ability to create a vision, to speak and listen powerfully, to build constituencies and to make things happen. Keeping these things in mind, The Hunger Project has evolved a Panchayati Raj Workshop Manual to build the capacity among the Elected Women Representatives and conducted a women leadership workshop.

The Hunger Project's Women Leadership workshop aims at building capacity among Elected Women Representatives to the maximum. It adopts the above framework for building capacity.

The Hunger Project acts as a catalyst in women representatives and empowers them to bring necessary changes in their lives as

Framework of The Hunger Project's Women Leadership Workshop

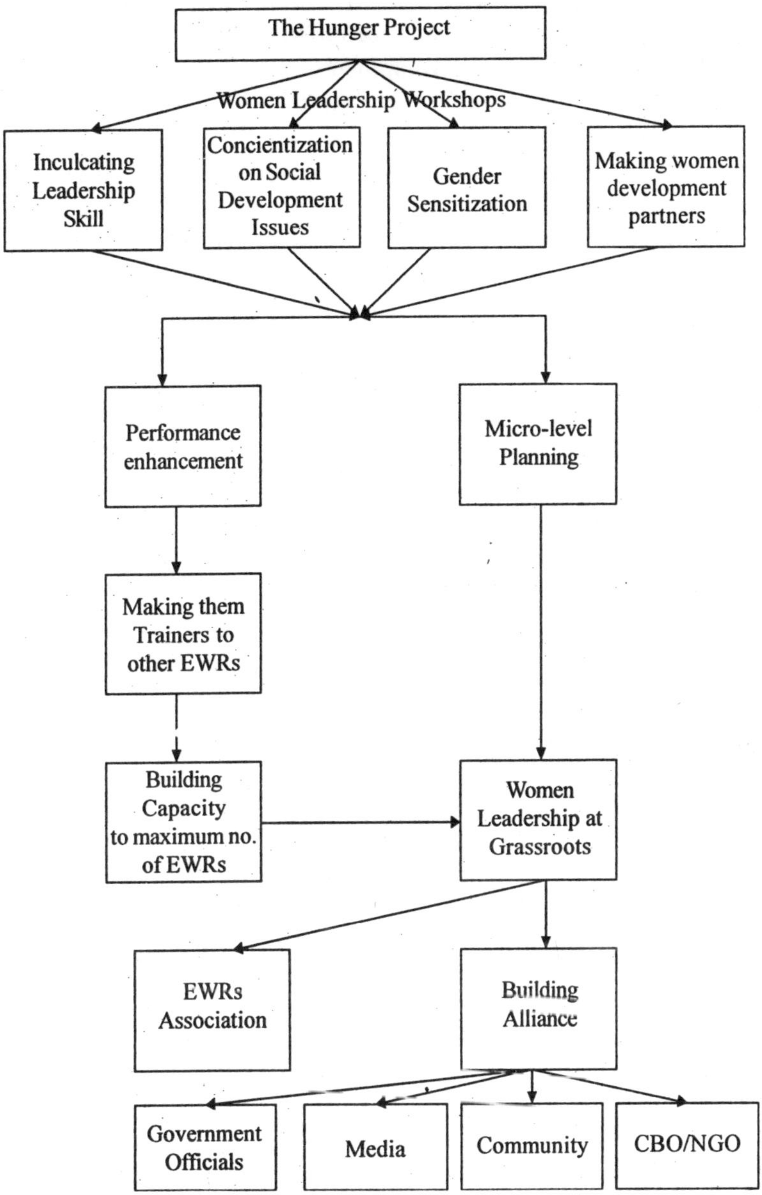

well as the life of the community at the grassroots, where they are elected as a leader. The Hunger Project also sensitizes and concretizes the mindset of the Elected Women Representatives on gender issues and social-development issues. The Hunger Project aims at not only creating vision for the Elected Women Representatives but also creates vision for the future of the community. To convert these visions into reality, the Elected Women Representatives are initiated to take the process of planning. In the planning process, they explore the different stages. In the first stage they were made to realize the present scenario and then they were made to create a vision for the future. The vision is a statement of the future that is possible to achieve and it brings them to a new level in the quality of life. Based on their vision, the Elected Women Representatives are assisted in creating a micro-level planning for their Panchayat to address the issues like malnutrition, under weight birth of the child, equal status for women and children, health of women and children, freedom from exploitation, education for all, income generating activities, food security, importance of realizing a plastic-free society, importance of caring pregnant women, steps to be taken by the Panchayats regarding health of all adolescents and children, personal hygiene, how to dispose human excreta safely, how to dispose solid wastes, importance of nutrition, role of women in social and economic development, realizing women subjugation is not their fault but it is because of the social conditions prevailing for many years and this is an opportunity to realize this and make other women in the society to realize this. The Hunger Project also educates women on the importance of building alliance with the media, CBOs/NGOs, Government Officials to carry out the activities successfully and also to access the information and to disseminate their successes and grievances to the other members of the society. In the meantime, the Elected Women Representatives realized the importance of forming informal groups among themselves to share their experiences and also to gain strength among themselves. This group, in the course of time evolved as a pressure and formal structure. Thus, the Hunger Project helps the women at grassroots to create a vision for the future of the village through PRIs and The Hunger Project made women leaders realize that they have equal opportunity, power and responsibility to ensure the well-being of the entire community and they can address all the social-development issues to improve the living condition of the village. The Hunger Project has given Elected Women Representatives an opportunity to build an alliance with other agents in the society to fulfil their commitment towards society.

Objectives of the Women Leadership Workshop

The main objectives of the programme is to enable the Elected Women Representatives to realize their commitments in the political space. This can be outlined as follows:

- Develop a sense of self-esteem and dignity.
- Make a shift from a mindset of "I cannot" to "I can".
- Instil a sense of political citizenship, fundamental rights and responsibilities that is crucial in making them effective leaders.
- Articulate a vision for their communities.
- Acquire the skills needed to be effective Panchayat leaders like familiarizing them with the rules and regulations, various schemes and programmes of the government, management of finance and accounts of the Panchayats etc.
- Emphasize the importance of the participation of women in regular meetings of the Panchayats and Gram Sabhas.
- Create a sense of solidarity with others (e.g. Self-Help Groups) committed to this cause.

Based on the above said objectives The Hunger Project is expccting to create the following results:

- Enhancing the leadership of Elected Women Representatives by eliciting leadership skill in action, and empowering them to bring about the necessary changes in their lives, their villages and their country, through the Panchayati Raj Institutions.
- *Dignity and self-hood:* Women taking the capacity building exercise a sense of self-hood, self-esteem, dignity, power and importance.

- *Subjugation and lack of progress:* That the women came to see that the subjugation that all women are subjected to is not their fault—but is a systematic, societal condition—and it is holding back progress in their country.
- *Personal role:* That the women have the feeling of not being able to back away from who they are and their key role for the future of their families and of India.
- *Personal potential and ability:* That the women come away with the feeling that this can be done, that they will do it.
- *Grounding and connectedness:* That the women are located in their villages and in India, and feel a sense of connectedness to the other women in the country.
- *Political citizenship:* That the women experience being citizens of a great country with basic rights and responsibilities.
- *Opportunity:* That the women see that they have been chosen by their fellow villagers and entrusted by the constitution to lead their villages to achieve a healthy and productive life. They have the opportunity, power and responsibility to ensure the well-being of everyone in their villages.
- *Vision:* That the women create a vision of the future, and work to make this vision a reality by exploring the statutes in the planning process.
- *Support structure:* That the women leave the capacity building programme with a system of on-going support and empowerment in place, including the creation of women's collectives and access to powerful information etc.

Capacity Building: Tamil Nadu Experience

Collaboration

The Hunger Project collaborated with the Rajiv Gandhi Chair for Panchayati Raj Studies in Tamil Nadu to carryout the capacity building programme for Elected Women Representatives. The Hunger Project felt that the achievements of the Elected Women

Representatives after the workshop would be recognized by the government only, if they collaborate with each other. It aimed at giving training to the village Panchayat women Presidents. In Tamil Nadu out of 12,613 Village Panchayats, 4,329 are presided over by women. The Hunger Project has targeted 1,000 Village Panchayat Women Presidents in the first phase. Before starting the exercise, the Chair Person of the Tamil Nadu Hunger Project contacted the Director of Rural Development (DRD) to invite the Women Presidents to Gandhigram Rural Institute, where the training was given. Women in the rural areas are not allowed to participate in any programme on their own because of the patriarchal implications and family responsibilities. Further, this programme is designed as a residential programme for five days at Gandhigram. The DRD was requested to issue orders to all the District Collectors to mobilize the women leaders. And the DRD, also requested the District administration to make this opportunity for conducting capacity Building Exercise to Elected Women Representatives. The District Panchayat Secretary was requested to be the nodal officer to help the Hunger Project in ensuring the attendance of Elected Women Representatives. All the District Collectors took earnest efforts to mobilize the women leaders. A few District Collectors, especially the District Collector of Ramnad Mr.Vijayakumar requested the trainers to include the computer-literacy package in the training programme. Mr. Hitesh Kumar Makwana, the District Collector of Pudukkottai District wanted to emphasis on Rural Sanitation in the programme. All District Collectors passed orders and gave instructions through the Assistant Director of Panchayat and the Block Development Officers to the Elected Women Representatives to attend the training programme. The Extension Officer of the Panchayat accompanied Elected Women Representatives of each block to ensure the attendance of the elected women representatives.

Methodology

It was a fully residential programme. The Elected Women Representatives had to stay for five days in the campus of Gandhigram Rural Institute. Of the five days, three days would be devoted to Panchayat administration and two days to social development issues. Subjects such as the bases of decentralization of powers in the context of the globalization of the economy, Panchayat, finance, common property resource management, people's participation, micro-level planning, economic development, accounting and auditing procedures, Gram Sabha and its implications, social justice and the implications of reservation of seats for women and Dalits were covered in three days. Social development issues such as sanitation, water supply, gender bias, child care, pre- and post-natal care, school enrollment, child labour, RCH and other issues were covered in the remaining two days of the five-day programme.

Originally, the capacity building programme initiated by The Hunger Project was only for three days. In order to create a cordial atmosphere efforts were taken to introduce the women leaders to each other and began to get to know each other as people with common struggles and experiences. Then their role as political citizen and social citizen were explained. The vision building exercises, opportunities of Panchayati Raj Institutions and steps in the planning process and making vision a reality were taught. Thirdly, the development of an on-going support structure was discussed. The Rajiv Gandhi Chair for Panchayati Raj Studies which has committed itself towards the empowerment of Elected Women Representatives extended the training programme for two more days to sensitize women on social development issues and management of Panchayats.

Trainers delivered lectures in the beginning of each sessions. After the lecture there was a discussion among the trainers on the lecture. Apart from these lectures, focused-group lectures were also given in the particular topic and they discussed intensively. Role plays, games, one to one discussions also were arranged. The trainers were divided into groups to prepare a vision document for the Panchayat. Doubt clarification sessions on Panchayati Raj Administration were conducted in the late evenings. The trainees also came up with their own solutions for various problems in group discussions. It is very difficult to understand the government rules and orders even by the literates. So, special sessions were arranged for them to understand and interpret those government rules and orders. Role models like the President of Kuthambakam Village Panchayat Mr. Ilango, the President of Keerapalayam Panchayat Mr. Panneerselvam were invited to share their experience and this motivated the Elected Women Representatives. The Dindigul District Watershed model was considered as one of the best models in Tamil Nadu. So, field visit was arranged to the watershed areas in Dindigul. Apart from this, many innovative models of Rural Development

Table 1 : Capacity Building Exercise of the Elected Women Representatives.

Day	*Contents of the Programme*
1	1. Registration and Personal counselling. 2. Principles of Decentralization, 73rd Constitutional Amendment Act. 3. Tamil Nadu Panchayat Act, 1994. 4. Gram Panchayat Administration: Duties, Responsibilities and Power. 5. Gram Sabha and People's Participation.
2	1. Multi-level planning in Gram Panchayat Discussion. 2. Integration of Panchayat Plan and Sectoral Programme. 3. Common Property Resource Management. 4. Protection of Natural Resources.
3	1. Financial Management, Finance and Financial Resources. 2. Maintenance of Accounts and Records and Audit Procedures. 3. Social Development and Social Justice. 4. Vision Building Exercise. 5. Leadership Building.
4	1. Status of Indian Women/Rural Women • Social Citizenship • Society and Family Related Issues Faced by Women • Problem Solving Process • Gender Equality Role of Individual. 2. Total Rural Sanitation. 3. Social Development • Listing of issues • Role of Women in Social Development • Role of Panchayat in Social Development. 4. Reproductive Child Health. 5. Role of Panchayat in Economic Development.
5	1. Computer Orientation. 2. Exposure Visit to Village Panchayat.

have been developed in Gandhigram Rural Institute and Gandhigram Trust and the trainees were taken to these places to get inspiration. Overall, the workshop was a participatory exercise where trainees were not treated just as "learners" but as "leaders-in-the-making".

Apart form the above-said input, the trainers briefed the Elected Women Representatives about the changes which they need in their behaviour, like how to keep their surroundings clean, use the toilets in their houses, how to sit in the meetings, how to behave in the crowd, interact with officials and how to ask questions in the meetings and also the trainers regularly interact of with them about the new culture that they have to bring about in their Panchayats.

Resource Materials

The Hunger Project considers this workshop not only for training women as leaders but they also want to provide all necessary information to the women leaders to run the Panchayat administration successfully to bring overall development in their Panchayats. The participants were given a manual written by Dr. G. Palanithurai entitled "New Panchayat Raj System in Tamil Nadu : Rules and Schemes". This manual consists of the updated Tamil Nadu Panchayats Act, Government rules, Government orders pertaining to Gram Panchayat administration, State and Central Government schemes for rural development. Apart from this manual, a small booklet containing the roles and responsibilities of the Gram Panchayat Presidents were given for easy understanding of the administration. The Charter of the new Panchayati Raj Institution system was also given to the trainees. While handling classes the trainers used flip charts and OHPs. To realize their roles and importance of being grassroots leaders, a film entitled "Namma Ooru Panchayat" was screened.

Resource Persons

The retired higher level officials of Rural Development were engaged in this programme to teach about the Panchayat administration. Apart from them, the professors of Gandhigram Rural Institute were asked to cover the focused topics like gender, governance, and social development issues, health and computer literacy. The Hunger Project Staff of Tamil Nadu dealt with the vision exercise and they stayed with the trainees throughout the exercise for provide overall personality development. They also counselled them personally and made them realize their potentials and strengths.

Table 2 : Number of Elected Women Representatives who attended the Capacity Building Programme.

Sl. No.	*Name of the District*	*Total No. of Women Presidents*	*No. of Presidents attended the programme*	*Percentage of Women Presidents*
1.	Pudukottai	172	140	81
2.	Dindigul	105	100	95
3.	Tiruchirappalli	132	131	99
4.	Sivagangai	153	112	73
5.	Ramanathapuram	147	116	79
6.	Theni	48	43	90
7.	Karur	49	49	100
8.	Virudhunagar	144	103	72
9.	Tuticorin	140	67	48
10.	Cuddalore	229	168	73
11.	Tirunelveli	147	104	71
12.	Thiruvarur	147	62	42
13.	Erode	130	50	38
	Total	**1743**	**1245**	**71**

Source: Computed.

Implications

The main purpose of the Capacity Building Exercise was to bring a change in the perspective of Elected Women Representatives and in their style of functioning. After getting the orientation and sensitization towards their endeavour, the Elected Women Representatives have started realizing their roles and responsibilities they would assume. They have been performing amazingly in spite of hurdles and obstacles.

Feedback from the Participants

Ms. Kala of Nuthulapuram Panchayat of Dindigul District in Tamil Nadu, who was helped by the reservation policy got exposure to the rules and regulations by establishing contacts with the officials. It has enhanced her leadership qualities. After getting the chance to attend the Capacity Building programme she fully understood the power and authority vested in her and does not allow herself to be used as a dummy of the dominant forces. Though reservation has brought forth the new dalit leadership, enormous investment needs to be put in enhancing their literacy levels and capacity building through periodical training to improve their performance.

Ms. Jesumarry of Michealpattinam Panchayat, Ramnad District felt that she gained the following aspects after attending the Capacity Building programme:

(a) how to speak before large gatherings
(b) how to conduct herself in a public place
(c) how to manage a crowd
(d) how to get information about the available rural development schemes
(e) how to get insights into administrative nuances
(f) how to maintain Panchayat records
(g) how to differentiate between government orders and notifications.

She felt that capacity building for women village Panchayat leaders and gender sensitivity training to their husbands and male counterparts are very important. She also felt that when women become effective local body leaders transparency and efficiency would improve. Gender sensitive training to their husbands would change their perception of female leaders.

Capacity building is not limited to building the managerial and communication skill alone. It includes changing the mindset of the leaders towards the issues of women, children and other marginalized segments[7]. Through the initiative of The Hunger Project, the Gandhigram Rural Institute's concept of preparation of a development plan was undertaken in K. Rayavaram village Panchayat of Pudukottai District. To attend the orientation programme, **Ms. Rani**, President of the village Panchayat along with the Self-Help Group (SHG) leaders visited Gandhigram, where they had an exposure to the various Khadi and Village Industries schemes. Their SHGs, after returning, asked her to help them in getting training in the activities. She met the district officials and succeeded in getting permission for a number of SHG members to undergo training in paper bag production. The trained women in turn gave training to the fellow members. She helped the women of her Panchayat to earn their livelihood.

Likewise, **Ms. Padmini**, Panchayat President of Konamoolai of Erode District is the best example to demonstrate that a women leader with a passion for public service, with a sense of commitment and honesty, can deliver the goods to the society effectively by realizing their responsibilities. She had a vision for the development of villages by taking up sanitation, water supply and environmental problems in the Panchayat. She effectively addressed the issues of women and children. Further she felt that a Panchayat could work effectively only with the active participation of the people and hence she started working for mobilizing the people for development by conducting the activities of the Panchayat administration transparently.

Ms. Easwari, Panchayat President of Appipalayam Panchayat in Karur District observed that the training and orientation given by Gandhigram Rural Institute and NGOs like Human Rights Foundation and AREDS helped her in understanding the significance of the village commons and link of livelihood with the village commons. She took about sixty villagers, farmers, young men and women to Kodaikkanal Anglade Institute of Natural History for an orientation and awareness in ecology, environment and protection of nature. As a woman hailing from family of farmers, she also realized the importance of protected drinking water and sustainable water for irrigation. Being the President, she wanted to ensure the same to one and all.

The experience of **Ms. Chinnammal,** Orathupatti Village Panchayat President of Sivagangai District is entirely different. She reiterated that if people were mobilized and organized at the grassroots without any cleavage, the government would abide by the wishes of the people, if the people are divided, the officials will take advantage of their division. She said that she has realized the power of the people only through training; and added that the Panchayat leaders have to be accommodating and should have patience in tackling the problems. The Panchayat leaders also have to be assertive, especially the women leaders.

Ms. Chandrika *Sarvesan*, the President of Siruthondanallur Village Panchayat of Tuticorin District said that in Tamil Nadu if women leaders, especially at village Panchayat level, are able to work to this level and win appreciation from all quarters, it is because of the training provided by Gandhigram Rural Institute. Because of the training, they are able to bring out the potential of women, and to support women leaders whenever they are in difficult situation. Now a stage has come to stand on their own feet by forming a federation of Elected Women Representatives.

Ms. Ponni Kailasam, President of Annaikuppam Panchayat, Tiruvarur District stated that all her assertiveness was gained only due to the motivation given by the Capacity Building programme. She came to know the logic of reservation of seats for women in local bodies and realized that women have to work rigorously to retain this position and do things which ought to be done. The reservation provided a political opportunity for women to participate in public activities. The Elected Women Representatives should speak out courageously without fear and shyness. They have to fight against the patriarchal society. They have to frequently approach government officials to solve their problems. Women have to work for the removal of proxy politics. She got these ideas from the Capacity Building programme which increased her confidence.

Ms. Tamil Selvi, Tiruvenkatapuram Panchayat President of Tirunelveli District after knowing about the method and procedure of removing encroachments has taken steps to remove all the encroachments in her Panchayat. Now her Panchayat has become free from encroachers. If someone asked her about the removal of encroachments she humbly says that it is her duty to do so.

Ms. Uma Rani, Panchayat President of Reddimankudi, Pulampadi Union of Trichy District has done wonderful work for children's education. She identified the dropouts of her Panchayat, who were all working in Andhra Pradesh and Maharashtra as child labourers and took earnest measures to bring them back to her village and provided them opportunities to continue their education. The training that she received enabled her to do such an exemplary work.

The women leadership workshop has created enormous changes in the personality of the Elected Women Representatives and it has brought about changes in their Panchayats. They have started collaborating with SHGs and them to clean the villages. This exercise, has created job opportunities for a few SHGs by preparing Bio-manure. Elected Women Representatives created awareness about personal hygiene among women. They constructed toilets in the Balwadis, Schools and houses like Michelpattinam, K. Rayavaram, N. Panchatti Gram Panchayats. They also provided 100 per cent protected drinking water supply to all houses. They have planted trees on both sides of the Panchayat roads. They have purchased nail cutters to distribute to the Balwadis and helped children to keep their fingers clean in Orathupatti Gram Panchayat. They have created awareness among villagers on the use of plastic in Panchayats. K. Rayavaram Panchayat has banned the use of plastic in their village by passing a resolution in the Gram Sabha. They have provided all basic amenities like laying roads, putting street lights, supplying safe drinking water, arranging for public health and sanitation in Athankaraipatti, Noothulapuram, Konavelanpatti Panchayats. They have abolished illicit liquor from some of the Panchayats.

The above-said experiences show that women can perform amazingly after assuming power if they are properly capacitated to exhibit their skills. Based on the several experiences of women in governance, Dr. G. Palanithurai[8] listed the following points which are vital and relevant in the Indian context:

First, women will usher in a different approach to governance.

Second, women perceive the concept of development, comprehensively rather than narrowly. They have a broad vision about the development process.

Third, Elected Women Representatives play an important role in pushing the women's issues forward for public discussion and decision-making.

Fourth, Elected Women Representatives ensure more participation of people in the process of development and governance. Women leaders at the grassroots in the Indian context always stand for simplicity, transparency and accountability.

Fifth, Elected Women Representatives have varied sets of skills and they have enhanced the leadership qualities of others. Women have developed skills to carryout works despite the limited resources and differences of opinion with their family members.

Sixth, Elected Women Representatives are the path finders in solving social problems.

Seventh, Elected Women Representatives tend to maintain secular values in dealing with matters of governance.

All these things can be made possible, if Elected Women Representatives are trained properly. The efforts taken by The Hunger Project with Gandhigram Rural Institute show that the leadership skills of Elected Women Representatives are entering into a paradigmatic shift from subordination to self-governance. Even though the Hunger Project has trained 1245 Elected Women Representatives of village Panchayats, visible changes could be obtained only from 50 per cent of the Elected Women Representatives. If there is a proper follow-up, all the capacitated Elected Women Representatives could be made role models for the whole country.

Conclusion

The main aim of the capacity building programme through women leadership workshop was to develop the skills, habits, knowledge and aptitudes in selected fields and also to increase their effectiveness and prepare the trainees for future position. The Elected Women Representatives who were trained through this programme are now acting as resource persons for trainees in the State Institute of Rural Development. The impact of the training of a Woman Panchayat President results in the uplift of her village Panchayat. This can be seen in many village Panchayats headed by the trained Elected Women Representatives. While observing their performance after the capacity building programmes one can notice the following changes in their functioning:

- They are well-versed in accounting procedures.
- They are working towards social justice and gender equality.
- They have gained leadership qualities like vision, values, strategic thinking and planning, augmentation of resources, accountability, relationship building, transparency, gender consciousness, empowering the disadvantaged and marginalized people, managing the Panchayat system by collaborating with higher level officials.
- Managing Common Property Resources.
- Understanding the importance of SHGs.
- Learning how to carryout micro-level planning.
- Ensuring more concentration on environment protection.
- Knowing schemes and programmes for rural development.
- Learning the importance of participation of people in development process.
- Learning how to work for the welfare of the society even with limited money and power.
- Women leaders have shown the way to others in innovations and have developed strategies to build alliances to overcome barriers.

The capacity-building exercise shows that the Elected Women Representatives can convince the policy-makers that the Panchayats can perform beyond expectations. Women leadership at local level is a space for development and not a space for politics. They realized the importance of training and continuous flow of information. Finally, one can conclude that empowering women through such a type of capacity-building exercise addresses the social issues and ensures socio-political uplift of the whole country.

NOTES

1. G. Palanithurai, *Empowerment of Women : Problems faced by the Elected Women Representatives in Tamil Nadu,* Gandhigram : Rajiv Gandhi Chair for Panchayati Raj Studies, 2001.

2. G. Palanithurai and V. Ragupathy, *Building alliance and capabilities among the Elected Women Representatives of Grassroots Institutions,* Gandhigram: Rajiv Gandhi Chair for Panchayati Raj Studies, 2003.

3. S.Wieringa, "Women's interests and Empowerment: Gender Planning Reconsidered", *Development and Change,* 25, 1994.

4. Amrita Basu, "Gender and Governance : Concepts and Contexts", in Martha Mussbaum *etal.* (Eds), *Gender and Governance,* New Delhi: UNDP, 2003.

5. G. Palanithurai, *Capacity Building of Grassroots Leaders,* Gandhigram: Rajiv Gandhi Chair for Panchayati Raj Studies, 2004.

6. Social Watch India, *Citizens Report on Governance and Development,* 2004, New Delhi: Social Watch India, 2004.

7. G. Palanithurai, "Role of Elected Women Representatives in Evolving Alternative Governance at Grassroots", *Social Change and Development,* Vol.3, July 2005.

8. G. Palanithurai, "Women in Governance for Development at Grassroots", *Indian Journal of Public Administration,* Vol. 1 No.1, Jan. - Mar. 2004.

8

CAPACITY BUILDING FOR PANCHAYATI RAJ FUNCTIONARIES IN KARNATAKA THROUGH SATELLITE

K. SUBHA, B.S. BHARGAVA AND MANGALA A. NAYAK

Decentralization was considered as the best form to promote participation and efficiency. Involving all the sections of local people in deciding what is best suited to them, so as to improve government decisions and increase democratic participation became the crux of the system of governance adopted by the country viz., Democratic Decentralization. The Constitution (73rd Amendment) Act, 1992 which was brought into force from 24th April, 1993, finally established India's Panchayati Raj Institutions (PRIs) on a sound footing.

In Karnataka, the 1985 Act was superseded by a new Act of the State, viz., The Karnataka Panchayati Raj Act, 1993, which incorporated the essential features of the 73rd Constitutional Amendment and established elected bodies at the three-tier—the Village, Taluk and District levels so that there is "*greater participation of the people*" and more effective implementation of rural development programmes in the State. The Act displays the following salient features:

- Establishes a three-tier Panchayati Raj System in the State based on the population as ascertained at the last preceding census of which the figures have been published. It envisages elected bodies at all the three levels.

- It provides for reservation of seats in favour of Scheduled Castes and Scheduled Tribes in proportion of their population and for reservation of one-third seats for women at all levels.
- It provides for reservation of offices of chairpersons at all levels in favour of Scheduled Castes and Scheduled Tribes and women.
- It also provides for reservation of seats and offices of chairpersons at all levels for the persons belonging to Backward Classes.
- It envisages constitution of State Election Commission, the Finance Commission and District Planning Committee.
- It also provides for Gram Sabha at the village level, which is obligatory on its part to convene a meeting at least once in six months. All the adults who are in the voter's list of the village are the members of Gram Sabha.

One of the initiatives towards strengthening decentralization is capacity building and training. So capacity building must be given utmost importance and priority. Although India has provided the much-needed scope for effective participation of the people in decision-making through the Panchayati Raj System, yet the statistics on their participation are dismaying, and to a large extent they still remain outside the mainstream. Increased participation in rural government cannot be achieved without capacity building. It is the building up of the capacity of human resource development for the rural government institutions like the gram panchayats where the capabilities of the elected members should be increased by way of training programmes and awareness programmes to function properly in their institutions. Given the socio-economic profile, in terms of low income/poverty, illiteracy, ill health and backwardness, and inclusion of the excluded communities in elected local institutions, capacity building programmes assume importance.

Training and human resource development for building up the capacity of any institution have to be looked at in the broader context of organizational reform, the imperatives of decentralized and responsive government and the operating environment of any institutions created by State Governments. Capacity building has to subsume the increased capabilities of higher-level and the governments on the one hand, and the various partners in civic society on the other, including elected representatives and citizen groups. In general, and in concerned literature, dimensions of capacity building are referred to as—it is ensuring that people have the capacity to be creative and effective to achieve impact with time and change; empowering all the SHG/NGO partners in development processes to manage social, economic, political and cultural aspects of life; awareness of social, political and economic reality and its analysis; developing a proper gender, caste and class perspective; communication skills/technical skills/negotiating—bargaining skills; organizing people for self-reliance; fullest participation of people; ability to assess needs and to identify solutions independently; vision/ mission/goals formulation; perspective building; capacity through and for; knowledge and perspective, skills, action and resources.

Similarly, methods of capacity building and training experimented and referred to as—participatory training; lecture-*cum*-interactions; panel discussions; individual and group assignments; audio-visual aids—films, slides, charts, etc. field visits/exposure visits; workshops; role-play, street plays; brain storming, mock up exercises; case studies; network and satellite training. Capacity building issue attracted the attention of Government as well as other research and voluntary organizations, which have had concern for the success of Panchayati Raj (PR). The Government of Karnataka has been making continuous efforts in this direction for the last one decade or so. Non-Government Organizations (NGOs) like SEARCH, Bangalore, Institute of Social Sciences (ISS), Bangalore, Institute for Social and Economic Change (ISEC), Bangalore, and many others, located at different places in the state do conduct capacity building programmes from time to time.

As per the Karnataka Panchayati Raj Act, 1993, three consecutive elections have taken place—1993, 2000, 2005 elections. Many training programmes were conducted during the first term of elections. After second term of elections it got accelerated, more and more members came in and training was given to the elected members of PRIs in full swing for strengthening and upgradation through capacity building mechanism. The following table shows the membership pattern in PRIs:

Table 1 : PRIs in Karnataka (2005).

Tiers	*No. of Panchayats*	*No. of seats (members)*
Zilla Panchayat	27	1005
Taluk Panchayat	176	3683
Gram Panchayat	5650	91600

It can be observed from the table that training for the elected members of the Panchayati Raj Institutions is a tremendous task because of its spread and number. It is clear by now that this paper tends to examine capacity building of the elected representatives of the PRIs in Karnataka, in the context of the 73rd Constitutional Amendment. Its main focus is on a very innovative and novel method of capacity building, and the programme is being organized by Abdul Nazeer Sab State Institute of Rural Development (ANSSIRD), Mysore, to impart training through satellite.

The main concern since 1993 is to train the rural leadership in the art of running these institutions, so that the rural local government is strengthened and it becomes viable enough to deliver the goods as desired by the objectives of Panchayati Raj and sustain the values of the system. This is truer for women leaders as they are new entrants to the field, illiterate and unexposed to the world around them. The need for systematic training and orientation is necessary to empower all elected members specifically the women members to exercise their authority. Empowerment gives women the capacity to influence decision-making process, planning, implementation and evaluation by integrating them into the political system. Awareness should also be developed in times to come as the fate of the State and National political system depends on the emerging leadership at the grassroots.

Capacity building actually means developing adequate skills to perform the given role and function efficiently depending on the capacity of the individual to understand the given situation, to work effectively, to tackle them and prepare future plans. To develop this skill, training is imperative—like training for prospective candidates, elected members and officials, intermittent refresher courses for the Panchayati Raj functionaries and other types designed to suit the local needs. Studies show that at local level the newly elected leaders have more responsibilities for which it is only through capacity building that leaders can be prepared to shoulder their responsibilities. Capacity building will concentrate on three aspects, namely training in skills, attitudinal training and volunteer participation and will focus on PRI members, PRI staff and the people.

For the success of vast training to all elected members the Abdul Naseer Sab State Institute of Rural Development has taken the great initiative to train the elected members in all aspects of functioning of the PRIs. ANSSIRD is working under the Department of Rural Development and Panchayati Raj, Government of Karnataka. ANSSIRD is primarily responsible for training elected representatives, functionaries, NGO personnel and members of the general public on various aspects of rural development. The training modes include face-to-face training programmes at the premises at Mysore, satellite based training with a studio, earth-station and transmission centre being located at Mysore and more than 210 receiving stations across the State, and cascade mode training for specific applications like computer software, etc. In the cascade mode, resource persons are trained at Mysore who in turn train participants at district and taluk levels across the state.

ANSSIRD has been designated as a nodal institute for undertaking training and capacity building of Panchayati Raj members. However, the planning for the training and capacity building programme was district specific. It also conducts capacity building programmes for officers of various development departments, representatives of voluntary organizations and Bank Officials. Conducting training research activities, evaluation and assessment of impact of various Rural Development Programmes are also being undertaken. The Government of Karnataka has constituted a Managing Committee with Additional Chief Secretary, Government of Karnataka as its Chairman, with representatives from Government of India and NIRD, Hyderabad and comprises 14 members. Director General of Administrative Training Institute is the Director General of ANSSIRD also.

During 2001-02, till March 2002, 58 training programmes had been conducted, in which 1115 trainees participated and out of which, 15 Adhyakshas and Upadhyakshas of Zilla Panchayats, 34 Women Adhyakshas and Upadhyakshas of Taluk Panchayats, 99 members of Zilla Panchayat, 118 members of Taluk Panchayats and under Rajiv Gandhi Pilot programme 30 members of Raichur Zilla Panchayat. Total 1411 trainees were trained. The focus of training programme was largely on local issues; the programme was the largest one of its kind held for the grassroots level leadership, encouraging them to contribute to mainstream development. The Rs. 30 crore programme, which covered representatives of Panchayati Raj Institutions in the State's 176 taluks, is also one of the major efforts to decentralize power and decision-making. It is the most important rural development programme by the Mysore-based ANSSIRD.

Background of the Programme

Between November 2002 and March 2003, ANSSIRD, Mysore, undertook stage 1 of an exciting satellite-based interactive training and communication programme with elected representatives of gram panchayat. The programme took place in three phases during 2003; ANSSIRD reached out to over 18,207 members from 1310 gram panchayats in 44 taluks of Karnataka. This training and interaction programme was of particular significance because of its innovative use of modern communication technology coupled with participatory training methodology to reach out to people spread over great distances. The objective of this interaction, which has been the outcome of months of intensive planning and preparation, was to create a ground well for democratic decentralization through people's participation in local planning. It aimed at provoking gram panchayat members, especially women and representatives of disadvantaged groups to take a deeper look at their own situations and struggling, to find solutions to their problems, as also to enable them to think constructively, i.e. in terms of small but constructive activities that they can initiate individually or as collectively.

The Satellite Based Training and Communication (SATCOM) Centre was established and commissioned in April 2002. Consequently various departments have made use of the setup for training participants on various subjects across the state. The advantage of reaching out to large numbers simultaneously at low costs is unmatched. The Satellite Based Training and Communication System comprises an earth station, digital transmission studio and one-way video, two-way audio communication on INSAT-3B satellite's extended c-band transponder. At the studio, dedicated anchors and panelists conduct live or pre-recorded presentations, discussions and talkback sessions, and transmit them through the earth stations linked to the studio. To make the participants feel at home, the set is designed to look like a typical panchayat session, where the panelists squat on the floor against a rural backdrop. Considered an effective strategy to ensure participation of women members and those from marginalized sections, the interactive sessions are eye-openers. They dispel ideas that rural folks are ignorant and don't take responsibility for their localities.

One of the main users of the setup is the Rural Development and Panchayati Raj department—for training the elected representatives across the State. 80,000 Gram Panchayat members have been trained for a period of 8 days each during October 2002-January 2005. Besides Gram Panchayat members, Taluk Panchayat and Zilla Panchayat members have also benefited from the SATCOM centre. The Satellite Based Interactive Communication System is an integral system of providing training and communication support for the developmental activities and thereby accelerate the effective implementation of development programmes which has maintained uniformity in all the taluk headquarters by the Abdul Nazeer Sab State Institute of Rural Development. At the outset of the programme out of 175 Taluks, 102 Taluk Panchayats had installed Dish Antennas, i.e. DRS (RX) to receive satellite waves and 47 Taluk Panchayats had purchased TV Sets. In other Taluk Panchayats installing of dish and purchasing of TV Sets was undertaken. Thus the Taluk Panchayat meeting hall was being converted as training hall. By this procedure training was imparted to maximum number of members at a time.

Objectives of the training and capacity building programme

- Enable gram panchayat members, particularly women and representatives of disadvantaged groups, to understand their own context and possibilities.
- Provoke them to take a deeper look at their own situations and struggling to find solutions to their problems.
- Enable them to think constructively, i.e. in terms of small but constructive activities that they can take or facilitate others to take.

As reported in a daily newspaper the Abdul Naseer Sab State Institute for Rural Development (ANSSIRD) has staged street plays in more than 5,000 villages across 44 taluks in the State to create an awakening about the Panchayati Raj System and Decentralization of power. The training and capacity building activities was conducted in all the gram panchayats of all taluks and in every District of the State. The trainings were conducted in phases. Training of panchayat members was conducted in four phases, each phase of two days duration. Two gram panchayats in each taluk was identified for initiating the processes of preparation of village plans. The street plays are part of a training programme organized by the institute to bring about a qualitative change in the functioning of gram panchayats and their members. They are not only aimed at creating an awakening about the panchayati raj system among the general public, but also to enable members of gram panchayats to understand their context in the decentralization process and inspire them to chart out their role in social transformation.

As stated earlier, the institute launched a satellite-based programme for the benefit of 18,000 gram panchayat members in 44 taluks. There are 88,000 gram panchayat members in all taluks of the State. The satellite-based programme and street plays are part of an elaborate training programme for gram panchayat members that began in November 2002. 44 taluks were covered in the first phase of the training programme. The taluks were divided into five zones—Mysore, Bangalore, Dharwad, Gulbarga, and Mangalore. The street plays, which would commence in the Mysore zone, were expected to continue for more than two months. A total of 600 amateur theatre artistes from voluntary groups in the State had been enlisted for the programme. The artists had been divided into 50 troups, each comprising 12 artists. The street plays had been specially written by well-known scholars, including the former Chairman of the Nataka Academy, C.G. Krishnaswamy, and the writer, H.L. Keshavamurthy, on the right to information, corruption, conservation of natural resources, accountability, and people's planning and participation in the process of decentralization.

An estimated 540 villages in Mysore Zone comprising Mysore, Mandya, Chamarajanagar, Hassan, and Kodagu districts were covered under the programme. Two villages under each of the selected gram panchayat had been chosen to stage street plays. Apart from enhancing the confidence of gram panchayat members, particularly women, to enable them deliver speeches and participate in panchayat meetings; the programme dwells on issues of social importance such as education, equality, and health. The message through films was considered to be an attractive medium for gram panchayat members. These films were developed in the workshop mode, which are neither pre-scripted nor use lectures from experts. They reflect the experience of gram panchayat members.

The format of the films included workshop discussions, individual interviews, and dramatized plays. For the training programme, 12 films had been developed with the assistance of UNICEF. Many NGOs had been involved in developing them. The films were to be transmitted from the Satcom Centre located at the institute in Mysore and received at district and taluk stations. The centre has a "one-way-video and two-way audio" system. One of the films, The First Step, aired during the first phase of the training programme, seeks to focus on the history of panchayat raj from the colonial rule to the 73rd Amendment to the Constitution. The film highlights the importance of decentralization, extending power to the people, and issues related to reservation.

Another film, *Learning to Speak,* deals with illiteracy, caste, and gender impediments. It also seeks to enlighten members of gram panchayats about tampering with the allocation or rotation of seats and reservation for the posts of chairperson and vice-chairperson, which often occurs on account of illiteracy, gender, and caste bias. *Marching Together* is a film related to gram panchayat meetings, including notice, agenda, ordinary and special meetings, quorum, sitting fees, recording and reading of resolutions, etc.

The film, *In Sitamma's Footsteps*, to be aired during the fourth phase of the programme dramatizes the anti-arrack movement that grew out of the literacy programme in Nellore District of Andhra Pradesh. The film raises the issue whether gram panchayats are intended to merely implement the schemes designed and conceptualized elsewhere or whether they have a role in the overall development of the people.

The Outcome of the Programme

It will not be an exaggeration to say that the programme could achieve cent per cent success in meeting its objectives. Though there were some constraints like elections and related activities and extreme climatic conditions like heavy rains, the programme went on well and could be completed involving the required number of members. The programme stressed the importance of grama sabha. The members realized the meaning, significance and purpose of gram sabha. They learnt that it is through grama sabha that they could make administration accountable and transparent. Therefore, conducting gram sabhas should be a priority for the members. The members have felt that they should take initiatives to make gram sabha an integral part of the Panchayati Raj System. Transparency in policy-making was one of the important concepts the elected members learnt. The orientation about powers and functions of the panchayats, their financial resources and funds was able to create confidence among the participants to do their tasks as responsible representatives of the people. Financial autonomy and adequate resources are essential for performing the duties of the panchayats. It is obvious that the members realized and felt the need to mobilize resources.

Members could see that adequate finance is the backbone to success of programme aimed at rural development. Their priority would, therefore, be to draw-up measures to strengthen the finances of the panchayats by way of collection of taxes. In course of conducting capacity building programme by ANSSIRD since the very beginning, many issues and practical problems have cropped up, which need serious consideration and appropriate remedies. Some of these are given below:

Issues and Problems

(i) The technology is quite expensive.
(ii) Lack of time for interactions with the participants.
(iii) Members have to come to taluk headquarters. In other words, it has not reached each gram panchayat.
(iv) Whether the training should be given in the beginning of the term they are elected or after one year after they are elected.
(v) Power cut, electricity problem at some places.
(vi) Timing of the programme is not convenient for most of the members.

Based on our visits to ANSSIRD at Mysore and attending relay of some programmes in the studio, and discussions with its officials and informal interviews with the elected members of a few panchayats and reading the scanty materials available in the ANSSIRD office, we developed our perceptions about the organization, its functioning and its impact. Some of the observations may be made as follows:

(i) The elected members have started realizing the importance of decentralization, grassroots governance and people's participation. They have realized that it is through this that the Panchayati Raj bodies can prepare and formulate schemes in a scientific way by involving the local people. One can surely say that these members have found new meanings to the word 'Participation'.
(ii) Also, leadership is necessary to influence people to co-operate towards a common goal and promote collective response. This shows very clearly that political development and democratic growth depend on the local leadership and

its functioning in the PRIs. As development progresses, the complexities increase and will demand more professionalism. The direct implication of this is the need for capacity building in the light of the socio-economic and political conditions of elected members.

(iii) Continuous efforts should be made to train the leadership with a broader perspective than before. Comprehensive and meaningful training programmes have to be designed specifically for rural women so that they perform their constitutional duties and responsibilities as elected members of the PRIs.

(iv) The programme discussed in this paper could bring out the hidden qualities of women members more so that they gain self-confidence, develop communication skills and raise issues. Still government, NGO, Academic and people themselves should be committed and completely involved in strengthening women's participation in rural local government.

(v) A strong information system is essential for participation and planning. More emphasis has to be laid on proper information system in the light of participatory democracy and the process of empowerment.

(vi) New and rigorous policies are needed which ensure that the growth pattern benefits the poor, needy and disadvantaged and that the resources are invested in building human capabilities on a priority basis.

(vii) Among other constraints, resource constraints pose great hassels in the process, but whatever the constraints human capacity building should command the highest priority. Simultaneously measures should be taken to restructure budget so that there is additional resources.

(viii) Participation is needed as a right to create a fair and just society. The 73rd Constitutional Amendment has given the necessary venue for participation for women so that they have a voice in decisions. The need of the hour is to invest in accelerating human development through capacity building. Only this can integrate the hitherto unexposed sections of society in the process of development and democracy in an effective manner.

(ix) The members expressed in one of the interviews that this programme was more effective and they would motivate the other members of their panchayat who could not attend the training and they stressed that the reservation to women has promoted greater participation and this programme has really strengthened and has made them knowledgeable and articulate to take effective decision.

(x) Due to the Rotation System as per the PR Act, the same constituency will change and new entrants of elected representatives come in after every five-year term is complete. So capacity building has to become a continuous process to strengthen the decentralized governance at the grassroots.

(xi) To cover such a huge programme concerted efforts by the Government and the organizations of the civil society is more important.

(xii) It is one of the innovative programmes and first of its kind in the country and it is hoped that it would cover whole of the country.

It is increasingly recognized that 'ANSSIRD's successful blending of technology and training has caught the attention of administrators at home and abroad. It appears that technology has taken a wider role though it is more expensive. To us, it should be a continuous process to have success of such an innovative programme.

REFERENCES

Capacity Building in Panchayati Raj, India Panchayati Raj Report, Four Decades of Decentralized Governance in Rural India, 2001, Ch. 9, pp. 89-103, Vol. 1, NIRD, Hyderabad.

Deccan Herald (Daily), Bangalore, October 18, 2005.

Palanithurai G. (Ed.), 2004, *Dynamics of New Panchayati Raj System in India,* (Volume IV, Empowering Women), Concept Publishing Company, New Delhi.

Satellite Based Communication and training programme for Gram Panchayat Members—Stage l, and website of ANSSIRD, Mysore.

Subha K., B.S. Bhargava and Mangala Nayak, January-June 2001, *Women in Panchayati Raj Institution: Political Empowerment through Capacity Building*, SAJOSPS.

9

CAPACITY BUILDING OF ZILLA PARISHAD FUNCTIONARIES IN HARYANA

MAHI PAL

Introduction

The State Panchayati Raj Acts which were legislated in conformity with the 73rd Amendment Act, 1992 have provided the sustained structure in the form of the Panchayats at district and sub-district levels to take up various activities for local development with social justice with effective people's participation. But the experiences of the functioning of the Panchayati Raj Institutions (PRIs) show that these institutions' Actors in the form of elected representatives who were expected to use effectively the Panchayati Raj System (PRS) for decentralized development were not only unaware of their powers and functions but also did not know about how to conduct the business of the Panchayats. The experiences of the working of elected representatives when these bodies came into being just after the implementation of the 73rd Amendment Act in 1995 could be expressed in their own words : "swords are given but how to use them not known". Further "The pen is given but how to use it not known". Meaning thereby that they have been elected to the Panchayats, but they do not know how to use the institutions of

Panchayats for their voters' development. After elapsing almost a decade, there found not much change in the enhancement in their understanding about the utility of the PRS and roles of these people in the functioning of these bodies except with some exceptions here and there.

In above context, it was highly desirable to start the process of capacity building of the Panchayat functionaries at all levels of the PRS. Hence, in order to not only build up their skills and enhance their knowledge but also change their attitudes, the Haryana Institute of Rural Development (HIRD) is organizing training courses for the capacity building of Panchayat Functionaries numbering more than 60,000 at three levels (i.e. Gram Panchayats, Panchayat Samitis and Zilla Parishads) in decentralized manner after assessing their training needs by organizing a series of meetings with various stakeholders involved in the process of decentralized planning and development. During training needs assessment exercise, the suggestions like training at the door step of the elected representatives, to and fro TA to the trainees for attending the training courses and involvement of the elected representatives who were knowledgeable as trainers were emerged. The HIRD tried to put these suggestions into practice during the course of the training. The training programmes for all the Panchayat Functionaries are being carried out by the HIRD with the help of State Community Development Training Centre (SCDTC) and nine Teams recruited for this purpose. The training for the elected representatives of the apex tier (i.e. Zilla Parishad) of the PRS has got over which was organized by the HIRD. The training to Gram Panchayat and Panchayat Simiti Functionaries is being imparted by the Trainers Teams at Block Headquarters and SCTDC at Nilokheri, respectively. The Zilla Parishad Functionaries (ZPFs) denote chairpersons, vice-chairpersons, Members and Account Officers/Accountants of the Zilla Parishad. The training progamme for the capacity building of the Panchayat Functionaries has been sponsored by the Ministry of Rural Development, Government of India. The present paper deals with the capacity building strategy adopted by the HIRD for ZPFs and the experiences gained from this exercise.

Capacity Building Module

The capacity building module for the ZPF has been prepared keeping in view their requirements in their day to day functioning. Requirements of these functionaries have been coached into five heads which have been outlined below. Reading materials which contains the following has been given to the ZPFs in the form of a book named as *Haryana Mee Panchayati Raj Avam Grameen Vikas* (Panchayati Raj in Haryana and Rural Development).

Main Features of the Haryana Panchayati Raj Act, 1994

The main features of the Haryana Panchayati Raj Act *inter alia* includes: meaning, relevance and conduct of the meetings of the Gram Sabha; conduct of the meetings of the Gram Panchayat (GP), powers, authority and duties of the GP and its representatives, constitution and importance of the Sub and Local Committees at GP level; duties of the Gram Sachives; finances of the GP; and proper keeping and preservation of the record and property of the GP. Functions, powers and duties of the PS and its chairpersons/ vice-chairpersons and members; functions and role of the Executive Officer of the PS, conduct of the business of the PS; constitution and functions of the Subject Committees; and power of overseeing the functioning of the GP under its jurisdiction. Functions, powers and duties of the ZP and its chairpersons/vice-chairpersons and members; functions and role of the Chief Executive Officer of the PS, conduct of the business of the ZP; constitution and functions of the Subject Committees; and power of overseeing the functioning of the GP and PS in the district. Relevant Articles of the Haryana Panchayat Act which establish the organic link between and among three-tiers of the PRS; Management and preservation of the common properties of the GP are also under this head. The purpose behind giving provisions pertaining to all the tiers of the Panchayats was to provide a holistic view of the PRS in the State because ZPFs are also expected to oversee and supervise both PS and GP.

Functions of the 16 Departments transferred to the Panchayats

The Government of Haryana devolved certain powers and functions of 16 Departments by issuing notifications in 1995 and 2001. This part of the Module contains a brief of the devolved functions at GP, PS and ZP.

Role of the Panchayats in Rural Development Programmes

In this part of the Module the salient features of various Centrally Sponsored Programmes like Sampooran Grameen Rozgar Yojana (SGRY), Swaranjayanti Grameen Rozgar Yojana (SGSY); specific focus on the strategy of the formation of the Self-Help Groups; Rural Housing Pradhan Mantri Gramodaya Yojana (PMGY); Rural Water Supply; Rural Sanitation; Haryali; and various State sponsored schemes being implemented by the Panchayats. It may be mentioned that while giving details of these schemes simultaneously specific role of various tiers of the Panchayat have been given in the Module. For example, in case of SGRY specific role has been assigned for GP, PS and ZP, but for proper implementations of the Programme ZPFs should know the role of other two tiers of the PRS also.

Decentralised Planning

This part of the training module *inter alia* includes: meaning of development; concept of planning and decentralized planning; different components of the decentralized planning such as participation, accountability, transparency, effectiveness, prioritization; different steps to be taken under decentralized planning such as socio-economic analysis of local situation; role of the District Planning Committee in formulation and implementation of the decentralized planning and finally role of the Panchayati Raj Institutions (PRIs) in formulation and implementation of the decentralized planning. Besides, salient features of the People's campaign for the 9th Plan in Kerala and measures to be adopted for effective participation of the Gram Sabha in formulation of the decentralized planning have also been included in this part of the Module.

Social Development and PRIs

The contents under social development *inter alia* includes: literacy and education; health, mal-nutrition and its impact on women and children; children health particularly pre- and post-natal cares; adverse sex ratio and its adverse impact on rural society; information about vaccination; major programmes for the development of women and children and rural sanitation. Details of the specific role of the PRIs at different levels have been given in the Module. It may be mentioned that major focus in the training programme was given to social development aspect of the rural development keeping in view the intensity of the problems in rural areas. In addition to above, the importance of the coordination between elected representatives and officials for smooth working of the Panchayats at district and sub-district levels was also told in the training courses.

Methodology for Conducting Training Courses

The period of training was for two days. The course was residential. The first session of the training course was started with the introduction of both trainees and the faculty. This was followed by the experiences sharing with the participants. The experience sharing exercise was proved very useful in knowing the Strength, Weaknesses, Opportunities and Threats of the functioning of the Panchayati Raj as a system of local governance and the extent of the understanding of its Actors in the form of PRFs about their roles and responsibilities in local development. This session not only gave an assessment of the status of the awareness of these functionaries which in turn proved very useful for the entire faculty for taking different sessions to focus the relevant issues in their lectures and interaction with the Participants, but also found useful in creating an conducive environment for healthy discussions and deliberations during training period. The participatory (i.e. Trainees centred) approach of training was practiced in delivering the training to the participants. More focus was given on interaction with them so that relevant issues and problems could be culled out from discussion for giving possible solution to them in the course of two day training.

Extent of the Participation of the PRFs

Before presenting the extent of participation of the ZPFs, let us throw some light on the methodology adopted by the HIRD for inviting them to attend training courses. The Haryana Government issued order to all the Deputy Commissioners and Zilla Parishad for the participation of the ZPFs in the training courses being organized by the HIRD in its campus. Account Officers of the ZPs were also invited with the purpose to make them understand various aspects of the PRS as well as to coordinate with the elected representatives of ZP for ensuring their participation in the training courses. It was also mentioned in these orders that to and fro fare for participating in the courses will also be reimbursed by the HIRD. Besides these orders, personal contact through phones at times were also made by the faculty of HIRD and the Director with the Additional Deputy Commissioners, AOs and Chairpersons and Vice-Chairpersons of the ZPs for requesting them to attend the training so that more and more ZPFs could participate in the training courses. Nine courses of two days for 19 ZPs (2 or 3 ZPs in each course) were planned. One course could not be held as none of the participants came from concerned ZPs. Hence, in total 8 courses of two days were held for ZPFs.

Table 1 presents the extent of the participation of the ZPFs district level and category level. It may be seen from the Table that out of total elected representatives 25.48 per cent participated in these courses in spite of HIRD's best efforts for ensuring maximum participation of the elected representatives. If we see category-wise we find that of the total 21 per cent male and merely 4.48 per cent of female participated in these courses. The main reason for dismal participation of women was the proxisim which prevails in the State because their husbands rarely want that their wives got outside exposure as chairpersons and members of the ZPs. There was no participation of both elected and officials from Hissar, Mahendergarh, Rewari and Sonepat districts. In case of Sirsa only one official participated in the training. There was no participation of women elected representatives from Bhiwani, Faridabad, Fatehabad, Gurgaon, Yamunanagar and Kaithal ZPs. If we see participation of elected representatives across the districts, we find that maximum participation was noticed from Karnal district and the lowest from Yamunanagar and Fatehabad districts. Elected women representatives' participation was highest from Kurukshetra District and the lowest was from Jind district from where only Chairperson of the ZP participated.

Four reasons could be attributed for the dismal participation from some districts in the training camps. One was that only one and half years are left for the new elections for the Panchayats. These elected representatives might have thought of not much use of the training from their angles. But the other side of this was that those who participated in the training courses have said that those who did not come to participate in these courses were looser because the intent and contents of the training was found very useful. But had the training been held just after the holding the elections of Panchayats in the manner it is being held now, their participations would have been higher. Second reason was that mostly elected representatives have their affiliation with different political parties and they were associated with Assembly elections in Rajasthan State. Third one was political because the Members of different political background found the training course a better forum for highlighting the deficiencies of the working of the Chairperson of a particular district. This might have hesitated the Chairpersons and his/her group Members to attend the training course. In other words, they hesitated from the exposure of their deficiencies as a chairperson or member of the ZP. Fourthly, the administrative machinery of the ZP also discouraged the ZPFs to attend these programmes thinking that awareness among these people may create problems for them.

Experience from the Capacity Building Exercise

In all the training courses, the first session was devoted to with the participants in which every trainee was expected to participate and expressed her/his experiences in terms of work she has done, the difficulties she encountered and the remedial measures taken by her/him. It may be mentioned that participants were found well satisfied after attending the course because they were told a number of new things pertaining to grassroots governance, planning and development which would be very useful in their work as people's representatives in Panchayat Bodies. During two days training course, a number of suggestions and issues cropped up which helped the faculty in subsequent deliberations and interactions with the participants. Some of them even have policy implications. The experiences of these training courses are given below:

During experience sharing and discussion, it was found that elected representatives of ZP who were having some experiences either Member or Chairpersons of the Cooperative Societies or any Social Organisation or associated with such organizations were found more assertive and knowledgeable about the Panchayats than the others. It is interesting to note that when elected representatives of the Faridabad and Kaithal ZPs were arguing that no meaningful powers have been given to the ZP. One of the members of the ZP told with audacity that : "We have to identify our own strength and try to overcome our weaknesses. The power vests with the ZP as an institution and not with the individual. If there is any problem before the Member, the same may be put before the ZP meeting and then see the results because Additional Deputy Commissioner (ADC) is the Chief Executive Officer of the ZP who is next to the Deputy Commissioner of the district. He will take the necessary action in the matter. But for that we have to become knowledgeable and have to know how to put the issue in the meeting and participate in the conduct of the business of the house." It was also found that those who were knowledgeable in terms of knowing the details of various schemes were implementing them more effectively than the others. In contrast, where those who were not knowledgeable either the MP/MLA or Bureaucrats holding the balance in local governance. Secondly, where coordination (better word in Hindi for this is *Talmail*) between elected representatives and bureaucrats was tuned, various works were done smoothly. Hence, the key factor was *Talmail* between these two Actors at ZP level for the better implementation of the Panchayati Raj System. In order to bring about proper coordination between non-officials and officials, it was suggested that joint training programme for both should be organized so that the gaps which exist in terms of knowing each other roles could be discussed. One Member of the Kaithal ZP said categorically that here in the HIRD they found very congenial atmosphere and the Faculty Members including the Director talked them in friendly manner. Had such environment been at the district level, there would have been smooth functioning of the Panchayats not only at the district level but also at sub-district levels.

In general the participants said that the Central and the State Governments are not interested in strengthening the PRS because innocuous functions have been given to them. Twenty Nine subjects listed in the 11th Schedule of the Constitution are expected to be devolved to the Panchayats but what is reality is a household name. During the training course, they have been trained, of course, the Panchayats have not emerged as a Institution of Self-Governments as envisaged in the Constitution, but the powers to the Panchayats given in the Panchayati Raj Act and subsequently given through Executive Orders have not been assimilated by them. Are you aware the extent of functions and powers given to the ZP? Are you aware the extent of supervision and control the ZP have on the lower two tiers (i.e. PS and GP) of the PRS? Their answer was no. That is why this training is conducted to make you people aware about under which sections elected representatives have the power to govern ZP properly and also help the rest tiers of the PRS in their good governance. One important thing noticed from the experiences of the these training courses is that there is a urgent need for creating awareness among Gram Sabha members about their rights and responsibilities by way of organizing Gram Melas locally because these people washed away their hands after casting their votes to their candidates. One interesting thing was also noticed that these elected representatives instead of organising themselves to press the Government for more devolution to the Panchayats from the State and Central Governments wanted the HIRD to write to the State and Central Governments on the basis of the recommendations of the training courses. This shows, their unwillingness to unite themselves through forming associations for building pressure on the Governments for more devolution to the Panchayats. In other words, a very little urge for power was found among them.

The concept of powers according to them was the full autonomy in utilizing the funds earmarked to the ZP and power of the transfer of officials from one place to other at whim. In case of funds even some of the participants suggested that Chairperson of the ZP should have been authorized to countersign the cheque as the Sarpanch at GP level practices. To this, they have been trained that the money which comes under various schemes is being distributed in different parts of the district as per decision of the ZP and the officer who signs the cheques in fact is implementing the orders of the ZP. Hence, countersigning is not important. What is important is knowledge about the working of the administration. They were told that even the Ministers at State and Central level never sign the cheques.

It was also told by the elected representatives that concerned Officials of the Line Departments did not come to attend the meeting of the ZP. Sometimes even the ADC depute the Junior Officer in the ZP meeting. To this, it was apprised to them that the presence of the ADC is a must for the meeting of the ZP. Without him meeting of the ZP was not valid. About the Line Departments, they have been told that a copy of the agenda should be sent to the Head of the Offices at district level. Initially the concerned Officers might not come first time due to some reasons. But if proper and sustain follow-up is followed, their regular coming to the meeting will become a routine matter.

They also said that District Rural Development Agency should be merged with the ZP as has happened in other States. All the elected representatives have to be united for this. We from the Institute's side also write in the report of the training to the State Government for merging the DRDA with the ZP in order to strengthen the PRS in the State. In the beginning of each course, they have been categorically told that training in term of capacity building is all about 'ASK', i.e. Aptitude, Skill and Knowledge. But at the same time they were told that if one has these three things, she enjoys the powers not only in the Panchayats but in any sector/ field.

The issue of irregular holding the meetings of the ZP also cropped up. It was told by one of the Chairpersons of the ZP that concerned file for fixing date of the meeting of the ZP was pending with the ADC for 20 days. To this, the participants have told that as per the Panchayat Act holding regular meetings of the ZP is the responsibility of the Chairperson. What is required is that the Chairperson should invite the agenda from different Members of the ZP and ask his/her Chief Executive Officer (CEO) who is ADC to issue agenda to all for discussion in the Meetings. In one training course, one Member of ZP apprised that in his district CEO has been transferred four times in three years. Happening such a frequent transfer of the CEO is injurious to the health of ZP governance. Some of the Members of some ZPs expressed that since their Chairperson is illiterate and inexperienced proper supervision and overseeing could not be done by them in proper managing the affair of the ZP.

The ZPFs also requested the HIRD that it would be very useful to them if regular exposure visits are organized to understand the experiences of other states where the PRIs have been functioning well. To this, it was told by the Institute that if resolutions for this may come to us at least from 10 ZPs such type of visits could be arranged on regular basis for their exposure and awareness about the best practices in other States in the field of the Panchayati Raj.

The issue of the implementation of the Sampooran Rojgar Yojana (SGRY) was also discussed in all the training courses which was obvious as it is the main programme being implemented by ZP. When asked about the manner in which the Scheme is being implemented by them. They said that they merely indicate the item of work and place of work under the Scheme. The implementing agency which is either PS or GP took the further action in the matter. However, some of the ZP Members said that in their ZP itself is the implementing agency. Generally, it was found that the amount received under the SGRY is being distributed among the different Members equally. However, this is not the right practice because as per the guidelines of the SGRY action plan comprising various activities to be undertaken is to be prepared under the scheme, it was told to the participants. Some of the Members particularly in the district of Gurgaon expressed the anguish that money allocated under the SGRY is being misused by the implementing agencies and they approached from post to the pillar but in vain. Due to lack of proper formulating of the Action Plan under the Scheme from the GS and onward overlapping of works are also being happening in the field. The participants were also opined that a copy of the order of the release issued under different programmes from the Central

Government and the State Government should also be sent to the ZP so that this body will also know the quantum of funds coming to the district.

Although order from the State Government for constituting the District Planning Committees have been issued long back, these Committees have not seen light of the day so far. ZPFs said in unison that meetings of these Committees are not being held at all, then what is the use of these Committees. They expressed in anguish that this Committee should be operationalised immediately so that meetings of it should held regularly in future.

The interesting point emerged from the training course was that some Members suggested that they should also be invited in the meetings of the GS in his/her constituency. It is really heartening to note that the Members of the ZP are interested to participate in the meetings of the GS on their own. However, in the Panchayat Act such provision is not there but if the ZP Members want to participate in the Meetings of the GS, the ZP'CEO can instruct the Executive Officer of the PS (i.e. Block Development and Panchayat Officer) to make available the dates of the GS Meetings to be held twice during May 15 to June 15 and November 15 to December15 every year to the ZP for giving the details of the same to the ZP Members for their necessary action. In fact, participation of the ZP Members may strengthen the direct democracy which is only being practiced at GS level in Indian federal structure. However, specific instructions in this regard should be issued from the State Government enabling ZPFs to participate in the meetings of GS.

It was also expressed by the ZPFs that for having a organic link between ZP and the State Government, there should be a Coordination between them. For this purpose there may a State level Council under the Chairpersonship of the Chief Minister so that the ZPs may air their grievances for the rectification of the same.

Conclusions

Eight training courses of ZPFs held in the HIRD were found very useful by the Participants. They were of the opinion that though such type of training should be held just after the holding the elections, but even than the inputs given to them and methodology of delivering training were appreciated by them. Lack of awareness about their powers/functions among the ZPFs was found one of the important inhibiting factors in performing their role effectively. Rarely anybody have gone through the Panchayat Act. The participation of women elected representatives was very low in comparison to their counterparts. The Panchayats elections in Haryana are due in first quarter of the next year. The type of training being given to the Panchayat Functionaries now should also be repeated after the next elections of the Panchayats with the same intent and contents to enable the Panchayat leaders to perform their role with clarity and effectively.

Table 1 : Statement showing the Extent of Participation of PR Functionaries of Zilla Parishad in Haryana.

Sl. No.	*Name of the District*	*Total Nos. of elected ZP representatives including President and Vice-President*	*Categorywise Participation*		*Total elected represe-ntatives*	*Officials partici-pated*	*Grand Total*
			Male	*Female*			
1.	Ambala	13	4	2	6	1	7
2.	Bhiwani	24	5	-	5	1	6
3.	Faridabad	18	5	-	5	2	7
4.	Fatehabad	13	1	-	1	2	3
5.	Gurgaon	24	4	-	4	-	4
6.	Hisar	23	-	-	-	-	-
7.	Jind	20	5	1	6	-	6
8.	Jhajjar	15	6	2	8	2	10
9.	Panchkula	10	2	1	3	1	4
10.	Mahendergarh	15	-	-	-	-	-
11	Rewari	13	-	-	-	-	-
12	Rohtak	13	7	2	9	1	10
13	Sonepat	21	-	-	-	-	-
14	Sirsa	17	-	-	-	1	1
15	Yamunanagar	14	1	-	1	2	3
16	Kurukshetra	13	2	3	5	1	6
17	Kaithal	17	7	-	7	3	10
18	Karnal	19	11	2	13	3	16
19	Panipat	12	6	1	7	-	7
	Total	**314**	**66**	**14**	**80**	**20**	**100**

10

CAPACITY BUILDING IN PANCHAYATI RAJ INSTITUTIONS WITH SPECIAL REFERENCE TO WEST BENGAL

Y. BHASKAR RAO

> "The Panchayati Raj System, a system of local self-governance is the backbone of democracy in India. However, it has been found that there is a lacuna, a key issue in the functioning of the Panchayati Raj System—the lack of meaningful participation by elected representatives, especially women, Dalits and backward classes. In spite of the 73rd Amendment, they have not been able to exercise their powers due to generations of subjugation. Many elected representatives are unaware of their duties as per the 73rd Amendment."
>
> —*"The Thimbaku Collective-Panchayati Raj, 2006"*

Context

The Constitution (73rd Amendment) Act, 1992, which came into force on April 24, 1993, is considered to be a major landmark in the transition of political power to the grassroots democracy. It has provided not only the Constitutional status to the Panchayati Raj Institutions but also enhanced responsibilities. It has been observed that the state legislature enjoys wide discretion. "Significantly enough, only the function of preparation of plans for economic and social development is provided for and not for the implementation of the plans they prepare. The omission appears to be deliberate. Further, only 'schemes' relating to the items of the Eleventh Schedule are to be implanted by the Panchayats and such schemes need not necessarily be those prepared by the Panchayats. It is wrongly presumed by many that the 29 'functions' of the Schedule are conferred on the Panchayats under the Constitution." By providing one-third reservation for women and proportionate reservation for other socially excluded and deprived sections (tribals, dalits etc.), the Constitutional framework for local governance mechanisms in India has enormous potential for affirmative action. One of the most important roles for these local governance institutions is to plan for local development and ensure social justice in consistence with the citizen's needs and aspirations.

Capacity Building is the Need of the Hour

Capacity building of any organisation is directly related to provide an opportunity to the constituents of the organisation to acquire the knowledge needed for smooth and successful operations of the organisation. The process should not merely end at that, but should ensure that the knowledge imparted is utilized by the recipients in their day-to-day functions and also that the relevant knowledge is refurbished at regular intervals so as to keep them abreast with the latest changes. However, the primary concern for any capacity building measure is to locate and focus on the training needs of the trainees. In other words the intervention should be topical, customized and user-friendly. Thus, the importance of a realistic training need analysis in respect to the capacity building initiatives in the PRIs need not be emphasized. It was with this in mind that this micro-study has tried to develop a sketch of what the constituents of the PRIs needs, where it is needed and when it is needed.

From the early years, panchayats were given a range of fairly serious responsibilities and tasks, such as the organization of relief and reconstruction after the severe floods of 1978. The involvement of the panchayats in such relief work substantially reduced the distress of the people of the affected areas that were usually associated with such calamities. Panchayats were also entrusted with the management of rural employment programmes—first the Food for Work then RLEGP, and more recently the Jawahar Rozgar Yojana as well as various other schemes and projects in the rural areas. In 1980, the West Bengal Government entrusted the panchayats with the implementation of as many as 27 rural development programmes. Among the programmes devolved, some were of major national importance. The list included some of the major developmental schemes, such as the Rural Reconstruction Programme, Rural Water Supply, Rural Housing Scheme, distribution of mini-kits for agriculture, and Programme of Reconstruction of School Buildings etc. In the implementation of these programmes, the Panchayats made a significant departure in the termination of contractor system.

Approaches for Capacity Building

In recent times, various strategies have been adopted to build the capacities in Panchayati Raj Institutions. Methods should be created for the sake of empowering the SC/ST and women elected representatives and lower level staff of Panchayati Raj Institutions. Whenever the capacities for the officials and non-officials of PRIs, are enhanced the change of scenario would occur in the rural areas. For instance, the given below approaches would be the best model for creating capacities among the institutions and their actors of implementation.

PRIA's Model

In a vast country like India, this democratic decentralisation has enormous challenges. In rural areas, nearly a-quarter million local bodies exist. Nearly three million elected representatives are there in these local bodies, of which nearly one million are women.

- Panchayati Raj Institutions (PRIs) are to be viewed as institutions of local self-governance and not as mere implementers of centrally determined development programmes. Bottom-up comprehensive planning based on micro-planning exercise is to be the basis of self-governance. PRIs should not be allowed to become a third tier of development administration.

- Emphasis must be placed on active participation in decision-making by women and other weaker sections with a view to enhance their role, status and leadership in local self-governance.
- Interventions in strengthening PRIs should focus on building, promoting and empowering new leadership of women, dalits and tribals.
- PRIs should assert their access to and control over local natural and human resources as well as other development resources that are available with state and national governments.
- Strengthening PRIs will entail clarity of their roles, systems of governance, accountability and transparency and inter-linkages.

The experience of functioning of these local bodies in the past 10 years in India makes it clear that effective local self-governance is still a distant dream and requires enormous interventions to realize its potential. This is particularly so because such democratic decentralization is coming after nearly 50 years of centralization in the state machinery, public resources and bureaucratic structures. As a result, hierarchies of government departments and agencies have generated vested interests and exercise their responsibility to apply public resources in an unaccountable manner. On the other hand, nearly five decades of state-led model of development delivered from the top has created a sense of passive dependence on government agencies, programmes and resources among citizens in rural and urban areas.

In this framework, capacity building efforts address the needs for enhancing capacity at the level of individual and organized collectives. In the framework presented above, different elements and processes of Capacity Building for local self-governance in the Indian context are elaborated and illustrated.

PRIA's focus on interventions to strengthen local self-governance has targeted the lowest tiers of this structure. Therefore, the interventions aimed at (1) Capacity Building of civil society—citizen leaders, community-based organizations, small voluntary organizations, Gram Sabhas, etc. to develop an effective voice on decision-making about access to and use of development resources; (2) Capacity Building, sensitization and policy advocacy within the governance institutions—three-tiers of PRIs, district administration, line departments, etc., to respond to the voice of the new leadership from civil society; and (3) enabling linkages (interfacing) between the voice (of civil society) and response (of governance institutions) to demonstrate innovative exemplars of transparent and accountable use of development resources in favour of the marginalized and excluded.

The Hunger Project Model

One of the keys to ending hunger is to strengthen local democratic institutions, so that people can directly participate in meeting their basic needs. In recent months, the Government of India has hosted a series of seven high-level round table meetings. The meetings are presided over by the Minister of Panchayati Raj and attended by over 30 Ministers of State for Rural Development and Secretaries of Rural Development from the States and Union territories across India.

The Hunger Project was chosen to be the nodal agency to co-ordinate the VIIth and final round-table that focused on the issue of "Capacity Building and Training of Panchayati Raj Institutions (PRIs)". The following Key outputs were produced to facilitate discussions at the round-table.

- State-wise fact-sheets on the status of training and Capacity Building were collected from 22 States and 5 Union territories of India. The State Offices and partner NGOs in the States were instrumental in compiling this information.
- A Draft National Approach towards Capacity Building and Training of PRIs was prepared. Two rounds of discussions

were held with more than 35 NGOs across the country. Representatives from Samavesh (Madhya Pradesh); RSCD (Maharashtra); RLEK (Uttranchal); PRIA (Delhi); ISS (Delhi); URMUL (Rajasthan); Gandhigram University (Tamil Nadu); UNNATI (Gujarat) contributed and co-produced this draft with The Hunger Project.

- Complied a small booklet containing experiences and learning from some of the leading state programmes.

UNDP Model

Eradication of extreme poverty and hunger through PRIs is certainly possible by target year 2015. More than a billion people still live on less than US $1 a day; Sub-Saharan Africa, Latin America and the Carribbean, and parts of Europe and Central Asia are failing short of the poverty target. To promote gender equality and empower women the Millennium Development Goals (MDG) determined some achievements during February 2006. They are as follows:

- On going awareness generation activities on issues concerning Panchayati Raj through information fairs, wall writing/wall paintings, Mahila Sammelans. Village and Hamlet level meeting are being conducted in all the project states and districts.
- Cluster, block and district level forums and networks of elected women created in various project districts.
- Institutional mechanisms such as Panchayat Information Centres, Information Kisoks, Panchayat Resource Centres (PRCs) are established and are providing continuous field-based support in the form of information and human assistance to the elected women representatives and the communities in the project districts.
- Monitoring of select government schemes for basic services by Elected Women Representatives is being done.
- A Panchayat jurisprudence study covering all states has been carried out, and consultations held with judiciary, civil society, and the government. The Ministry of Panchayati

Raj started using the findings of the study for reviewing the State Panchayat Laws.

- Media involvement is being fostered; press meeting and media workshops have been held in project states; distribution of material concerning Panchayati Raj through the media has been undertaken.

NIRD Model

During the February 2006, the National Conference on "National Training Design for training of elected members and officials of Panchayati Raj Institutions" was held at NIRD, Hyderabad. During the deliberations, they have prepared an agenda for training plan for the PRIs. The training plan essentially involves, preparation of a training strategy for the State covering the issues of:

- Preparation and submission of a Training Calendar and Budget thereon,
- Development of Training Modules/Pilot Testing,
- Conduct of TOT,
- Launching field-level training programmes,
- Preparation and delivery of supplementary reading material,
- Community/Social Mobilization,
- Identification of Institutes/Organisations within State and networking with them,
- Identification of Resource Persons at each level.

In addition to the conventional training methods of interactive lectures and class room sessions, participatory strategy of training will be used so as to build on experiences and environmental realities in which Panchayati Raj functionaries operate. The following training methods will be useful and practical and it will be selected on the requirement of each training module:

- Braining Storming
- Case Material
- Case Studies

- Simulation Exercises
- Role Play
- Field Visits
- Individual and Group Assignments
- Panel Discussions
- Lecture-*cum*-Discussions
- Audio Visual Aids
- Films and Charts
- Video Cassettes and Posters.

Moreover, the best and innovative practices will be developed across the States as a case study presentation. Training methods will be used in such a way that an illiterate representative can learn the identified content.

Besides, exposure visit of elected representatives may be organized to show the best and innovative practices in various states.

Working Experience of West Bengal

What was of significance was the relative importance given to the elected representatives rather than the local bureaucracy, which was much greater in West Bengal than anywhere else in India. The Zilla Parishad was given representation on the governing bodies of the institutions that governed various public schemes. Further, the Sabhadhipati was made the Chairperson of the District Rural Development Agency; the most important government official in the district, the District Magistrate was the Vice-chairperson. The agency was thereby firmly tied into the Panchayat framework. Also, the rural power balance was shifted away from the complete domination of the bureaucracy towards the framework locally-elected and locally-accountable people's representatives.

There are many actors in the political and the bureaucracy field, without certain skills, knowledge and technical knowledge in the field of rural development. Particularly, the elected representatives of PRIs, were mostly illiterate without basic knowledge about the structure available, geographic and demographic situations at the grassroots levels. Taking into consideration of all these facts, the government and NGOs and other civil society bodies were taken care of in creating more awareness among the elected representatives. Even after 13 years of the 73rd Amendment Act implementation, the revenue committee expressed, that there is no much improvement or performance in PRIs because, a good training to the elected representatives of PRIs was provided not only in West Bengal but also across the country.

Indeed, one of the more interesting features of the West Bengal experience has been the extent to which the institutions of elected local government have been used not only to participate in but to actively further various initiatives and programmes of the State Government. These responsibilities placed upon the Panchayats, and the consequent expectations generated, have sometimes been so heavy that they were extremely difficult to fulfil. For example, a 1994 directive of the ruling party (the CPIM) to its own Panchayat members, which was also widely circulated among the general public so as to get greater public response, listed a formidable, even daunting, set of tasks for the members of the local bodies. Ordinary citizens, in turn, were encouraged to insist that the Panchayat members actually did fulfil these various duties and responsibilities. The Panchayat members were instructed to be concerned with and even be responsible for the management of the following activities:

- Forestry, management and land reclamation.
- Public health, community disease prevention, public health campaigns.
- Improvement in land use patterns and farming techniques.
- Rural diversification, especially into fishing, livestock-rearing and poultry, etc.
- Monitoring of literacy campaigns, continuing the progress of increasing literacy and ensuring universal school attendance.
- Monitoring the Public Distribution System for food, checking ration card use, and keeping watch on the activities of Fair Price Shops.
- Monitoring the IRDP, and encouraging diversified use of energy sources such as gobar gas.

- Preventing electricity theft, ensuring correct meter reading and billing.
- Organising the repair and expansion of rural roads, the cleaning of water tanks and ponds.
- Decentralised planning for the medium-term, through an inventory of available resources and systematic listing of possibilities for the future.
- Raising own resources for development and enthusing local people to contribute to community infrastructure.
- Focusing on and prioritizing less privilege groups such as Scheduled Castes, Scheduled Tribes and women in all general activities, as well as in special programmes designed for them.
- All this to be carried out with a proper class perspective and with sensitivity to the specific needs of the local working people.

In addition, Panchayats were duty bound to hold regular meetings. Not only of their own Panchayats, but also of the Gram Sabhas and Gram Sansads for periodic ratification and support for their activities. With such an exhaustive list of proposed activities, it is surprising to note that the Panchayats received very little in terms of resources or administrative support with which to carry out all of these functions. The most recent version of the ruling party's directive for Panchayat members contains a more realistic listing of priorities in terms of activities, with health and sanitation, education, water resource management and women's empowerment being at the top of the agenda.

One of the remarkable features of the local government institutions in rural West Bengal in particular is that now the range of activities they have been involved in has expanded, and even been fulfilled at least partially, while the resources they have received, and their capacity for autonomous resource raising, have been constrained. In addition, the Panchayat bodies do not have administrative or functional control over many of the social sector delivery institutions, such as in health and education. Government educational institutions, including primary schools, are under the administrative control of the line department and associated bodies; Panchayats may only supervise and monitor the much more recently started experimental schools, the Shishu Shiksha Kendras. Similarly, public health institutions such as Primary Health Centres are also not under the control of the Panchayats, although they are clearly expected to work closely with them for example, in public health campaigns.

The law provides that the Sabhadhipati or Sabhapati is responsible for the financial and executive administration of the Zilla Parishad or the Panchayat Samiti, as the case may be. But this is not reflected in the financial and account rules that have been framed (as well as the orders and clarification issued). This has meant that instead of the power of bureaucracy being curbed and the controlling powers of the Panchayat and its elected representatives being established, there could be a counter-tendency of strengthening the bureaucracy. The District Magistrate, the Sub-Division Officer and the Block Development Officer have been appointed the authorities under those provisions of the Act relating to control over the Panchayat and its office-bearers. Obviously, this has negative implications for both the capability of the Panchayat and its accountability to the local people rather than to the bureaucracy. The legal-administrative framework may, therefore, need to be altered in order to preserve and strengthen the basic goals of decentralisation.

Some Panchayat members do feel that direct control over local institutions of public service delivery would assist in making them more responsive to local people's needs, and there is certainly a case for increasing local Panchayat's roles in both public health and education systems. Nevertheless, the relative success of Panchayats, particularly in some districts, of success in terms of even partially fulfilling these many roles, is a tribute to the motivation of those involved as well as a comment on the huge potential for decentralized governance.

Decentralized Planning and Capacity Building

The Planning process should begin from the bottom, the gram sansad. Gram Panchayat is the key unit to prepare the planning of the village. There is a District Planning Committee (DPC) which is informed for every district with Sabhadhipati as its chairman, Karmadhyakshas of standing committees of ZP, Sabhapatis of Panchayat Samitis as its members. Therefore, the committee requires appropriate knowledge to prepare agenda. Plans, budget estimates for the village development which leads to the improving of the socio-economic development of the people. There is dire need to improve the capacities of the elected representatives through organising many rural training programmes in the State.

As the Panchayati Raj Institutions stabilized and matured, their greater involvement in the planning process became an imperative necessity, if their capabilities were to be tapped for accelerating rural development. A number of reforms were introduced in the planning process from 1983 onwards to ensure the participation of the local bodies in the planning process. At the apex of the institutional structure were the State Planning Board (SPB) and the state planning department. Even though SPB was an advisory body for the formulation of the state plan, it played a leading role in guiding and coordinating the lower level planning machinery. At the district level there were two tiers; the District Planning and Coordination Committee (DPCC) more of a deliberative body, and the District Planning Committee (DPC), its executive arm. The DPCs were to prepare the plan, which would be approved by the DPCCs. The Block Planning Committee (BPC) was the planning agency at the block level.

The Chairperson of Zilla Parisad headed the key institution of the decentralized planning structure, the District Planning Committee (DPC), and the District Collector was its member-secretary. It had a mixed membership of non-officials and officials. It was the duty of the DPC to integrate the local plans prepared by block and municipalities within the overall guidelines indicated by the State Planning Board. The District Planning Committee was empowered to approve schemes up to Rs. 5 lakhs while schemes of higher value and inter-district schemes would require the approval of the State Planning Board.

The Block Planning Committee, headed by the Sabhapati of the Panchayat Samiti, comprised Chairpersons of all the standing committees of the Samiti and also of Gram Panchayats as well as the block-level officers of various development departments. The Block Development Officer (BDO) was its member-secretary. This committee prepared block-level plans and approved block-level schemes costing less than Rs. 50,000. Schemes involving more expenditure, and inter-block schemes, had to be submitted to the DPC for approval. A small planning committee at the block-level was meant to prepare schemes and send them to the BPC for discussion and appropriate action; review and coordinate plan schemes being implemented within the block.

Standing Committee (Sthayee Samiti)

Accordingly, 20 standing committees were working at block-level and Zilla Parishad level. Various communities like SC, ST, OBCs and women headed these committees, as their socio-economic background reveals that they do not have any requisite qualifications to handle the institutions. An important approach is to bring SC/ST and women into the political structure and support in the backward and forward linkage through providing capacities for the elected representatives.

The Standing Committee is a powerful organ of the Panchayati Raj System in the State. The Panchayat Samiti and the Zilla Parishad, each operates through the Standing Committees constituted at the level and exercises functional control over the development bureaucracy.

Standing Committee of the Panchayat Samiti

Panchayat Samitis operate through ten standing committees. Each standing committee consists of the following members:

(i) Sabhapati as ex-officio member.
(ii) 3-5 members elected by the Samiti members from among themselves, and
(iii) A number of government/quasi-government officers appointed by the State Government as its members (without right to vote).

No person other than the Sabhapati or the Shakari Sabhadipati can be a member of more than three committees. The standing committee draws up, implements or caused to implement, monitors and reviews implementation of sectoral programmes. There are 10 standing committees as mentioned below:

(i) Finance, Establishment, Development and Planning
(ii) Forest and Land Reforms
(iii) Agriculture, Irrigation and Cooperation
(iv) Public Works and Transport
(v) Public Health and Environment
(vi) Education, Culture, Information and Sports
(vii) Cottage and Small Scale Industries, Relief and Social Welfare
(viii) Fisheries and Animal Resources
(ix) Food and Supplies
(x) Power and Non-Conventional Energy Sources.

Each standing committee is to be headed by a Karmadhyaksha (Chairman) to be elected by the members of the committee. But any Pradhan or any government officer—member cannot become Karmadhyaksha. The Sabhapati of the Panchayat Samiti will be ex-officio Karmadhyaksha of the finance, establishment, development and planning committee. The Extension Officer, Panchayats is the Secretary to this committee. The members of each committee elect one among the officer-members to act as its Secretary.

A Karmadhyaksha of the standing committee of the Panchayat Samitis performs the following functions:

(a) Be responsible for the financial and executive administration in respect of the schemes and programmes and the purview and control of the committee.
(b) Be entitled to call for any relevant information, return statement, account or report from the office of the Panchayat Samiti.
(c) Be entitled to require the attendance at its meeting of any officer of the Panchayat Samiti, and

(d) Exercise such other powers, perform such other functions and discharge such other duties as the Panchayat Samiti may prescribe.

Besides, there is a Coordination Committee for every Panchayat Samiti. It consists of the Sabhapati, the Shakari Sabhadhipati and the Karmadhyakshas of all standing committees and the Executive Officer of the Panchayat Samiti. The Secretary of the Panchayat Samiti acts as the Secretary to the Coordination Committee. The Coordination Committee is responsible for coordinating the functions between a standing committee and the Panchayat Samiti and among the different standing committees of the Panchayat Samiti and for monitoring of activities of the Gram Panchayats in respect of the schemes for which the Panchayat Samiti allots funds to Gram Panchayats for the execution of such schemes. It meets atleast once in a month in the office of the Panchayat Samiti.

Standing Committee of the Zilla Parishad

Like Panchayat Samitis, the Zilla Parishad also functions through ten standing committees by the same subjects and nomenclature. A Standing Committee of the Zilla Parishad consists of the following members.

(i) Sabhadhipati and Sahakari Sabhadhipati ex-officio;
(ii) 3-5 members elected by members of the Zilla Parishad from among themselves; and
(iii) A number of government/quasi-government officers appointed by the State Government as its members (without right to vote). The members of the standing committee elect one chairman to be called Karmadhyaksha (Chairman) from among themselves. But the Sabhadhipati will be the ex-officio Karmadhyaksha of the standing committee of the Finance, Establishment, Development and Planning. The Secretary of the Zilla Parishad acts as the Secretary to all the standing committees.

Besides, there is a Samanway Samiti (Coordination Committee) consisting of the Sabhadhipati, the Sahakari Sabhadhipati, Karmadhyaksha of the Standing Committees, the Executive Officer and the Additional Executive Officer of the Zilla Parishad. The Secretary of the Zilla Parishad acts as the Secretary to the Samanway Samiti. It meets at least once in a month. The Samanway Samiti is responsible coordinating the functions between a standing committee and the Zilla Parishad and among the different standing committees and for monitoring of activities of the Panchayat Samiti in respect of the scheme for which the Zilla Parishad allots funds for execution of such schemes.

Institutions to Build Capacities

The West Bengal Panchayat (Amendment) Act, 2003 has made it obligatory for a Gram Panchayat to act upon any recommendations of a Gram Sansad relating to priorities of any list of beneficiaries or schemes or programmes so far as it relates to the area of Gram Sansad. The Gram Unnayaan Samiti, Block Sansad and Zilla Sansad are also introduced in the West Bengal Panchayat (Amendment) Act, 2003, and Gram Sansad may constitute a Gram Unnayan Samiti having jurisdiction over its area. The Gram Sabha is responsible to prepare the budget estimates and approve its improvement. It is very crucial at Gram Panchayat level so, there is a need for providing capabilities for each and every structure to be strong as per their PR Act.

Gram Sansad

The concept of Gram Sansad incorporated by the West Bengal Panchayat (Amendment) Act, 1992, has been widely acclaimed by political observers as an epitome of participatory principles. It consists of registered electors of a constituency—single member or double member—within the area of Gram Panchayat. Thus a meeting of Gram Sansad implies a meeting of the electors of a constituency. In a sense, it is the legal entity at the grassroots level below the Gram Panchayat.

Under the law, the Gram Panchayat is required to convene at least two meetings of every Sansad in a year, annual meeting in the month of May and half-yearly meeting in the month of November every year. In addition to these two statutory meetings, a Gram Panchayat may hold extraordinary meeting of a Gram Sansad at any time if the situation, so warrants, of the situation so directs.

The main function of Gram Sansad is to guide and advise the Gram Panchayat in regard to the schemes for economic development and social justice, identification of beneficiaries for various poverty-alleviation programmes, constitution of one or more beneficiary committees for ensuring active participation of people in implementation, maintenance and equitable distribution of benefits of one or more schemes in its area. A Gram Sansad may raise objection to any action of Pradhan or any other member of Gram Panchayat for failure to implement any development work properly.

Further, it is mandatory for a Gram Panchayat to place in the meetings of Gram Sansad the budget and audit report of the accounts of Gram Panchayat for deliberation, recommendation and suggestion of Gram Sansad.

The West Bengal Panchayat (Amendment) Act, 2003 has made it obligatory for a Gram Panchayat to act upon any recommendations of a Gram Sansad relating to prioritization of any list of beneficiaries or scheme or programme so far as it relates to the area of the Gram Sansad. However, if Gram Panchayat decides in a meeting that such recommendations are not acceptable or implementable under the existing provisions of the Act, rules or orders, such decision of the Gram Panchayat shall be placed in the next meeting of the Gram Sansad.

Gram Unnayan Samiti

The provision of Gram Unnayan Samiti has been introduced very recently by the West Bengal Panchayat (Amendment) Act, 2003. A Gram Sansad may constitute a Gram Unnayan Samiti having jurisdiction over its area. Gram Unnayan Samiti shall be responsible for ensuring active participation of people in implementation and equitable distribution of benefits of Rural Development Programmes within its jurisdiction. It shall be accountable for its functions and decision to the Gram Sansad. Gram Unnayan Samiti may also constitute such number of functional committees as may be required. The manner of Constitution of Gram Unnayan Samiti along with its functional committees and the conduct of its function and responsibility shall be prescribed in the rules. The State Government has constituted a committee to frame draft rules, which are likely to be ready shortly.

Gram Sabha

The concept of Gram Sabha was introduced by the West Bengal Panchayat (Amendment) Act, 1994. A Gram Sabha consists of registered electors of a Gram Panchayat area. So the jurisdiction of a Gram Sabha is the whole area of a Gram Panchayat. The difference is that Gram Panchayat is an institution of elected representatives of its area, whereas Gram Sabha is a forum for registered voters of a Gram Panchayat.

It is the duty of a Gram Panchayat to convene a meeting of Gram Sabha in December every year. The Gram Panchayat will submit in the meeting of Gram Sabha its budget for the next year, annual plan and audit report of Gram Panchayat and its receipt and expenditure report for the last year. The agenda of Gram Sabha will include the subjects already discussed in Gram Sansad. Gram Panchayat is bound to consider the decisions of Gram Sansad and Gram Sabha. Non-compliance of decision by Gram Panchayat will be reflected in audit report.

Role of the Leader of the Opposition and Members in Opposition

The leader of the opposition and members in opposition have been assigned greater responsibility in the function of Zilla Parishad and Panchayat Samiti by the West Bengal Panchayat (Amendment) Act, 2003. In the newly elected bodies, the leader of the opposition in Zilla Parishad or Panchayat Samiti has become an ex-officio member of Finance Standing Committee (Artha Sanstha Unnayan Parikalpana Sthayee Samiti) of Zilla Parishad or Panchayat Samiti, as the case may be. Other members in opposition in Zilla Parishad or Panchayat Samiti have been included as members in each of the nine other Standing Committees in Zilla Parishad or Panchayat Samiti, as the case may be. In case of any shortfall in the number of members of recognized political parties in opposition, the independent member in opposition shall be chosen for membership in a Standing Committee to fill up the vacant seat.

Innovative Practices

A number of innovative practices have also been incorporated in the West Bengal Panchayat (Amendment) Act, 2003, which is known as 'District Council'. It is a watchdog and a monitor of the people's aspirations and development. The Act has a provision by which the elected representatives will be the whole-time functionaries like regular employees of the State Government. Keeping in view, the facts of innovativeness of the structures available in West Bengal, it is necessary to create a model 'Training Action Plan' to be maintained and separate funds also be created to built capacities among the elected representatives and functionaries of the PRIs.

District Council

The District Council for Panchayats has been introduced by the West Bengal Panchayat (Amendment) Act, 1994 and its basic role is of a watchdog and a monitor. Chairperson or Adhyaksha of District Council is the leader of the recognized political party in opposition having largest number of members in Zilla Parishad. All members of the Zilla Parishad including the ex-officio members, elected Chairperson, and other five members.

The Additional Executive Officer of the Zilla Parishad acts as Member-Secretary to the Council. Three other officers appointed by the State Government are—District Panchayat and Rural Development Officer, Parishad Accounts and Audit Officer, and Executive Engineer-I, PWD posted in the district.

The District Council is empowered to exercise according to the Section 214A(2)—to examine the accounts of the Panchayats within territorial jurisdiction, in relation to the budget approved by such

Panchayats, the annual report of such Panchayats and such other accounts of such Panchayats and the District Council may think fit;

(a) to satisfy itself, while scrutinizing the accounts of the Panchayats, that—
   (i) the money shown in the accounts as having been disbursed where legally available for, and applicable to, the service or purpose to which they have applied,
   (ii) the expenditure conforms to the rules governing such expenditure and also the financial proprieties of such expenditure, and
   (iii) every re-appropriation has been made in accordance with such rules as are applicable;

(b) to consider the inspection of reports on the annual audit of accounts of any Panchayat within its jurisdiction, conducted by the auditors appointed under Section 186, and to examine the replies thereto furnished by the respective Panchayats;

(c) to examine the accounts of stores and stocks maintained by the Panchayats within the area of their respective jurisdictions;

(d) to pursue relating to the unsettled objectives raised in any inspection report on audit of accounts of such Panchayats and refer such matters to the authorities concerned suggesting corrective actions;

(e) to suggest ways and means to remove the difficulties, if any experienced by the Panchayats in giving effect to any provision of this Act or the rules made thereunder within their respective jurisdictions.

The term of office of the members of the District Council is for the entire period of the term of office of the members of the Zilla Parishad unless a member of the District Council is restrained by any other provision of this Act from continuing as a member of the Zilla Parishad.

The District Council shall determine its own procedure and shall have the right to obtain a copy of every inspection report on audit of accounts of any Panchayat within the area of its jurisdiction and may call for any record of any Panchayat within such area to be produced for its inspection.

Without prejudice to the generality of the provisions in sub-section (4), the State Government may, by general or special order, provide for—

(a) the procedure for convening of the meetings of the District Council and the procedure for the meetings;
(b) the powers and duties of the secretary of the District Council;
(c) the terms of office of different members of the District Council and the travelling allowances admissible to such members.

Any elected or nominated member of the District Council may resign his office by tendering his resignation in writing to the Sabhadhipati of the Zilla Parishad or the Mahakuma Parishad, as the case may be, and such resignation shall take effect from the date on which Sabhadhipati accepts it.

Any casual vacancy in the office of any member of the District Council shall be filled in such manner as may be prescribed and the member elected or nominated to fill such casual vacancy shall hold office for the remaining portion of the term of the Zilla Parishad.

The District Council enjoys the unique position of overseeing all the financial transactions, maintenance of accounts, and inspection reports for all the tiers of the Panchayati Raj Institutions. Thus this body has the capability of identifying the lacunae, weaknesses, loopholes and deficiencies in the system and suggesting ways for their removal and improvement.

Whole Time Functionary

The Sabhadhipati, Sahakari Sabhadhipati and Karmadhyaksha and of Sthayee Samiti of Zilla Parishad; and the Sabhapati/Sahakari Sabhapati of Panchayat Samiti have been made whole-time functionaries of their offices by the West Bengal Panchayat (Amendment) Act, 1992 and it is mandatory for them to submit declaration in writing that on being elected, they shall be whole-time functionaries and shall not hold any office of profit or shall not carry on or be associated with any business, profession or calling in such manner that is likely to interfere with due exercise of their powers, functions or duties. They are not paid remuneration instead of 'honoraria' for holding the office while Karmadhyakshas of PS and Pradhan/Upa-Pradhan of GP is given honoraria.

REFERENCES

Capacity Building of Panchayati Raj Institutions; UNDP, India, February, 2006. (www.undp.org.in).

Government of West Bengal, SIPRD, Kalyani (2000): *Report on Gram Sansad Meetings,* 18-30, November, 1999 (in Bengali).

I.C. Srivastava, "Empowering Panchayats for Good Governance", *Yojana,* Vol. 44, No. 10, October, 2000, p. 29.

Jayati, Ghosh, *West Bengal Human Development Report,* 2004, UNDP, India, Development and Planning Department, Government of West Bengal, pp. 50-57.

K.B. Srivastava, "Capacity Building in Panchayati Raj Bodies", *The Administrator,* Vol. 42 (4), October-December, 1997, pp.162-163.

Kaustur Kanti Bandyopadhyay; Capacity Building for effective democratic local governance, Experience from India.

K.B. Srivastava and A.C. Jena, *Panchayati Raj System in West Bengal,* Hyderabad: NIRD, 1995, pp. 243-246.

Local Self-Governance, the Timbaktu Collective Panchayati Raj, 12.5.2006 (www.timbaktu.org./panchayatihtml).

Maithresh Ghatak and Maitreya Ghatak (2000), 'Grassroots Democracy: A case study of the Operation of the Panchayat System in West Bengal', Paper presented at conference on the Real Utopias Project, January 14-16, University of Wisconsin, Madison.

N.C. Saxena; What is meant by People's Participation: *Journal of Rural Development,* Vol.17(1), 1998, pp.111-113.

National Training Design for Training of Elected Members and Officials of Panchayati Raj Institutions: Submitted to the MOPR, GOI, CPR, NIRD, Hyderabad, February 2006, p. 33.

Prabhat Dutta and Panchali Bhattacharya Sen, 'Participatory Rural Governance in India', *Indian Journal of Public Administration,* XLVI (1), January-March 2000, 38-49.

Prabhat Dutta and Panchali Bhattacharya Sen, Participatory Rural Governance in India, *Indian Journal of Public Administration,* XLVI (1), January-March, 2000, 38-49.

R.C. Choudary, *Participating Development: A Case for Civil Society and Panchayati Raj Collaboration: Emerging Institutions for Decentralized Rural Development*, Hyderabad: NIRD, 2002.

R.C. Choudhary and S.P. Jain, "Panchayati Raj in India: An Overview" in Chaudhary and Jain (Eds.), *Patterns of Decentralized Governance in Rural India*, Hyderabad: NIRD, 1998, Vol.1, pp.1-22.

Samirendra N. Ray (1998): 'Decentralized and Participatory Rural Development in West Bengal in a Comparative Perspective: Some Conceptual and Operational Issues and Problems', paper presented at the State-level Seminar on Decentralization, Devolution and Participation, organized by State Planning Board, Government of West Bengal, November 20-22, 1998.

Society for Participatory Research in Asia (1997): 'Local Self-Governance: Myth or Reality of Gram Panchayat and Grama Sabha', Seminar on Strengthening Panchayati Raj Institutions in India, New Delhi: India International Centre.

Society for Training and Research SIPRD, Kalyani (1999): Panchayats and Rural Development, Working on People's Participation in Development, December 15-16, 1999, Calcutta.

S.N. Mishra and Chaitali Pal, "Good Governance: The Context of Democratic Decentralization", in Mishra, Suresh and Rajvir S. Dhaka, (Eds.), *Humanizing Development Trends in Public Administration*, New Delhi: Sustainable Development Foundation, 2001, p.151.

The Hunger Project Hosts Ministerial Round-table on Capacity Building in Panchayati Raj, December 17-19, 2004, Jaipur (www.panchayat.nic.in).

V.K. Ramachandran, 'On Kerala's Development Achievements', in Jean Dreaze and Amartya Sen (eds): *Indian Development: Selected Regional Perspectives*, New Delhi: Oxford University Press, 1996.

11

CAPACITY BUILDING FOR NEW WOMEN LEADERS THROUGH AAGAZ ACADEMICS—A NEW LEADERSHIP SCHOOL

THE HUNGER PROJECT

The Story

Year 2005 has been the first pilot year for moving with the leadership schools from concept to reality. Now, almost a year down, one can say with reasonable degree of comfort that the leadership schools are indeed a reality. The challenge now is to deepen the quality, plug the existing gaps and manage the growth as an institution, a collective, for it to have a more significant impact. That in a nutshell is the story of the first year. However, as it is often said, the devil lies in the detail. And thus we share the detail below to find out where the devil is, such that we learn to be able to better deal with it in the coming year.

The thinking around the leadership schools began way back in 2004.[1] Ideas are like plants, which grow slowly and quietly, from a seed into a tiny green sapling and eventually taking on larger life and forms. It is difficult to say when exactly are they born, so with the leadership schools. Yet for the purposes of this report one could use January 2005 as a reference point. It was the first time when the collective of anchors actually sat own to discuss what shape the leadership schools would take. RNE (Royal Norwegian Embassy) funding for the programme began from August 2005. Thus the programme was funded for almost 6 months, from THP's (The Hunger Project) other sources. This has an implication on the fund utilization. However, since the plant is healthy and growing, the report will indicate and suggest areas where the remaining funds could well be utilised.

About Aagaz Academy—Centre for Women's Leadership

Aagaz Academy—Centre for Women's Leadership is an institution of learning designed to strengthen transformative leadership abilities amongst the women representatives elected to the local governance structures. Its purpose is to recontextualise the experience and skills of women leaders so that they are able to exercise their rights to participate effectively in the socio-political and development processes to end hunger, poverty and injustice from India.

We aspire towards a world where women Panchayat leaders become actors of their own development and exercise their socio-economic, political and cultural rights in a way that sets the path for a society free from hunger, poverty and injustice.

About the Course

The Course has been conceptualized as a process of co-learning that leads to an unfolding of potential that is inherent in the participants. Some of the basic premises of the course:

- Builds on the experiences of group.
- Methodology of learning being as important as the content.
- The learning space enables exploration, experimentation and evolving alternatives.
- The focus is not so much on "giving information" as on learning how to "access information".

The course duration is over a period of two years, with 20 days of indoor, structured training in year one, and seven days of structured learning in year two. The faculty will visit the participants at least three times over this period to help strengthen the practice of leadership in the field, and address challenges that are faced by elected women representatives.

Components of the Course

Personal Empowerment—From "I cannot" to "I can"

This is about understanding oneself, better as an individual, woman, a member of a society with caste, class and religious identities and how these identities impact women's role as a leader.

Constituency Building—From "I" to "We"

The most important aspect of vibrant local governance is a Gram Sabha—a collective of people at the village level. This component of the course helps participants develop an understanding of Gram Sabha as a group(s) of people and builds deeper understanding of group dynamics. It focuses on mobilizing Gram Sabhas to become active participants in building effective self-governance.

Technical Skills

This component helps build an understanding of the Panchayat Act and Government schemes. It helps to work and manage technology like computers, phones, mobiles, etc. Comprehending the administration structure, writing applications, handling budgets, Panchayat finances, enhancing communication skills and functional literacy are also part of this component.

Participant Profile

The batch consist of women Sarpanchs and Panchs who have already participated in the Women's Leadership Workshops (WLWs) conducted by The Hunger Project in the past. The participants are women who have expressed a desire to explore deeper learning processes and have exhibited a potential at being able to practice transformative leadership in their families and communities. A mixed group of literate, semi-literate and illiterate women, these elected representatives will be from Chhindwara, Seoni and Hoshangabad districts of Madhya Pradesh.

Benefits of the Course

The course will help the participants

- To enhance their own personal effectiveness by developing confidence in their own ability to transform social conditions.
- Have a deeper understanding of the functioning of Panchayats and build skills for effective local self-governance.
- To develop skills required for effective communication, decision-making, public speaking and other life skills.
- To strengthen solidarity networks amongst women leaders so that they are able to build spaces for co-learning, mentoring and supporting each other across the social structural divisions of caste, class, religion and age.
- To help women emerge as effective leaders in their constituencies for ending hunger, poverty and injustice.

Background

The Hunger Project has been working towards strengthening the leadership potential of elected women leaders in Panchayats for the last five years. It has been able to provide training support to more than 30,000 women leaders through WLWs with the help of more than 90 local NGOs across 14 States. There are now more than 700 trained women facilitators across the country who have been trained by The Hunger Project to support the learning needs of elected women representatives.

The journey so far has been very enriching. Our experience has reaffirmed that when rural, poor, dalit and tribal women leaders are empowered they are able to provide a leadership that is essentially transformative in its character. They question and challenge the *status quo*; they prioritise basic needs, they think first of the weakest and they extend their hands across social boundaries to collaborate with others. When women take on the mantle of leadership they address issues that affect the entire community and village—issues of food security, education, health, girl child, sanitation, water, electricity and basic human survival.

It is this belief and experience that has guided. The Hunger Project to envision the next step of supporting the elected women representatives. Today in this country there does not exist any institution of support dedicated to the rural, poor and illiterate women. It is this gap that the Aagaz Academy is committed to fill. Aagaz Academy is a unique collaboration of several NGOs under the leadership of The Hunger Project. 'Aagaz' meaning a new beginning, hopes to support these women in practicing transformative leadership at the grassroots that would lead ultimately to social transformation—ending hunger, poverty, inequity and injustice from their families, communities and the country.

SECTION I
Identifying Anchors, Building Teams

If the beginning then is January 2005, then one needs to assume the anchors were well in place by then. Because the identification process had happened already, and seven anchors were identified, talked with and who had agreed to be part of this process. For most of the anchors, the participation was almost spontaneous, as it was also somewhere part of their own journey in their lives. Before I go on, let me explain here who an anchor is. An anchor is like a core leader, facilitator and administrator for the leadership school. The anchor puts together a team to support the learning processes, takes responsibility to build the curriculum and other learning processes within the agreed framework; leads the entire learning process with the participants, and takes responsibility to effectively manage all aspects of it—logistics, documentation, publicity, follow-up etc. The anchors for each school, along with core team from THP, thus together form the collective where the reality of leadership schools has been nurtured through careful and reflective deliberation.

The seven anchors have come with a very varied experience and skill base. And in these entire multiple and diverse context of individuals (anchors) and institutions (institutions hosting anchors) the idea of "strengthening elected women leaders' leadership" found a strong relevance and resonance. The different contexts within which the idea thus got rooted, has impacted both ways. The contexts have lent richness to the idea of leadership schools as it moved into the realm of reality. At the same time, the idea has enriched the contexts by lending new dimensions to the work being done on the ground. Since being part of a larger collective was very important, it was agreed that once the anchors are identified, the MOUs would be signed with the institutions, as well as with the specific anchors. This was to ensure that the individual commitment and zeal was protected and the participation of the same person enabled bringing up a strong collective of the anchors.

The anchors identified were:

Anita Mathur and Ganga Gupta, for Rajasthan

Anita joined in this process from her reality of being a consultant. In fact, she is the only anchor who is not from within an institutional context, and this has had implications in the ultimate running of the leadership schools. The financial arrangements had to be different. There was need to provide greater support to her, given that the institutional support available in other contexts (and which is not always costed or visible) was not present in her case. However, she is a founder member of Astha, a well-known and well-respected NGO of Rajasthan. And is herself well known and respected for her more than two decades of work with communities as an activist, trainer and a significant woman leader in Rajasthan. Given this, together it has been possible to provide the required support to this leadership school and its anchor team.

Ganga had yet another reality. At the time of signing the contract, Ganga was working with Urmul Trust in Bikaner. However, after a short while, Ganga made a choice of leaving Urmul Trust after a long-term association of almost twenty years and work with THP, which offered her a national canvas. Though the decision was independent of the leadership schools, it had implications in that, this school thus became one which is now being implemented in a sense directly by THP.

Seema Sadiq and Siyaag Bhai from Madhya Pradesh

Both the leadership schools in Madhya Pradesh offered less complexity. Seema and Siyaag Bhai, both belong to institutions, IDYWC and SAMAVESH respectively. And both occupy senior positions, as they are co-founders of their respective institutions. Thus, in both the cases, getting institutional support and ownership to the idea has not been a challenge at all.

Siyaag Bhai has, so far, had the unique distinction of being the only "male anchor". And this has also brought in yet another diversity and richness to the group.

Nandini Narula and Anita Borkar for Maharashtra

Maharashtra has only one leadership school but two anchors. The reason behind this was that Anita Borkar was earlier not known to THP. Nandini, who is also a 'sakha'[1] to the leadership school helped in identifying Anita Borkar from Abhivyakti as an anchor person. The relationship since has established itself, and from this year on, Nandini will play other roles, such as an anchor for Training of Trainer processes, while Anita Borkar continues to lead the Maharashtra leadership school.

Philomina Vincent for Bangalore

This was perhaps the least complex identification process. Philomina has been known to THP, as well as to many individuals in THP as a woman activist, leader and a great facilitator for many years. So, when THP approached her, and she agreed, that was the beginning and the end of that story.

The anchors then over a period of time identified their own team members. Each anchor team now has four core members. A main trainer/facilitator and two other co-facilitators. One of the two is intended to be a current or ex-elected woman representative, and the other co-facilitator is meant to play the role of a process documentation person. The anchors are meant to work with this group as well as a team and such that they as well grown and learn in this journey along with the elected women representatives. There have obviously been some hiccups in identifying the rest of the team members, but as I write this, all anchor teams were in place with atleast clear four members on board. *(See annex)*

So with all the anchors in place, the most critical part in setting up the schools was done. The idea was that the anchors together, along with the core members from THP, would form a-team, and the rest of the reality would be co-created together. This indeed happened over the year, through four meetings, over Delhi, Bhopal and Bangalore; e-mails and phone calls. As I write this, the anchor team has emerged a strong cohesive group, able to work together, to create together, to share, to challenge and to learn together as a team. It is this team, which functions as the fountain-head of energy and creativity for the leadership schools. And as we expand and grow in our vision, it will be important to maintain and further strengthen this team.

SECTION II
Building the Curriculum—Content and Processes

The first meeting of the anchors and THP team, was held in January. One of the first things it attempted was rechristening the baby, or should I say the plant. Thus the leadership schools, came to be called as *Aagaz Academies*. The name is important because it becomes over a period of time our identity. And we did not wish the programme to be identified as a "one-off training programme". Training programmes are associated normally with a casual approach, not necessarily rigorous. The intention is to build this programme, as a serious, intense, rigorous and yet flexible, open and flowing learning process. A learning process that provides cutting edge quality to the elected women leaders, not as a one-time thing, but as an accompaniment through their five-year term, in different ways. Where the school plays different roles at different times, based upon the needs and demands of the women themselves, and in their professional contexts as gram panchayat leaders as well. The use of the word 'Academy' is meant to put it at par with academies meant to train the elite of the society and the word is associated with a certain value and esteem.

This is also where the choice of anchors becomes a very critical factor. Because in the end the quality of what we deliver, is determined by the quality of people who are delivering it. All learning processes in Aagaz are thus personally led by the anchors, or members of their team, and not delegated to "field staff" of participating NGOs, who are often highly committed but perhaps least trained in the entire hierarchy of the concerned NGO.

It was in this first meeting in January, that the idea of curriculum was unpacked. Conceptually it had always been clear that the entire learning process with the elected women representatives needs to be based upon the same ground as the womens' leadership workshops. This was not because that is what THP had been doing earlier. But because having implemented WLWs for nearly five years we had learnt that the basic grounding of WLW in a woman's experience of her own reality enables her to make the shift in her mind from "I cannot" to "I can". This, we think is perhaps the most critical, the most transformative, aspect in strengthening womens' leadership. True, it is not sufficient in itself. There needs to be more support provided with other kinds of intervention in terms of information on policies and other skills etc. But that without it, everything else is often rendered quite meaningless, unable to sustain itself.

The meeting unpacked what all could be covered under this aspect, which later got termed as "Personal Empowerment". This is one of the central and core pillars of leadership schools and it was agreed that it should form 35 per cent of the course component. Similarly, the other aspects were unpacked. "Constituency Mobilisation" which also received 35 per cent weightage, and "Technical Competence" for 30 per cent. Technical competence, here was not narrowly defined as in an understanding of the constitutional amendment and the act etc. Of course, those things are important, but other things include, knowing about your panchayat, block and district. Knowing who the other officials are and how to access them. Understanding the need to have the cheque books under one's control. Learning basic literacy and numeracy and learning to sign. Managing to ride bicycle, handle a mobile phone, using computers, etc. The Aagaz Academies intends to offer the latest available technology to women leaders, so that they can empower themselves by understanding how to use it or make use of it for their own purposes. *(A detailed curriculum design is available in the Annex-II.)*

The curriculum was not just what got offered in the 21 days, spread over three or four phases over the year. It was also about the nature of support that the faculty would provide to the women leaders in between. The time between two phases, is when the faculty team visits each and every person. To offer support, to learn about their struggles and to ensure that all of this feeds into the detailed design of the next learning process.

As I write this, in every Aagaz School, the anchor teams have already undertaken atleast one, and in some cases two rounds of both in class as well as in the field learning experiences. Detailed notes for these are available for each academy, and for each learning participant.

These curriculums have been built through a very rigorous and interactive process. Two anchor meetings were around sharing and review of curriculums. Peer teams were set up to support each other. Each curriculum has been through several rounds of iterations. And finally, they have been approved by a team consisting of Country Director THP, senior team members and an external reviewer to the process. Detailed comments were then shared with the anchors, and finally, a curriculum "manual" was produced which is going to be made available in both Hindi and English, for general sharing and use by all. The curriculum manual is not just course design. But it is a statement of intent for the entire learning process as well. It also contains session-wise detail including the content, the process, the objectives, outcomes and the approach to be adopted.

The curriculums vary in their thrust, their strengths and their roadmaps. Each curriculum reflects the experience and strength of its anchor. However, they are all united in the core perspectives that they uphold. The three core perspectives that the curriculums are build upon are:

From I Cannot to I Can: a journey in understanding self, as a social construct and to use this understanding to empower oneself.

From I to We: that social change happens when individual changes get transformed into community changes and larger macro changes. And participants learn to deal with not just power within them but the power they have with large numbers of strong groups and constituencies.

Understanding Panchayats as little Republics: that local governance is not about having efficient and effective decentralised mechanisms delivering development to the local persons. It is about local people, taking control of their own development, and governing themselves such that they are able to direct, design and impact upon significantly their development processes.

SECTION III
Identifying Participants

The story here gets a bit more complex as new characters get introduced. And these are the partner NGOs. Each of the anchors and Aagaz Academies cater to an area—maybe two or three or more blocks over one or more districts. On the whole, the Aagaz Academies over the first year have been able to cover 120 panchayats, over 23 districts. This has been made possible because the Academies do not function on their own. They work with NGO partners who are also working with THP and who provide the basic, three-day womens' leadership workshops. These WLWs are then considered almost a foundation course. They are offered to large numbers of elected women representatives. And out of this group, women who have completed the WLW, are the participants for Aagaz Academies selected. A detailed selection criteria has been agreed to within the anchors and the respective partner NGOs.

Though it sounds simple, it is in effect a complex exercise, as processes have to be coordinated amongst a large number of stakeholders. In the first pilot year, several Academies had to postpone their phases because the WLWs had not been conducted on time, and thus the participants could not be selected on time. There was also the factor that the participant profile of the WLWs also determined the participant profile for the Academies. For instance, if most participants to WLWs have been ward panches and very few sarpanch, then the Aagaz participants would also be similar. Since Aagaz Academies aim to reach the most disadvantaged first, conscious effort had to be made to ensure the participants to WLWs were SC or tribal women, and from more disadvantaged areas. The results have been self evident. *(see the box)*. Again, the partner NGOs also play a crucial role in ensuring a more regular follow-up with the participants, for they are the ones who are available to them on a daily basis. It is thus important that the partner NGOs also be part of the Aagaz understanding, and build a sense of ownership towards the three core perspectives that inform the work of Aagaz. Performance on this aspect has been a little bit uneven, and it is intended that partner forums will be strengthened in the coming time.

Phase I: Participant Profile.

Total Participants	*Literacy*	*Caste*
241	71 - Literate 130 - Illiterate	27 - General 174 - SC/ST

SECTION IV
Taking Off, Aagaz Academies

The Academies finally took off, from July onwards. *(See box for detailed schedule)*. Each Academy was inaugurated in a special way. The idea was both, to make the women participants to feel special and warmly welcomed but also to be able to launch the Academy in a high profile kind of manner, to ensure there is a visibility to it at the local level.

District and State level government officials were part of this inaugration in Udaipur, Bikaner, Bhopal, Chindwara and Bangalore.

Most of them got good coverage in the local media, including the print media. In Bikaner, the radio channel aired an hour everyday about the programme.

Aagaz Schedule

Month	*Aagaz Academy*
July 2005	Bikaner, Phase I Chindwara, Phase I
August 2005	Udaipur, Phase I
September 2005	Bhopal, Phase I
October 2005	Bangalore, Phase I
November 2005	Chindwara, Phase II Bikaner, Phase II
December 2005	Udaipur, Phase II Bhopal, Phase II
January 2006	Bangalore, Phase II
February 2006	Nasik, Phase I Chindwara, Phase III
April 2006	Nasik, Phase II Bangalore, Phase III
May 2006	Udaipur, Phase III Bikaner, Phase III
June 2006	Nasik, Phase III

In all the Aagaz Academies the women participants were welcomed in their own special ways. The venues were chosen with great care, except in one case where there was limited infrastructure. But this was also an overall learning. That the physical environment is as important as the intellectual and the emotional in order to help women participants feel special. It was agreed that required investments needed to be made to ensure that women participants are dealt with as how one would deal with maybe District Collectors. Aagaz Academies have to give this message to elected women leaders that they indeed are very important leaders for their communities and for the nation.

All Aagaz Academies have had a very planned and structured engagement with the local government officials as well as the media.

Annex II gives a brief overview of the government officials who have been part of the Aagaz processes. Annex III gives an overview of the participation and coverage so far.

A total of 72 days of structured learning processes have been offered on the whole till now. Apart from this, there have been "interphase" processes, where faculty teams have gone out to meet every single participant between two successive phases. This has also been an opportunity where faculty teams have been able to provide support on a one to one basis, but also document the work that the participants have been able to accomplish in this while. The faculty teams meet not just the woman leader, but also the community representatives, as well as representatives of the NGO. This has been perhaps the most critical link for women leaders, ensuring that the phases are not looked upon as just ad hoc learning events. The inphase processes build a sense of flow, of learning as a continuous process, and assure women leaders that there realities are indeed informing the form and direction this flow takes.

SECTION V
Looking Ahead

As I write this report, all the Aagaz Academies are now running towards their last phase with the first batch. Abhivyakti in Nasik, which had a delayed start due to several reasons, is going to hold its second phase in April and the third one in June end or July beginning.

The planning for future includes, both those aspects that need to be strengthened, as well as beginning groundwork for the year two of Aagaz Academies.

The partners' engagement needs to be cemented further, by them understanding better the overall purpose behind the Aagaz Academies. A meeting with partners will need to be organised, especially in Rajasthan and Madhya Pradesh, where this linkage has been less strong. Maharashtra has only one partner, a network. And in Karnataka, the relationship with partners has been exceptionally strong.

The capacities of some anchor teams need to be strengthened. It is part of the challenge offered by the context as well, that the capacities of anchor team members in some states maybe need to be strengthened. At the same time, in the new States where Aagaz Academies are planned, such as Bihar, there would be a similar challenge. It has thus been decided to start a ToT, to train new anchor team members and support the existing ones where they need to be supported. One or two of the existing anchors will hold these learning processes as well.

In May, Bihar is going in for Panchayat elections; and Assam goes in for elections in October this year. Aagaz Academies have been planned in both these states. Identifying possible partners, anchors, etc. will need to begin, so that the womens' leadership workshops can happen in time and Academies are poised to function at the earliest opportunity after the elections have been concluded.

Overall, in our journey so far, the mood is very upbeat. In every single Academy, without exception, women participants have responded with such enthusiasm, and eagerness. It leaves no doubt in our minds that we are indeed hitting the right note. The challenge is to sustain this effort and let it build up such that it can have a significant impact on the lives of women leaders, and on the functioning of their panchayats.

NOTE

1 In 2004, as THP was building the concept of leadership schools, it identified 'Sakhas' from across the country. Sakhas were individuals, men and women leaders, who contributed their experience and wisdom in helping shape up the concept of leadership schools.

ANNEXURE I

ANCHOR TEAMS

Aagaz Bikaner

Anchored by Ganga Gupta

Training team:- Kamla Ranga, Tara Devi, who was Sarpanch of the Samarda Village Panchayat, Asha Kiran, Dilip Singh (PD person).

Aagaz Chindwara

Seema Sadiq, Anchor

Training team:- Rafiq Khan, Vishnu Dayal, Maya Dhurve, (ex-Janpad Upadhyaksha), Tejinder Bhogal (PD person).

Aagaz Bangalore

Anchored by Philomena Vincent

The training team comprises of M.M. Kumaraswamy, Kalpana Sharma, Dr. Shashi Rao (PD person).

Aagaz Bhopal

Anchor, Ram Narayan Siyag

Training Team:- Sangeeta Patidar, Ranjender Bandu (PD person).

Aagaz Udaipur

Anchored by Anita Mathur

Training Team:- Sumitra Menaria, Ashwini Paliwal, Kali Bai (ex-sarpanch), Indira Pancholi (PD person).

ANNEXURE II

Curriculum Design

Personal Empowerment—From 'I cannot' to 'I can'
Understanding SELF & Understanding SOCIÈTY

- Self-understanding/awareness— As Individual
  As Woman
  As Leaders—I can do—'what' and 'how'
  —Appreciation of self
  Analysis of self
  Alteration of self - ACTION
- Identity - as a woman 'self-contained' and also understanding differences amongst women: married/single/deserted/ widow.
- Understanding of *gender*, caste, class, religion and how these differences are not just out there but inside individuals as well. Especially understanding how patriarchy exists within us and how to deal with it.
- Understanding Leadership—transformative process leading to dismantling of patriarchal injustice and oppression.
  Leadership— Styles
  Types
  Transformations
- Understanding SOCIETY
  Power Analysis and how it operates at all levels: Social structures/institutions
  Political Structures/Institutions

Technical Competencies

(Skills and information needed to perform their roles better)

- The macro perspective on Decentralisation and Self-governance
- Panchayat Acts, 73rd Amendment
- Government schemes and policies
- Planning
- Budgets
- Negotiating skills
- Rights and entitlements as per Constitution
- Functioning Literacy
- Manager
- Legal Literacy
- Mobilising the Gram Sabha: How a panchayat is expected to function
- Resource Mobilisation
- Lobbying
- Definition of Development: Human Centric (HDI's) *vs.* infrastructure
- Reading (minimum literacy package), Writing, using TV, VCD, Computers, Mobile Phones
- Geographical lay-out of area
minimum administrative setup/lay-out
structures, who reports to whom
telephone numbers and information
centres at block-level
- How to monitor village-level institutions
- Applications— how to write
Procedures
- Cheques
- Simple communication skills
- Micro-Planning (PRA/PIA)
- Public-Speaking skills
- Media Literacy and how to negotiate with the media
- Policies enabling/detrimental to women: Lobbying/Advocacy

Constituency Building

(Need for nurturing and broadening constituency base)

- From "I" to "We"—including standing committees
- Ensuring schemes reach the truly needy—
  BPL lists
  PDS shops
  Mid-day meals
  Food for Work Programs
  Social security schemes
  Education of girl child
- Expected roles of elected representatives
- Addressing issues of— Women
  Poor
  Disadvantaged
  (feminization of poverty, violence, caste discrimination)
- Religion-based— discrimination
  Violence
- Transparency/Downward accountability—across not only downward
- Organization— Building (in context of Gram Sabha also)
  Dynamics
  To keep it active and alive
- Change from (transition):
  Voter as Receiver to Leader/Elected Representative as decision-maker
- Accountability - across not only downward
- Focus on girl child Mid-day meal, school education
- Formation of youth groups
- Formation of adolescent groups

ANNEXURE III

Overview of State Government involvement in the Academies

Aagaz Academies have had a very close interaction and exchange with Government officials right from the beginning. There are three clear strategic areas of involvement. These are primarily:

- Participation in development of the curriculums and the concept of Aagaz Academy.
- Participation in the running of the Aagaz Academies.
- Participation in terms of signing of certificates of achievements for the women, thereby giving a note of recognition to the Aagaz Academy processes.

Ms. Amarjit Ahuja, Principal Resident Commissioner and Additional Chief Secretary, Government of Rajasthan; ex-Joint Secretary, Ministry of Rural Development is on the board of Aagaz Foundation, and has closely been involved in the development of the concept and curriculum of Aagaz Academies.

At State levels, as well as Nationally it is expected that the highest level officials of Central and State level Ministry of Panchayati Raj would be signing the certificates of honour and participating in the graduation ceremony planned for the first batch in November of 2006.

At the level of each Academy, all Aagaz Academies have had interactions with several officials, State level as well as district and block level as part of their co-learning processes. This interaction has happened in both forms. By the officials participating in the Academy sessions as resource persons and having extended discussions with women; as well as by elected women participants visiting the offices of the officials and holding discussions with them on various issues.

Given below is detailed information from a few Academies that demonstrates this interaction.

Aagaz Academy in Bhopal, Madhya Pradesh anchored by SAMAVESH

The officials who participated in the Academy sessions include:

Collector, Dewas District
Deputy Director, Panchayats, District Dewas
CEO Janpad Panchayat, Dewas and Ashta, Sehore Ditsrict
ICDS Supervisor
Food Officer (responsible for PDS)
District Hospital, Health Officer
Ms. Nirmala Buch (former Chief Secretary, Madhya Pradesh)
Member, M.P. Human Rights Commission

The elected women representatives from the Academy in Bhopal visited the offices of the following officials:
Office of the Collector
Offices of District Panchayat
Offices of Janpad Panchayat
Women and Child Department
PDS District Office
PHED
SC/ST Police Station
District Hospital
Tribal Welfare Department
District Education Centre
District Planning Office
District Land Record Office
District Office Panchayat and Social Justice

Aagaz Academy Udaipur in Rajasthan is anchored by an individual working closely with other NGOs. The Government officials who visited the academy and interacted with the elected women elders include:
The CEOs for Rajasmand District, Sirohi District and Udaipur District
Deputy CEO/Officer, Zilla Parishad Udaipur

Collector Rajasmand District
Superintendent Police, District Sirohi
Block Development Officer, Khamnor Block, District Rajsamand. And Badgaon Block, District Udaipur
Tehsildar for Khamnor Block, Rajasmand District and for Abu Road Block, Sirohi District
Sub-Divisional Magistrate for Sirohi

For **Aagaz Academy in Chindwara, Madhya Pradesh** anchored by IDYWC, the Government official with whom the Academy participants interacted include:
Sub-Divisional Magistrate, Amarwara Block, Chindwara District
Director Panchayat Training Centre, Pachmarhi
State Panchayat Minister
Training Incharge, Panchayat Training Centre, Pachmarhi

Apart from this the Academy as well utilised the Government infrastructure, by hosting its second phase (6th -10th November) at the Sanjay Gandhi Institute in Pachmarhi

Aagaz Academy in Bikaner, Rajasthan had the involvement of the following officials:
Collector, District Bikaner
Development Officer, Panchayat Samiti Loonkaransar Tehsil
Sub-Divisonal Magistrate Loonkaransar Tehsil
Director Agriculture Extension Department, Bikaner District
Collector, District Bikaner
District Revenue Officer, District Bikaner
District Police Superintendent, District Bikaner
Women and Child Development Department, Bikaner
Womens Counselling and Security Centre/Women Police Station, Bikaner

Apart from this, the second phase of Aagaz Bikaner was held in the premises of Government owned, Shri Radhakrishnan Shikshak Sadan (A Teachers' Training Centre) in Bikaner.

Aagaz Centre	*Dates*	*Coverage*		*Partner Institutions*	*Sarpanch/ Panch*	*Literate/ Illiterate***	*Dalit*/ General*
		No.	*Geographical*				
	19–25th July	40					
	26 Nov.– 2 Dec. 2005	30					
	Feb. 2006						
Aagaz Academy, Chindwara IDYWC (9,83,000)	25th–29th July	35	District – Chindwara Seoni, Hoshangabad Panchayats-21	IDYWC, Chindwara SOPAN, Seoni Grameen Sewa Samiti, Hoshangabad	14–Sarpanch 21–Panch	21– Literate 14–Illiterate	3–General 32–SC/ST
	6th–10th 31 November, 2005				14–Sarpanch 17–Panch		

Contd. ...

Aagaz Centre	*Dates*	*Coverage*		*Partner Institutions*	*Sarpanch/ Panch*	*Literate/ Illiterate***	*Dalit*/ General*
		No.	*Geographical*				
	February 2006						
	Apr. III/IVth wk 2006						
	2nd–7th Sept.	48					
	Dec. 2005	43					
	Feb. 2006						
Aagaz Academy, Bhopal Samavesh (5,38,000)	2nd – 6th Sept. and 25th–29th Sept.	39	Districts–Sehore, Dewas, Harda Blocks – Ashta, Sonkach, Khategaon, Khidkiya Panchayats-24	Pushpa Kalyana Kendra, Sehore Samavesh, Dewas, Harda	20–Sarpanch 19–Panch	5– Literate 34–Illiterate	0–General 39–SC/ST

Contd. ...

Aagaz Centre	*Dates*	*Coverage*		*Partner Institutions*	*Sarpanch/ Panch*	*Literate/ Illiterate***	*Dalit*/ General*
		No.	*Geographical*				
	Dec. 27–Jan. 2	31			17–Sarpanch 14–Panch		
	Feb. 2005						
	Apr. 2006						
Aagaz Academy, Bangalore Aikya (9,85,500)	14th–20th Oct.	39	District–Bangalore (Rural) Mysore Mandya Chamarajnagar Coorg Tumkur Hassan Panchayats-34	ASEDA, Kolar BWS, Kolar WLARS, Hassan and Tumkur SAKTI, Bangalore (Rural) Vidyaniketan, Bangalore (Rural) SUMANA, Mysore ODP, Mysore, Coorg, Mandya and Chamarajnagar	5–Sarpanch 4–Up-sarpanch 28–Panch	32–Literate 7–Illiterate	6–General 33–SC/ST/ Others
	Jan. 27–Feb 3	32			5–Sarpanch 4–Up-sarpanch 28–Panch		

Contd. ...

Aagaz Centre	*Dates*	*Coverage*		*Partner Institutions*	*Sarpanch/ Panch*	*Literate/ Illiterate***	*Dalit*/ General*
		No.	*Geographical*				
	March 2005						
Aagaz Academy, Nasik Abhivyakti (8,47,500)	Feb. 2–7, 2006	23	Districts–Jalgaon, Dhule, Ahmednagar Panchayats–18	Janarth Adivasi Vikas Sansthan (Uttari Maharashtra Lok Vikas Manch–20 NGOs)	3–Sarpanch 20–Panch	9–Literate 14–Illiterate	2–Tribal 3–Nomadic 18–Maratha Caste

Contd. ...

Consolidated Status

Aagaz Centre	*Days*	*Coverage*		*Partner Institutions*	*Sarpanch Panch*	*Literate Illiterate***	*Dalit*/ general*
		Nos.	*Geographical*				
6 (52,57,400)	Phase 1–36	224	Districts–22 Panchayats–138	19	50–Sarpanch 10–Up Sarpanch 162–Panch 1–Panchayat Samiti member	80–Literate 144–Illiterate	45–General 179–SC/ST/ other
	Phase II–31	167			43– Sarpanch 9–Up Sarpanch 114–Panch 1–Panchayat Samiti member		

* SC/ST figures included other backward castes, Muslims and Christians
** Are all provisionary figures

APPENDIX

NATIONAL CAPABILITY BUILDING FRAMEWORK FOR PANCHAYATI RAJ ELECTED REPRESENTATIVES AND FUNCTIONARIES

I : INTRODUCTION AND BASIC PRINCIPLES UNDERLYING THE FRAMEWORK DESIGN

Introduction

The Constitution provides for the devolution of powers and responsibilities to Panchayats including the 29 matters listed in the Eleventh Schedule. Most States have enacted State Panchayati Raj Acts and Rules, in which they have indicated subjects with regard to which functions would be devolved to Panchayats. However, effective devolution has to still be accomplished, primarily through a process of activity mapping to ensure the concomitant and simultaneous devolution of functions, funds and functionaries to Panchayats at all three levels. The greatest challenge facing all stakeholders is to ensure the capability of Panchayats to effectively perform the responsibilities entrusted to them. The absence of training continues to be used as an alibi for non-devolution of functions, or for dis-empowering Panchayats, despite the well-grounded fact that the exercise of responsibilities is, in itself, the optimal mode of training.

Effective implementation of the provisions of Part IX of the Constitution will require building of the capability of Panchayats in the fullest meaning of the term, which will encompasses training, provision of adequate functionaries, technical assistance and a host of other support to Panchayats. The Seventh Round Table of State Ministers of Panchayati Raj held at Jaipur in December 2004 adopted several action points relating to the subject of training and capacity building of elected representatives and officials of Panchayats at all levels. These action points provide the underpinnings for the design of a National Capability Building Framework (the Framework) for Panchayati Raj Elected Representatives and Functionaries, which is aimed at comprehensively building effective and sustainable capability of all Stakeholders in Panchayati Raj, particularly elected representatives, office-bearers such as Presidents, Vice-presidents (Sarpanches and Up-sarpanches), Chairpersons of Standing Committees and officials connected with subjects devolved to Panchayats under State legislations.

The overarching objective of the Framework is to achieve the goal of Panchayats becoming institutions of self-government, in the letter and spirit of Part IX of the Constitution. The implementation of the framework is aimed at creating a grounds well in favour of democratic devolution to Panchayati Raj Institutions. The Framework aims to break through the deadlock of whether capacity building should precede devolution of functions, funds and functionaries.

Objectives of the National Framework

The four basic objectives of the National Capability Building Framework are as follows:

(a) It aims at enabling Panchayat elected representatives to upgrade their knowledge and skills to better perform their responsibilities towards the Panchayat. In particular, it aims to expose them to the modalities of implementing several programmes equitably, particularly cutting across the inequalities of caste and gender. Programmes under the Framework will enable Panchayat elected representatives to comprehend their own situations and find answers to their problems through the medium of the Panchayati Raj system. It will enable them to think constructively, in terms of small but significant actions they can take or facilitate others to take. It will also equip them with the operational skills required for day-to-day performance of executive duties of the Panchayat.

(b) Key officials associated with the functions devolved to Panchayats and who are working under or closely with them require appropriate orientation so as to effectively serve and facilitate the Panchayats in the performance of devolved functions. On the one hand these officials represent a vast pool of detailed technical knowledge pertaining to the departments they serve and therefore, can play a important facilitatory role in advising Panchayat elected representatives and imparting to them their wisdom. On the other, these officials also would greatly benefit from imbibing lessons drawn from the grassroots level experiences of elected representatives, who will bring to mutual interactions their significant local knowledge of ground level nuances. The Framework aims to (i) equip these officials better to function as technical advisors and trainers, and (ii) orient them to respect, be more receptive and learn from the ground level experience of elected Panchayat representatives.

(c) The Framework aims at improving the vigour of practice of grassroots level democracy through promoting the effective functioning of the Gram Sabha. This will provide a space for the community, particularly the poor, to assert their demands through participative planning, to monitor the implementation of such plans and to hold their Panchayat to account through the instrumentalities of the Right to Information and Social Audit.

(d) The Framework would include special efforts to sensitise the media, political parties, representatives in the legislatures, civil society organisations and citizens to looking at Panchayati Raj as an effective level of local government.

Basic Principles Underlying the Framework

The Framework is grounded on the following basic principles:

First, implementation of the Framework is a continuous and sustained process. Capability building cannot remain limited to a few erratic and non-regular episodes of training. It is a multifaceted exercise aimed at promoting effective functioning of Panchayats, of which training is but one facet, which must be periodically repeated as a longer and continuous process of transformation and development with the active participation of all the stakeholders involved.

Second, the focus of training under the Framework is not upon information alone. It is a process of exploration, discovery and growth; a process in which trainers and participants are involved in a common inter-learning situation, where both are enriched.

Third, training cannot provide ready made answers to all problems. Trainers do not need to fill every gap, answer every question, plan every event and deal with every problem, but must provide space and time for trainees to reflect on and analyze their situation and seek solutions to their problems.

Fourth, mutual learning, assimilation and retention to meet diverse requirements happens best in an environment which:

- Uses several modes so as to sustain interest,
- Is non-hierarchical and non-threatening, encouraging people to be active in an informal atmosphere,
- Where trainers are not lecturers, but facilitators, friends and counsellors, who can evoke and stimulate thinking and accept criticism from the trainees,
- Promotes and facilitates the individual's discovery of personal potential and capabilities,
- Recognizes peoples' right to sometimes make mistakes,
- Accepts differences,
- Encourages openness, self and mutual respect,
- Encourages togetherness among learners,
- Brings trainees and trainers closer.

Fifth, all participants in the Panchayati Raj system bring with them well honed knowledge about grassroots reality experience and native wisdom, which must be respected and should constitute the base for their further learning. There are various sections that need specialized training, such as SCs, STs, and Women. Members of SC/ST communities, Women and marginalized groups should invariably be given special attention in all training efforts. No member can be, even inadvertently, scorned or maligned on account of his/her social and economic background.

Sixth, participatory approaches reduce stress and enhance effectiveness. Therefore, the training programme should be designed to ensure participation of all members—not just a talkative and domineering few—through activities that are interesting and relevant, that provide scope for thinking and doing, involve creativity and arouse curiosity, and also provide mental exercise and the right degree of challenge.

Seventh, the training team should comprise a group of like-minded individuals, selected for their commitment to secular values and principles. The training team should be objective and non-judgemental in outlook, a group with whom the trainees can feel free to communicate without fear of ridicule. The training team should function as facilitators, friends and counsellors, who can evoke and stimulate thinking and accept criticism from the trainees.

Eighth, the processes and logistics of the framework must be convenient and relevant to the ground reality of elected representatives. It must enable Panchayat members, particularly women and representatives of disadvantaged groups, to understand within their own context how to increase their overall exposure, learning and comprehension through regular participation in these training programmes.

Ninth, the programme must aim at maximum initial coverage within a limited period of time, so that all stakeholders can quickly settle down in to playing their roles and commence their work.

Tenth, training for PESA areas should be designed in keeping with the cultural traditions and special needs of tribal people.

Eleventh, the framework has to constantly develop and evolve on the basis of regular impact assessment. Training must become a two-way process so that feedback is ploughed into reforming of content and process of training. In turn, this should yield systemic changes in panchayat and government functioning.

The Stakeholders

The Framework is targeted to reach the following:

Elected Panchayat Representatives

There are about 22 lakh representatives elected to the three levels of Panchayats. These comprise of Ward Members and Territorial

Constituency members, those elected to leadership positions as Presidents (Sarpanchas, Mukhiyas, Adhyakshas) or Vice-presidents (Up-sarpanchas, Up-mukhiyas, Upadhyakshas) and Chairpersons of Standing Committees.

Officials Working with Panchayats

It is estimated that there are about 8 lakh key officials at various levels, who deal with or work under the Panchayats. Most of them are poorly trained through their line departments, who often do not keep aside enough funds for the purpose. They require orientation training that is primarily aimed at inculcating the right mindset amongst them towards Panchayat members, so as to foster a more harmonious relationship and for them to realize the opportunities presented by Panchayats. The main categories of such officials are as follows:

(i) Panchayat Secretaries,
(ii) Junior Engineers,
(iii) Anganwadi Workers,
(iv) Primary Health Workers,
(v) Public Health Workers,
(vi) Panchayats own employees such as bill collectors and clerks,
(vii) Agricultural Extension Officials,
(viii) Teachers and Education Administration Workers.

Pressure Groups within the Gram Sabha such as SHGs and CBOs.

Elected Representatives and Officials of higher levels of Government

Officials and Elected representatives of Professional cadres such as doctors and engineers need to be sensitized to become facilitators of Panchayats. There is also a strong need to sensitise policy-makers such as MLAs, MPs, political leaders and media to ensure that they provide a nurturing environment for the growth of Panchayats.

II : CONTENT OF THE FRAMEWORK

Introduction

Capability building of stakeholders in the proper implementation of Panchayati Raj cannot be treated as an isolated training exercise. The rightful position of Panchayati Raj as a potent instrument of rural local self-government aimed at decentralized planning and implementation, will need to permeate all capability building initiatives. This is particularly important as Panchayati Raj is an important cornerstone of governance reform. Keeping in mind this background, the Framework aims at segregating the training content and phasing the training programme into three parts, the details of which are given in Table 1 below:

Table 1:

	Theme	*Description of the manner of interaction*	*Area covered, in brief*	*Category covered*	*Duration*	*Time line for completion*
Part I	Building the right mindset for implementation of Panchayati Raj and learning basic functions	Course I (a): Foundation Course	Overview of Panchayati Raj	Elected Panchayat representatives: about 22 lakh Panchayati Raj Officials: about 8 lakh	4 days, *in toto*	Within 20 weeks of election
		Course I (b): Basic Founctional Course	Internal Housekeeping, including understanding of accounts, Social Audit, Right to information, Panchayat revenues	Elected leaders of Panchayats at all levels and Chairpersons of Standing Committees (5 per Panchayat):	4 days	Within 20 weeks of election. (Including foundational course, each office bearer would

Contd. ...

	Theme	*Description of the manner of interaction*	*Area covered, in brief*	*Category covered*	*Duration*	*Time line for completion*
				About 10 lakh: Panchayati Raj Officials; about 5 lakh		undergo 8 days of training)
		Course I(c): Functional Literacy Course	Give those who need to an exposure functional literacy	Illiterate of semi-literate elected representa-tives (about 8 lakh people)	One month, or as required, preferably at the village level itself.	6 months
Part II	Basic skill building for planning and implementa-tion	Course II(a): Sectorally focused training programme	Coverage of core functions of Panchayats aimed at improving capacities to deliver services and development programmes	Elected Panchayat representati-ves: about 22 lakh Officials associated with Panchayati Raj: about 8 lakh	At least 6 days (2 phases of 3 days each)	Within 40 weeks of election
		Course II(a): Computer Training	Training in basic computer skills and selected sofrware for Panchayat level training	At least 2 persons per Panchayat: about 5 lakh	At least 6 days, with local handhold-ing from the resource centre	Within 52 weeks

Contd. ...

	Theme	*Description of the manner of interaction*	*Area covered, in brief*	*Category covered*	*Duration*	*Time line for completion*
Part III	Consolidation through interaction and networking	III(a): Gram Sabha level campaigns	Awareness creation	Gram Sabhas, NGOs, SHGs and CBOs	At least 3 days a week	Coverage of all Gram Panchayats at least once a year
		III(b): Panchayati Raj TV channel and radio programmes		People at large	At least 3 days a week	All-India coverage
		III(c): Panchayati Raj Newsletter		Panchayati Raj members and individual subscribers	Once a month	All Panchayats
		III(d): Formation of networks of Panchayat elected representatives	Experience sharing	Elected Panchayat representatives: about 22 lakh		Within the first years after election
		III(e): Yearly refresher course		Elected Panchayat representatives: about 22 lakh	At least 4 days	Once a year for remaining 4 years
		III(f): Visits to identified 'beacon' Panchayats	On the site training	At least 10 lakh elected leaders of Panchayats	At least one full day each, excluding travel	At least two exposure visits every year

Contd. ...

	Theme	*Description of the manner of interaction*	*Area covered, in brief*	*Category covered*	*Duration*	*Time line for completion*
		III(g): Intermediate Panchayat level Resource Centers	Daily assistance to support Panchayat level planning and implementation	Elected Panchayat representatives: about 22 lakh	Every working day	To commence by 20 weeks, when members have finished Part I training
		III(h): Helplines			16 hours a day, every working day	
		III(i): Certificate courses	More intensive and academic study	Interested stakeholders	6 month course	For about 100 persons per State

Part I: Description of courses comprising Part I of the framework:

Part I comprise of a group of courses aimed at giving each participant a basic grounding in Panchayati Raj and skills required to get started. Part I would also build the receptivity required for effective assimilation of Part II. The details of the courses that comprise Part I are as follows:

Course I(a):

Basic foundation course; Building the right mindset for implementation of Panchayati Raj:

It is essential that everybody involved in Panchayati Raj, be the elected Panchayat representatives or officials at any level are fully conversant and believe in the ideals that underlie it. The bane of

the curriculum, as also the details of the curriculum itself, in respect of Part I is indicated below in Table 2.

Table 2:

Central Government	*State Government*	*District Training Team*
Course I (a) & I (b) (Foundation Course and Basic Functional Course)		
a. Preparation of basic material covering the nationally common aspects of Panchayati Raj, namely, (i) Constitutional provisions regarding Panchayati Raj and the current position, particularly with reference to the RT Action points, (ii) Principles of secularism, equality and human rights emanating from the Constitution of India, (iii) General awareness of gender equity and social justice, (iv) Status of human development, (v) Poverty alleviation, (vi) Participatory planning, (vii) Implementation and monitoring, (viii) Right to information and transparency and Social Audit, (ix) Importance of regular conduct of Gram Sabha. b. Comparative position of States in the implementation of Panchayati Raj. c. Basic awareness of the funds that are destined to go to Panchayats from the Government of India.	Salient features of the State Panchayati Raj Act and rules and regulations covering Panchayati Raj, Overview of the status of human development in the State, interalia, covering Gender equity and social justice and poverty alleviation, State specific details regarding participatory planning, particularly the broad approach to district level planning and consolidation of plans into the district level plan, Elements of Implementation and monitoring of programmes, Overview of States' approach to right to information, transparency and Social Audit, State specific provisions relating to Panchayat level maintenance of accounts,	Details of the implementation of Panchayati Raj within the district (such as the number of members, their qualifications, etc.), Answering district specific queries relating to planning and implementation, Overview of sectoral implementation of programmes in the context of the district, Role of Panchayats in promoting equity, Micro Planning at the level of each Panchayat, in the building up of the district plan, Techniques of Participatory Rural Appraisal (PRA) exercises.

Contd. ...

Central Government	*State Government*	*District Training Team*
Course I (a) & I (b) (Foundation Course and Basic Functional Course)		
d. Basic overview of Panchayat level financial management, including maintenance of accounts,	State specific details of own resource management and accounting,	
e. Awareness of the importance of own revenues of Panchayats and the need to collect them,	State specific details of relevant rules such as delegation orders, PWD code, rules of countersignature, treasury code etc.	
f. Awareness of the provisions of PESA.		
Course I (c) : Functional Literacy Course		
Basic materials on literacy, as designed for the National Literacy Mission. Designs etc. prepared by the Nehru Yuvak Kendra.	State specific material on literacy.	District level materials prepared for the literacy programme.

Training Methodologies of Part I and Logistics for Implementation:

The magnitude of the implementation of Part I is unprecedented—nearly 35 lakh people will be involved in it, either as trainers, or trainees, or both. All would need to be covered within 6 months at the most [20 weeks for Courses I(a) & I(b) and 26 weeks for Course I(c)]. Having considered the large target group and the tight timelines the logistics dictate (a) a mechanism of large scale rollout, such as satellite or distance training (b) intensive local support and facilitation, through face-to-face participatory training. Combining a distance mode, based on common films and presentation alternated with local discussions, interactive sessions and followed by question and answer sessions over satellite carries the following advantages:

(a) It allows broad standardization of content, at the state specific level,
(b) It allows for wide dissemination and rapid coverage,
(c) Local interaction can adapt the message conveyed over the introductory satellite based session into locally relevant lessons and exercises,
(d) Sharing of problems through the interactive mode builds a feeling of community among participants even though they are not face to face,
(e) With satellite training costs are also kept low, as Panchayat members do not have to travel very far to the site of training.

The details are as follows:

Interactive Satellite Training:

Interactive Satellite-based training uses a dedicated satellite channel (provided by the ISRO) for beaming programmes to specified centres for being viewed by trainees. Each reception centre is also equipped with a talk back facility (either through telephone connection or on the satellite channel itself), which enables trainees to ask questions to resource persons located at the central studio. Replies given by such studio-based resource persons can be heard over the entire network. Satellite transmission, when combined with face-to-face participatory training methodology provides a intermixed programme combining the triggers provided by a central audio-visual programme, with facilitation provided by appropriately oriented resource persons at the local training centres. Large number of trainees can be rapidly and effectively covered through this composite approach. Training can also be locally focused according to the group's needs. Training can start with the sharing of experiences amongst the participants in group discussions. Sessions can be interesting and retain attention, with inclusion of games, exercises pictures related to day-to-day life of the Panchayats, and elsewhere in related fields, so as to make it more interesting and with a more enduring impact. Keeping in mind these advantages, the Framework aims to cover all States with the infrastructure required for Satellite training, which essentially would comprise of Satellite Studios, reception centers (televisions, satellite dishes, telephones, uninterrupted power supply systems and miscellaneous civil works).

Local Face-to-Face Training:

All basic training for Gram Panchayat elected representatives and officials ought to be held, as far as possible, within the same Block/ Intermediate Panchayat area in which the Gram Panchayat is located. Such training could make use of the existing network of Extension Training Centres within the Block, as already provided by government. Local infrastructure such as school buildings or community centres could be used for holding training.

The local face-to-face training would be through resource persons specially oriented for the purpose. In order to ensure complete participation and attention, it is proposed to engage 5 resource persons for every training session. The strength of each classroom session is proposed to be limited to 20 participants at a time. Based on these calculations, the number of resource persons required has been worked out to 30,000. Details are given in Chapter 3.

Combining Satellite and Face-to-Face Training:

A suggested pattern of combining distance satellite transmission with local training facilitated by local resource persons is described below in Table 3:

Table 3:

Activity	*Agency*	*Responsibilities of authorities concerned*
Introduction to the film	Resource Persons at the training centres	Resource Persons at the Training Centres make a brief introductory statement about the film, or conduct an introductory activity without pre-empting what is in the film.
Screening the film	Satellite transmission	The film is screened through the Satellite Centre. Resource Persons at Training Centres ensure that the TV set is switched on 5 minutes before satellite transmission for viewing the film.

Contd. ...

Activity	*Agency*	*Responsibilities of authorities concerned*
General Responses	Resource Persons at the training centres	The first 5-10 minutes after the film is screened is for participants' general responses. Resource Persons at the Training Centre can invite participants to individually identify 3-5 of the most significant statements or scenes from the film and share these in a small group. This can be followed by a plenary, wherein participants would discuss themes identified by them. This provides an opportunity for participants to turn over the film in their minds, to let it sink in and take root.
Facilitated discussion/ activities	Resource Person at the training centres	Each film comes with a training package including a set of topics or activities to be facilitated by resource persons to encourage the participants to go beyond the film and to think of steps they might take in their own circumstances. Resource persons are also given techniques to nudge discussion in certain directions. Games and activities can be taken up to retain interest.
Question Answer session	Satellite transmission	Participants can ask the panelists at the SATCOM studio questions or discuss ideas that may have emerged during the general responses and facilitated discussions. Panelists could also initiate discussion on 2-3 issues.

Training in Mixed Groups

While training each category separately makes for easier design of the training programme, the advantages of training in mixed groups justifies the effort involved. With adequate care taken to ensure full participation, training different stakeholders together builds relationships between them in a non-threatening and informal atmosphere and can dispel pre-conceived notions that each have about the other. Training of officials with Panchayat members is essential to dispel misgivings regarding their role *vis-a-vis* Panchayat members, a fear that they will be subject to oppressive and indecisive oversight by Panchayats, and a fear of being accountable to a much greater level. It is envisaged that both Courses I(a) and I(b) will be of mixed groups of elected representatives and officials, special orientation courses would be arranged for such workers simultaneously with the orientation course for elected Panchayat representatives. Other mixed groups could also be created for combined training, as follows:

(a) *Second-term members and members of beacon Panchayats:* Panchayat members elected for a second tenure, and those from Panchayats which have a track record of efficient functioning will be identified for this programme. The overall objective is to provide for Panchayat representatives to (a) share their experiences of good practices, and (b) network with each other with a view to develop a common pool of knowledge. Such training could also include field visits.

(b) *Joint training of GP Sarpanches, and Secretaries:* GP Sarpanches are usually responsible for (a) passing bills before payments are made, (b) check measuring any public work before the measurement is accepted for payment, (c) accord administrative sanctions for development works, (d) ensure proper executive and financial management of the Gram Panchayat, and (e) signing cheques jointly with the Secretary for fund withdrawal. Gram Panchayat Secretaries are responsible for (i) proper custody of records and properties, (ii) clearing audit objections, (iii) preparing and placing budget, (iv) supervising the work of the GP staff. Joint training for GP Office bearers and Secretaries will enable them to understand their mutual responsibilities better.

(c) *Members of different levels of Panchayats:* This programme will put together members of the District, Intermediate and Gram Panchayats, so that they can better understand each others' roles in Panchayati Raj and the need for close coordination. Further variations on the same theme could include training of members and Chairpersons of Standing Committees of Panchayats at various levels together.

(d) *Training of staff drawn from different levels:* This training is to create a sense of team-spirit amongst staff involved in

Panchayati Raj and reinforce the point that Panchayati Raj is part of the larger goal for self-reliance and development. It aims at creating a different work culture and ethic suited to Panchayati Raj. This programme will also provide a forum for exchange and dissemination of good practices facilitated in different districts by individual officers.

(e) *Engineering, Auditing and Accounting Staff:* This is aimed at fostering a better understanding among engineering, accounting and auditing staff of the social, economic and human effects of 'projects'. This training will familiarize participants with the enhanced powers of Panchayats in planning and implementation of various programmes. It will focus on the importance of transparency and certification by the Gram Sabha before measurement is processed for payment. Training will also familiarize participants with the documentation involved in the implementation of works.

Part II: Description of Courses Comprising Part II of the Framework

Course II(a): Sectorally focused training programme:

Part II of the Framework focuses on Sectoral Training covering several aspects of programme planning and implementation, with an added emphasis on service delivery. The role of Panchayats as local self-governments central to planning and implementation would be a cross-cutting theme of training. While all matters listed in the Eleventh Schedule can be ideally included, it is proposed to prioritise major sectors and Centrally Sponsored Schemes pertaining to the core functions undertaken by Panchayats. An initial listing of these Schemes and the sectors that could be covered in Part II are given in Table 4.

Planning, implementation, supervision and monitoring, disclosure and accounting will be explained with reference to service delivery. The need for PRIs to function in concert for efficient implementation of schemes will also be explained.

Table 4:

Sector	*Scheme*		*Central Ministry Department*
Elementary Education	1	Sarva Shiksha Abhiyan	Department of Elementary Education
	2	Mid-day Meal Scheme	
Adult Education	3	Total Literacy Campaign	
Public Health	4	Drinking Water Mission	Department of Drinking Water Supply
	5	Total Sanitation Campaign	
Health	6	National Rural Health Mission	Ministry of Health
Child Welfare	7	Integrated Child Development Services	Ministry of HRD, Department of Women and Child Welfare
Poverty Alleviation	8	National Rural Employment	Ministry of Rural Development
	9	Scheme (including SGRY)	
Rural Housing	10	Indira Awas Yojana (IAY)	
Rural Roads	11	Pradhan Mantri Gram Sadak Yojana (PMGSY)	
Rural Electrification	12	Rajiv Gandhi Grameen Vidyutikaran Yojana	Ministry of Power
	13	Remote Village Electrification Programme	Ministry of Non-Conventional Energy
Tribal Development	14	Tribal Sub-plan	Ministry of Tribal Welfare
Natural Resource Management	15	Haryali	Ministry of Rural Development
	16	Watershed Scheme of Agriculture Ministry	Ministry of Agriculture
Industry & Rural Business Hubs	17	Various Schemes	Ministry of Food Processing, Ministry of Textiles
Disaster Management			SSI and Agro-Rural Industries

Curriculum for Course II(a):

Training under Course II(a) is envisaged to be through a series of interactive exercises that guide Panchayats and their staff through the step-by-step modalities of implementation. The core curriculum could be developed in workshop mode, by representatives of selected SIRDs & NGOs who have a proven track record in developing and conducting effective training programmes. This would cover the following aspects in respect of each sector or scheme covered, as given in Table 5.

Table 5:

5(a): Planning					
1	Broad overview of scheme guidelines or legislation concerned	2	Preparing a participative plan for the service concerned	3	Prioritising list of projects at Panchayat level
4	Scrutiny of the Panchayat plan and obtaining of approvals	5	Examples of how to converge different programmes	6	Preparation and updating a shelf of works
		7	Consolidation of Panchayat level plans into the district level plans		

5(b): Implementation					
1	Beneficiary Selection	2	Muster roll Maintenance	3	Payment of Wages

5(c): Supervision and Monitoring					
1	Measurement of Work	2	Quality Control	3	Certification of Work Undertaken
		4	Preparation of Annual Report		

5(d): Disclosure					
1	Meeting obligations under Right to Information	2	Public display of details of works	3	Conduct of Social Audit
		4	Grievance Redressal		

5(e): Accounting					
1	Overview of Panchayat Accounting	2	Maintenance of Statutory Registers	3	Management of Panchayat Funds
4	Treasury Procedures	5	Bank Procedures	6	Conduct of Audit

Responsibilities in designing of the detailed curriculum for Course II(a):

An activity mapping, giving the details of the responsibilities of the Central Government, State Governments and the District Training Team in preparing the curriculum, in respect of Course II(a) is indicated below in Table 6:

Table 6:

Central Government	*State Government*	*District Training Team*
Details of important programmes being implemented by Panchayats, obtained from the Central Ministries concerned and summarized into core content for Panchayat members.	State specific priority areas pertaining to the Sector concerned, which need to be addressed by all Panchayats in planning and implementation.	District level nuances, concerning planning and implementation of these sectoral programmes in Panchayats in the district.

Training methodologies of Course II(a) and logistics for implementation:

Emphasis on engaging District and Sub-district line Department Staff as resource persons: The investments in powering the roll-out of Part I would also stand in good stead for Part II. Resource persons readied for implementation of Part I will be continued for the implementation of Part II. However, since sectoral programmes are to be implemented, there will need to be a greater emphasis on operational details. Field level line department staff with the right attitude and aptitude will have a key role to play as trainers for Course II(a), for the following reasons:

(a) They usually have universal presence and are available,
(b) They have an intimate knowledge of local situations and the grassroots level reality concerning their sector,
(c) If properly motivated, many of them can break out of their routine activities and undertake something creative and useful, pertaining to their respective departments.

Course II(a) training would be led by departmental field staff, already selected into the district training teams. District and sub-district level functionaries shall be entrusted the responsibility of undertaking such hands on training for members of the Standing Committees in short-term courses. Such programmes could be arranged in courses of one day or half day, so as to ensure a balance between regular duties and additional ones of training.

Duration of Course II(a):

The programme for implementation of Course II(a) can be split into two phases as described below in Table 7:

Table 7:

Sl. No.	*Phase*	*Duration*	*Content*	*Remarks*
1	Phase 1	3 days	Cross-cutting aspects of sectoral programmes, such as accounting, fund management, disclosure, social audit, etc.	For all participants, as indicated in Table 1
2	Phase 2	3 days	Sector specific and scheme specific training	Participants will be segregated into groups, based on the Standing Committees that they belong to and attend the appropriate sessions

Depending on the scope and ambit of empowerment of Panchayats, States can adopt variations on this basic pattern.

Course II(b): Building ICT Skills:

Through Course II(b), at least two people per Panchayat will be equipped with computing skills. Training will be required for about five lakh persons.

Curriculum for Course II(b):

Training content would be aimed towards awareness generation and skill development in software proposal to be deployed at the Panchayat level. The curriculum for Course II (b) would consist of the operational aspects of the Panchayat Suite and other back end solution software applications from NIC. Special emphasis would be given to familiarization with the National Panchayat Portal (NPP, http://panchayat.nic.in). Training for selected persons would include operation of the software, as also include data entry skills.

Responsibilities in designing of the detailed curriculum for Course II(b):

An activity mapping, giving the details of the responsibilities of the Central Government, State Governments and the District Training Team in preparing the curriculum, in respect of Course II(b) is indicated below in Table 8:

Table 8:

Central Government	*State Government*	*District Training Team*
NIC to provide software and basic manuals.	State specific manuals to be created in association with State Informatics Officers of the NIC.	Local selection of resource persons for training.

Training methodologies of Course II(b) and logistics for implementation:

Training for ICT skills is best done in cascade mode. Care may be taken to ensure that sufficient resource persons selected for implementing the framework are skilled in IT. Training of trainers at the State level can be organized in a collaborative manner between the SIRD and the State Information Officer.

Part III: Strengthening and consolidation of capability through interaction and networking

In each State, the first year after election would be devoted to the roll-out of Part I and Part II of the Framework. However, so as to retain the momentum after Panchayat members and officials go back to work, there is a need for continuous interaction and providing them additional support when they are confronted with issues and decisions at the ground level. Several activities (not necessarily in the nature of courses) together comprise part III of the Framework, as follows:

III(a): Campaigns at the Gram Sabha Level:

The training of Panchayat members and Staff shall be complemented by a large scale community mobilization programme aimed at motivating people to improve the vigour of practice of democracy, especially through the Gram Sabhas. NGOs and CBOs would be involved in a big way both in spreading the message of participation as also in Gram Sabha level interactions such as beneficiary selection, social audit, etc. Within the general campaign, there would be particular focus on motivating Self-Help Groups, Groups such as Mahila and Youth Mandals and other activity based groups to participate in Gram Sabhas and act as more assertive pressure groups within it. Such campaigns would also aim at motivating people to serve in various Panchayat Standing Committees and participate more actively in planning and implementation of sectoral programmes.

Campaigns at the Gram Sabha level could also focus on important common concerns of the people and Panchayats, such as alcoholism, literacy, girls' education, domestic violence, dowry, water and soil conservation, organic farming, etc. through the performance of Kala Jatha Nataks and evocative songs, with the objective of triggering collaboration and common action between Panchayats and the people on a daily basis, instead of only at the time of conduct of the Gram Sabha.

Course I(a), namely, in satellite assisted face-to-face mode. The overall objective of this training shall be to provide a forum for Panchayat representatives to (a) share their experiences of good practices as well as learn from their failures, and (b) network with each other. Each training programme will be of 4 days duration and may be combined with experience sharing and field visits.

III(f): Visits to identified 'beacon' Panchayats:

Beacon Panchayats will be identified through a transparent and independent process so that the work that they have done can be showcased. Study visits of other Panchayats to these beacon Panchayats will be organized, so as to promote exposure to best practices and replicate models of development and good governance.

III(g): Intermediate Panchayat level Extension and Resource Centres:

It is envisaged that under the framework, there will be at least one extension centre at the level of each Intermediate Panchayat, so as to cater to the training requirements of all Panchayats within the area of the Intermediate Panchayat. Each Extension Training Centre would provide a space for training activities, for hosting the Field Resource Persons pertaining to the block concerned and for receiving Panchayat members for consultations and networking. The Satellite training facility will also be physically located at the Extension Resource Centre. Panchayat members would be facilitated for congregating at these resource centres for smaller level meetings and mutual support.

When Panchayats are entrusted tasks of planning and implementation, fundamental changes are required in departmental processes to better empower local officials to deal with local needs. Creating a pool of technically competent staff or other agencies at the Intermediate Panchayat level is another form of capacity creation for Panchayati Raj. To meet this need, each Extension Centre would be staffed with a few resource persons who would provide technical support to the Panchayats, as follows:

(a) An engineer to technically review Panchayat level infrastructure construction projects and provide support for preparation of estimates, procure tenders and monitor quality,

(b) An accountant to assist Gram Panchayats to follow prescribed financial guidelines, to provide assistance where needed, and to collate Panchayat accounts at the block level for transfer to the district,

(c) A social specialist, to assist Panchayats in conducting decentralized participatory processes for planning, mobilize the poorest and vulnerable groups to attend Gram Sabhas and Ward Sabhas.

Running of the resource centres could be organized either through (a) the District or Intermediate Panchayat, (b) the SIRD, supported by the district or Intermediate Panchayat, (c) a collective of the Panchayat members themselves, wherever such networks have been created and are strong, (d) an NGO, associated with the Panchayat member network or Panchayat Representatives. These arrangements would ensure that the O & M requirements are met through appropriate agreements. Whatever the model adopted, Panchayat members will be fully associated with the governing arrangements for the running of the resource centres.

Along with the establishment of Resource Centres, the Centre and States shall work towards upgradation of training centres, such as NIRD, SIRDs, and extension training centres at the district, block level and below.

III(h): Helplines:

Even after training of all stakeholders is completed, there would be a need to provide a speedy channel of clarification and information, to those involved in the implementation of the programme. Helplines can provide continuous online support to trained persons and link help seekers with providers while in the long-term, IT would provide an interactive mechanism of seeking and getting clarification, considering the low penetration of IT in Gram Panchayats, telephone helplines will be set up. Important points concerning setting up telephone helplines are summarized in Table 9.

Table 9:

Location:	Can be at the State level to start with, but district level would be ideal.
Minimum facilities:	At least one telephone line and one independent fax line is essential for each helpline.
Training:	Staff should be specially trained to take calls and answer them. They should have pleasing manners, must be helpful and fully conversant with all aspects of Panchayati Raj. The best Field level resource persons could be given helpline duties on a rotation basis.
Timings:	The helpline could be run for 16 hours, every day, in two 8-hour shifts. This is because persons seeking clarifications on phone often wait for STD rates to be low when making calls.
Publicity:	Wide publicity should be given to the helpline telephone numbers in all communications of the government. They should also be widely publicized in the press.
Availability of materials for clarifications:	The State will need to provide all material such as copies of legislations, rules, regulations, activity mapping, orders and circulars to the helpline. All information including those related to Right to Information should be available at the Helplines. The helpline could also provide assistance by way of quick clarification, in preparation of estimates, reference to Schedule of Rates, etc.
Faxing of instructions from the Helplines:	It is possible that from Gram Panchayats etc., details would be sought over phones in public STD booths, where there may also be fax availability. Therefore the helpline should be in a position to readily send faxes to those requiring it.
Logging of calls and replies:	Calls to helplines will provide invaluable feedback on the implementation of Panchayati Raj. Therefore, systems for lodging calls will need to be put in. On a daily basis, the gist of calls will need to be recorded in writing in special logbooks for the purpose.
Grievance redressal:	It is quite possible that helplines are also used by people to complain and record their grievances. Arrangments will need to be made to send the complaints received to the authorities concerned for redressal and to provide replies to the persons concerned.
Debriefing:	Wherever a State decides to have more than one helpline, a monthly debriefing of helpline staff may be conducted so as to get information on field activities. This will also provide an opportunity for staff to learn from each others' experiences. The logs can also be registered in a common repository during the debriefing, from where they can be used to prepare replies to frequently asked questions.

III(i): Formal Certification courses in Panchayati Raj:

A more formal training system will be required to provide formal certification of courses for training. Training programmes shall be designed especially for the secretarial and technical staff working with Panchayats through institutions such as IGNOU. Other stakeholders, including interested Panchayat elected representatives will also be assisted to undertake this course. Such training programmes will lead to formal certification on achieving prescribed standards of learning.

III : RESOURCE PERSONS FOR IMPLEMENTING THE FRAMEWORK

The predominant mode of rolling out Parts I & II of the framework is through combining satellite and face-to-face training. Cascade training is aimed at creating pools of resource persons at each level, from the National to the Block level, who are a lasting investment in the training chain. Since training is not envisaged as a one time effort, resource persons also cannot be selected on that basis that they will be required intermittently. This pool of resource persons will be created through a three step cascading process, comprising of national Resource Persons, State level Resource Persons and District and Sub-district level resource persons. In the case of IT training [Course II (b)] it is envisaged that only a two level cascading process will be adopted, namely, of State and District level Resource Persons.

Details of Resource Persons Required for the Programme:

Master Resource Persons:

Master trainers are key role players and should have the right attitude and aptitude for imparting skills concerning key development programmes. Variations in skills required would depend on the content, mode of roll-out and logistics of the programme. The basic qualifications for master trainers would need to be spelt out in advance and they would vary depending on the kind of design. The tasks of trainers at each level would considerably vary, depending upon their immediate tasks. At the National level and the State level, trainers are expected to train State level master trainers who would in all probability, come to the training programme carrying significant experience both in training as well as implementation of Government schemes. The approach at the National level would encompass communicating both the ethos of Panchayati Raj, as well as the processes invòlved. This would largely be the approach of State Master Trainers also.

Resource Persons at the District level:

The approach of District level Resource Persons would be strikingly different from those at the National level. Most individuals selected as Resource Persons at the District levels would also be stakeholders and participants in Panchayati Raj. Their roles at this level would be blurred—many trainers will also double up working in resource centres that provide ongoing assistance to Panchayats.

Number of Resource Persons Required:

The kinds of resource persons required for implementation of the programme are given below in Table 10:

Table 10 :

Sl. No.	*Category of resource person*	*Number required*	*Basis for calculation of numbers required*	*Broad work chart, including Course concerned*	*Responsibility of undertaking training*
Central level					
1	Satellite training anchores and presenters	96 (100)	At least 4 per State	To anchor State satellite transmissions for Parts I & II of the programme	Ministry of Panchayati Raj to provide baisc orientation, through a programme operated at a designated SIRD that is already using the system
2	National Resource Persons	150	Given in Table below	To undertake TOTs for State level master trainers, for courses in Parts I & II of the Framework	State to select persons, MORP to provide basic orientation course through a programme operated at a designated SIRD
	Total	**250**			

Contd. ...

State level					
1	Sate level Master Resource Persons	1850	Given in Table below	To undertake TOTs for District level master trainers in Parts I & II of the Framework	State to select and train in programme at SIRDs
2	District level Resource Persons	27500	Given in Table below		State Master Resource Persons to undertake training at district level
3	State level Master Resource Persons for IT	100	At least 4 per State	To undertake TOTs for District level Resource Persons	To be selected by NIC in consultation with State
4	District level Resource Persons	1800	At the rate of 3 per district		State to select and train in consultation with NIC.
	Total	**31250**			
Grand Total		**31500**			

The calculations in respect of the requirement of resource persons are detailed below in Table 11:

Table 11:

a	No. of elected representatives to be trained	2200000	
b	No. of persons per batch	20	It is envisaged that training batches will not be larger than 20 persons at a time, so as to ensure meaningful participation of all.
c	No. of training batches (a/b)	110000	On the basis of 20 persons per batch, more than 110000 batches will require to be trained.
d	No. of weeks in which each round of training is to be completed	20	It is envisaged that each round of training (whether foundation, sectoral or refresher) should not take more than 20 weeks to complete. In other words, in every State, each round of training will need to be completed in 20 weeks.

Contd. ...

e	No. of training batches per week (c/d)	5500	If 20 weeks is taken as the basis for completion of training, then each week, 5500 batches will require to be trained.
f	No. of field resource persons per batch	5	It is envisaged that for optimum results and interactivity, each batch will need to be assisted by at least 5 resource persons on site. It is envisaged that of these resource persons, at least 3 will be from full time trainers drawn from NGOs, ex-Panchayat or sitting Panchayat members, retired Government officials etc. At least two will be from line departments working at the district and the block levels.
g	Total number of field resource persons required (exf)	27500	The total requirement of resource persons for Panchayat level training.
h	No. of field resource persons per State master trainer	15	It is envisaged that each State Master Trainer would handle 15 field resource persons.
i	No. of state master trainers required (g/h)	1833	
j	No. of national master trainers per state master trainer	15	It is envisaged that National Master Trainer would handle 15 State Master Trainers.
k	No. of national master trainers required (i/j)	122	

Selection of Resource Persons:

Effective implementation of the Framework is critically dependent on the quality of Resource Persons at each level. Care will need to be taken to specially identify people with the right mindset, commitment and drive as Resource Persons. These could be drawn from Panchayat members themselves (or ex-members), NGOs, or could be government servants, both serving or retired. The process of selection has three phases as follows:

(a) a preliminary screening before selection for the orientation course,
(b) a rigorous orientation course,
(c) a post-orientation evaluation.

The details of each step are elaborated below:

Preliminary Screening of candidates before selection for the orientation course:

Criteria for preliminary identification and screening are as follows:

(a) Commitment to values of gender and caste equity and secularism and lack of prejudices based on caste, gender or religion,
(b) Experience in Panchayati Raj System may be desirable, but not compulsory,
(c) Ability to sympathetically communicate, particularly to draw out the withdrawn,
(d) Ability for multitasking, as Resource Persons will need to be equally at home in face to face trainings, satellite training, operating helplines and providing online assistance at the field level for Panchayat representatives.

The Induction Course:

The induction training programmes for selection of master trainers would be a rigorous and well-documented process, concentrating on sensitization of all Master Trainers to the special needs and concerns of Panchayati Raj. This will be a 2 month long course, aimed at testing various skills of participants particularly that of empathizing with the poor and ability to persevere in adverse conditions. It will include a village immersion stage. The induction course will also equip Master Trainers with a thorough knowledge of the entire gamut of the management of training processes, including funding and logistics.

Final Screening:

The induction course would be followed by a final screening that tests both knowledge, commitment and mentoring skills.

Line Department Staff as Trainers:

Line department staff could be inducted into the training system at all levels, namely, as National or State level Master Resource Persons or as Field level Resource Persons. Of the five resource persons required at each training batch, at least two could be such line department officials. These officials would come into the training system with some amount of prior knowledge and commitment. While ideally such persons should also be put through the induction course of 2 months. In case it is felt that they cannot be spared full-time for training, then they could be put through a shorter induction course (about 2 to 3 weeks) and then join the resource team batch.

Separate honorarium would be paid to such field level staff, who join the Resource persons teams. These will need to be fixed by the State. For the Purposes of standardisation of calculation of costs, the costs pertaining to honorarium have been subsumed into the costs of each training course.

Refresher Courses for Resource Persons:

There would be yearly colloquia for the interaction of Resource Persons. Exposure visits for trainers, especially to well performing States in Panchayati Raj, would also be part of the refresher courses for Master Resource Persons.

IV : DEVELOPMENT OF TRAINING MATERIALS

General Principles for guidance in preparation of training materials:

Training materials should be mostly illustrated. They must always be in the local language, preferably in the local dialect and simple. Local best and innovative practices should be captured in pictorial training materials. Folk resources should be used extensively. For the lower level functionaries the materials should be in question answer mode. Frequently asked questions, (Dos and don'ts) and a detailed glossary of the frequently used terminologies should be included in training materials. A handbook containing basics of PR system in simple language should be handed over to the PRI functionaries at the time of oath taking.

Print Material

Training of the magnitude envisaged will require the development of a variety of print material, which ought to be easy on the eye and preferably well illustrated. Print material could be of the following kinds:

(a) Reference handbooks for Panchayat members, staff and other stakeholders, which is best arranged in the form of answers to frequently asked questions.
(b) Charts, wall newspapers and posters on various aspects of Panchayati Raj, which can be displayed in Panchayat Offices and other public places.
(c) Newsletters for both circulation among stakeholders as well as the general public.

Film and Electronic Material

Some of the points that could underlie the development of film material for training are as follows:

(a) Format of the films could be workshop discussions, individual interviews and dramatised plays, derived from the experience of elected Panchayat members, discussing and thinking about what they bring out, and considering lessons for one's own Gram Panchayats.
(b) Films need not be pre-scripted and there need not be expert lectures. The films will reflect the *lived* experience of elected gram panchayat members.
(c) Gender and caste equality would be a cross cutting theme.

Wherever possible, NGOs could be involved in developing the film material.

Panchayat participation in programme design and management:

There is a need to encourage Panchayats to develop a sense of ownership of the training programmes and to play a major role in designing content and mechanisms of training. This could start with providing representation for Panchayat members in the Governing Boards and Task Forces within training institutions that address their needs. In the first instance, trained members should be encouraged to become resource persons for further training of Panchayat representatives Peer to Peer learning, both within and outside the State through regional or national tie-ups should be encouraged and supported. However, a more long-term approach would be to ensure that Panchayat member networks take over a large part of the management of training programmes—a kind of self-training system.

V : PROGRAMME MANAGEMENT, EVALUATION, AND DOCUMENTATION

Evaluation of training ought to be undertaken by those institutions that do not undertake training. Training institutions should undertake a self evaluation. The NIRD can be entrusted the task to become the nodal agency for identifying independent evaluators. The NIRD and its sister institutions should undertake periodic evaluations in order to ascertain whether Panchayat members have been trained on time and adequately and provide advise on course corrections. The NIRD shall prepare a matrix for both self-evaluation and impact assessment of training. The mechanism for monitoring and evaluation of Framework implementation would include both:

(a) quantitative and measurable outputs, in terms of activities such as numbers of training workshops conducted, attendance obtained, presence and participation of women and SC/ST representatives, use of radio/films, use of satellite training etc., and

(b) outcomes, in terms of
   (i) Quality of facilitation provided to Panchayats, particularly Gram Panchayats, in undertaking their responsibilities,
   (ii) attitudinal change or enhancement in the conduct of activities at the Panchayat level and quality of service delivery.

Monitoring of Outcomes:

Outcomes would need to be assessed against detailed analysis of qualitative parameters. Criteria for monitoring outcomes would also be chosen so as to clearly identifiable, observable, identifiable, verifiable and quantifiable. In this regard, there is a necessity for constant innovation in design of new research methodology, monitoring methods and indicators, so as to effectively gauge the impact of training. Some aspects that could be assessed to determine to what extent the potential of Panchayats has been unlocked are as follows:

(a) How training has enabled more effective community participation, particularly with reference to the conduct of Gram Sabhas, Ward Sabhas and Social Auidit,
(b) How training has affected the functioning of standing committees in the Panchayats,
(c) How training has catalysed partnering amongst functionaries, Panchayat elected representatives and people,
(d) Efforts undertaken by Panchayats to practice democratic processes in decision-making, both in the Panchayat itself and the Gram Sabha,
(e) How training has facilitated designing and approving participative plans,
(f) Taking numerous decisions involved with the implementation process, particularly compliance with Statutory procedures,
(g) Improvement in accountability, in terms of responding,
(h) Addressing public grievances,

(i) Participation by Ward Members in GP meetings and in decisions, and

(j) Participation of Gram Sabha members in decision-making of the Gram Panchayat.

Training Programme Management:

Programme management shall be decentralized and adapted for local needs. At the national level, the NIRD will work closely with the Ministry of Panchayati Raj in a joint management group that will oversee the implementation of the programme. A core team of full time managers of training shall be located at the State level, preferably at the SIRD. This State level Training Managing Committee will be responsible for giving policy guidelines regarding training, and reviewing and monitoring the implementation of the Capability Building Framework. Separate sub-committees to oversee specific aspects of programme management could also be set up, as given in Table 12 below:

Table 12:

Name of Committee	*Duties*
Curriculum Committee	This Committee can be responsible for developing training designs–including the content and process of training. It can also identify core and supplementary reading/ training material for development, production and dissemination.
Monitoring, evaluation and documentation Committee	This Committee would identify indices for monitoring and evaluation. It will also identify appropriate agencies to undertake documentation and evaluation of the various training programmes undertaken.
Finance and Accounts Committee	This Committee will monitor utilization of funds released for training. and ensure regular and periodic audit of the funds released. It will ensure timely submission of utilization certificates on training funds, as required.

At the District level, Peer groups of Panchayat representatives, resource persons and NGO representatives may be involved in the preparation of training, material, design of content, evaluation forms and post training performance of Panchayats.

VI : ESTIMATION OF COSTS OF IMPLEMENTING THE FRAMEWORK

Several aspects need to be taken into consideration while preparing the cost estimations for the Capability Building Framework. The costs of implementation of the Framework comprises of Capital and revenue costs. Ideally speaking, capital costs are to be invested during the first year of the implementation. As the training process under the framework will undergo continuous improvement and refinement. While training for the first year would be to give every stakeholder a basic minimum input required to operate the programme, experiences of the first year can substantially modify the training programme for the second year. Modules, training groups and training strategies, etc., will change, leading to modifications in cost estimations. Some costs are incurred once in every few years, such as preparation of printed and audio-visual material. They are proposed to be paid for in the first year. For the above reasons, revenue costs would be different for the first year and for subsequent years of training. The details of the components for which the costs are calculated are given in Table 13 below:

Table 13:

Capital Costs (to be invested up-front in the first year)	*Revenue Costs*	
	Items to be covered in first year	*Yearly items, from second year onwards*
Satellite training facilities	Induction course for Master Resource Persons	Refresher Courses for Resource Persons
Installation of Computer hardware in Panchayats	I(a): Foundation Course	III(e): Yearly Refresher Course
Intermediate Panchayat level Resource Centres	I(b): Basic Functional Course	III(f): Visits to identified 'beacon' Panchayats
Strengthening of NIRD	I(c): Functional LIteracy Course	III(a): Gram Sabha level campaigns

Contd. ...

Capital Costs (to be invested up-front in the first year)	*Revenue Costs*	
	Items to be covered in first year	*Yearly items, from second year onwards*
Strengthening of SIRDs	II(a): Sectorally focused training programme	III(I): Certificate Courses
	III(d): Formation of networks of Panchayat elected representatives	Monitoring of Outcomes
	II(b): Building ICT Skills	
	Film and Electronic Material	Action Research
	Print Material	
	Common items from first year onwards	
	III(b): Panchayati Raj TV channel and radio programmes III(c): Panchayati Raj Newsletter III(g): Intermediate Panchayat level Resource Centres III(h): Helplines Training Programme Management	

The costs in respect of the Capital costs are worked out in Table 14 below:

Table 14: Capital Costs.

Table 14(a-1): Costs for installation of Satellite training facilities in all States: (Option 1)

Item	*Cost per Unit (Rs. cr)*	*No. of Units*	*Level of Unit*	*Total Cost*
Satellite studio	5	24	One per State	120
Satellite receiving stations	0.007	240000	One per Gram Panchayat	1680
Miscellaneous civil works (electrification, training halls, etc.)				200
Total				**2000**

The above calculations are based on the eventual complete coverage of satellite receiving stations at each Gram Panchayat level. However, at the first instance, if satellite training stations are located at the block level, costs would come down considerably, as given in Table 14 (a-2).

Table 14(a-2): Capital costs for satellite training (Option 2)

Item	*Cost per Unit (Rs. cr)*	*No. of Units*	*Level of Unit*	*Total Cost*
Satellite studio	5	24	State	120
Satellite receiving stations	0.007	6100	One at each Intermediate Panchayat level	42.7
Miscellaneous civil works (electrification, training halls, etc.)				100
Total				**262.7**

The actual requirement may lie somewhere in between. In isolated locations, it makes sense to have satellite receiving stations at the sub-block level, even at every Panchayat level. In other locations, it would suffice if the satellite training centre is located at the Block Panchayat level.

Table 14(b): Cost of installation of Computer Hardware in Panchayats

Item	*Cost per Unit (Rs. cr)*	*No. of Units*	*Level of Unit*	*Total Cost (Rs. cr)*
Computer Hardware	50000	240000	One at each Village Panchayat level	1200

Table 14(c): Capital cost for strengthening of training infrastructure

Item	*Cost per Unit (Rs. lakhs)*	*No. of Units*	*Level of Unit*	*Total Cost (Rs. cr)*
Intermediate Panchayat level Resource Centres	10	6000	One at each Intermediate Panchayat level	600
Strengthening of SIRDs	100	24	One per State	24
Strengthening of NIRD	1000	1		10

Grand total costs of capital investments:

Table 15(a)

Item	*Total Cost (Rs. cr)*
Satellite Training *(Option 1)*	2000
Computer Hardware	1200
Intermediate Panchayat level Resource Centres	600
Strengthening of SIRDs	24
Strengthening of NIRD	10
Total	**3834**

Or

Table 15(b)

Item	*Total Cost (Rs. cr)*
Satellite Training (Option 2)	263
Computer Hardware	1200
Intermediate Panchayat level Resource Centres	600
Strengthening of SIRDs	24
Strengthening of NIRD	10
Total	**2097**

It may also be noted that the capital costs would vary on the basis of the extent of availability of existing infrastructure, such as extension training centres, satellite training facilities, etc. already existing in States.

Revenue Expenditure

As detailed earlier, revenue expenditure would vary from year to year, depending on the mix of programmes that are implemented each year.

Table 16: Costs for the first year are detailed in below:

Sl. No.	*Item*	*Number*	*Basis of Calculation*	*Total Amount (Rs. cr)*
1	Induction course for Master Resource Persons	31500	60 day course, at the Rate of Rs. 1000 per day per participant (Inclusive of all costs)	189.00
2	I(a): Foundation Course	3000000	4 day course at the rate of Rs. 150 per day for 22 lakh elected representatives and 8 lakh officials	180.00
3	I(b):. Basic Functional Course	1500000	4 day course at the rate of Rs. 150 per day for 10 lakh elected office bearers and chairpcrsons of Standing Committees and 5 lakh officials	90.00
4	I(c): Functional Literacy Course	800000	Rs. 1000 lump sum grant per illiterate person for 8 lakh illiterate persons	80.00
5	II(a): Sectorally focused training programme	3000000	4 day course at the rate of Rs. 150 per day for 22 lakh elected representatives and 8 lakh officials	270.00
6	III(d): Formation of networks of Panchayat elected representatives	24	One network per State, with basic start up costs given at Rs. 2 lakh per State.	0.48
7	II(b): Building ICT Skills	500000	Cap. of Rs. 2000 per individual for 5 lakh persons	100
8	Film and Electronic Material	25 films	At Rs. 10 lakhs per half-hour film	2.50
9	Print Material		Lump sum allocation	5.00
10	III(b):Panchayati Raj TV channel and radio programmes		Lump sum allocation	5.00
11	III(c): Panchayati Raj Newsletter		At rate of Rs. 10 per newsletter, 5 copies per Panchayat every month (i.e., 60 copies per annum per Panchayat)	15.00
12	III(g): Intermediate Panchayat level Resource Centres		Lump sum allocation of Rs. 3 lakhs per Resource Centre	18.00
13	III(h): Helplines		Lump sum allocation of Rs. 1 cr per State	24.00
14	Training Programme Management		1 per cent of total revenue cost	9.89
	Total			**988.87**

Table 17: Revenue expenditures in respect of each year from the second year onwards

Sl. No.	*Item*	*Number*	*Basis of Calculation*	*Total Amount (Rs. cr)*
1	Refresher Courses for Resource Persons	31500	4 day course, at the Rate of Rs. 200 per day per participant (Inclusive of all costs)	2.52
2	III(e): Yearly Refresher Course	2200000	4 day course at the rate of Rs. 150 per day for 22 lakh elected representatives	180.00
3	III(f): Visits to identified 'beacon' Panchayats	1000000	2 day course at the rate of Rs. 150 per day for 10 lakh elected office bearers and chairpersons of Standing Committees	30.00
4	III(a): Gram Sabha level Campaigns	800000	Rs. 5 lakh lump sum grant per district	30.00
5	III(I): Certificate Courses	100	At the rate of Rs. 10000 per course for 100 persons per year	0.10
10	III(b):Panchayati Raj TV channel and radio programmes		Lump sum allocation	5.00
11	III(c): Panchayati Raj Newsletter		At rate of Rs. 10 per newsletter, 5 copies per Panchayat every month (i.e., 60 copies per annum per Panchayat)	15.00
12	III(g): Intermediate Panchayat level Resource Centres		Lump sum allocation of Rs. 3 lakhs per Resource Centre	18.00
13	III(h): Helplines		Lump sum allocation of Rs. 1 cr per State	24.00
	Monitoring of Outcomes		Lump sum allocation	2.00
	Action Research		Lump sum allocation	2.00
14	Training Programme Management		Maintain the cost for first year	9.89
	Total			**318.51**

Detailed Projectisation for each State:

Currently, there is no standardization of types of programmes or their duration, between States. Therefore training proposals are received from States that only look at piecemeal training of Panchayat members. Consequently, the quality of training and the extent of retention of what is conveyed, varies widely. This framework is designed to ensure that there a broad minimum standards of capability building are acheived. Therefore, it is necessary that every State prepares a project report that looks at the implementation of every aspect of the framework. Technical assistance shall be provided by the Ministry of Panchayati Raj for the preparation of State specific Framework implementation project documents. State specific projects will follow the same sequence of courses and activities. However, there may be variations on the number of days devoted to training on certain matters, based on the extent of devolution to Panchayats. Similarly, in States that do not have satellite training facilities at present, an interim cascade mechanism of training may be adopted, while working toward the eventual goal of establishing a distance training network. State-wise projects will also undertake a census of facilities already available for training, so that only the incremental requirement needs to be met. All these matters will be captured in a State-wise needs assessment, which will form an integral part of the State Specific Framework design.

Resources for Funding the Programme:

Need for Convergence of Training Efforts:

The Central Government spends around Rs. 75,000 crore on implementation of Centrally Sponsored Schemes. Funds for training are sprinkled across several Ministries, each with a separate distinct design, stated objectives and target groups. Thus while a particular Ministry may sanction allocations for a training programme for staff or NGOs connected with implementation of the Ministry's schemes, Panchayat elected representatives who are vitally concerned with the implementation of the programme may be left out, or may be given an isolated brief exposure. Ministries might prepare a stand alone training programme for a one time training for all concerned including Panchayat members, which results in duplicating logistics and even infrastructure for training. Moreover, such sectoral training of different Ministries would have greater lasting value if they occur after a foundational course that prepares the ground and is followed by networking and other activities that consolidate what has been gained through training.

Creation of a Common Fund for Capability Building:

Against this background, it is now necessary for Central Government to ensure that instead of assigning separate funds for training to MoPR, it would immediately and irrevocably promote the agenda on capability building if 1 per cent of public expenditures on all CSSs are placed in a non-lapsable consolidated corpus, and assigned exclusively for implementation of the National Capability Building Framework. This would particularly apply to seven of the eight Flagship Programmes, which fall within the 29 matters identified in the Eleventh Schedule for devolution from State Governments to Panchayats and schemes that come under the umbrella of Bharat Nirman. This will facilitate smooth and continuous training of PRI elected representatives and functionaries at all levels. It would also enable the Central Government to issue consolidated sanction *in toto* for any State specific project for implementing the Framework, for which release of funds would continue to be done from year to year from the non-lapsable consolidated capability building fund.

Dissemination of the Detailed National Training Design:

The Detailed National Training Design for training of Elected Members and Officials of Panchayati Raj Institutions put together by the National Institute of Rural Development would be widely disseminated by the Ministry of Panchayati Raj and NIRD in their website for wider consultation, public opinion and feedback.

PREPARATION OF A NATIONAL TRAINING DESIGN

The Seventh Round Table at Jaipur held in December 2004 resolved, *inter alia*, that there should a national perspective plan on decentralized training and capacity building for all PRI functionaries with specific objectives timeframe and resources. The extract of all resolutions of the seventh RT are placed on file at Flag 'A'.

In pursuance of the above resolution of the 7th RT, the Ministry has been engaged in the preparation of a National Training Design for Panchayati Raj members. This matter was discussed through several meetings, including discussions with State Secretaries in Delhi, discussions in the Mysore SIRD and at NIRD Hyderabad. After these discussions, NIRD was asked to prepare a detailed design. They prepared a design document, which is Placed at Flag 'B'. At the Workshop of Writers and Thinkers, the Minister announced that Dr. SK Singh of NIRD would be in charge of the design of the Framework.

During discussions at Hyderabad on 1 and 2 July, 2006, a group of NGOs and others who were involved in grassroot level development were invited to give their views on what a national training design should contain. Incorporating these views, a broad policy statement was prepared, which was designed to be a kind of introduction and covering statement to the framework designed by the NIRD.

On 2-7-2006, after SPR had left Hyderabad, this document (Flag C) was discussed with the Minister. He made several observations, the gist of which are as follows:

- A more detailed work was required, into which all components of capacity building could be plugged in, so as to ensure that training was not a one-time event, but a larger process of growth and development.
- Certain aspects of the logistics of training, such as using district officials for training of Panchayat members needed to be given much more emphasis in the design.
- Capital costs of strengthening training infrastructure needed to be worked out in greater detail.
- The construction of the document ought to be in such a manner that it could be posed to any funding agency, which could then pick up components that they could support, without straying away from the grand design.

MPR also instructed the undersigned to start working on the same and prepare a draft that encompassed all these priorities.

Taking the above points into consideration, the undersigned began work on the development of the document while on leave from 3-7-2007 to 7-7-2007. The document has been completed and is placed at Flag 'D' for consideration. The salient features of the document are as follows:

This is designed as a more comprehensive approach at capability building rather than mere training, which has limited application and effectiveness. Therefore, I have called the document 'the national Capability Building Framework' rather than the 'National Training Network'.

After going through the detailed document prepared by the NIRD, I found that it was disappointingly, very limited in approach. Basically in spite of its voluminous calculations, it only worked out in detail the modalities of a one-time training for all Panchayat members and officials. Much of the data on the basis of which the calculations were made are outdated and inaccurate. Some of the logistics planned (such as 50 persons per training batch) were not conducive to better assimilation of what would be conveyed. These shortcomings have been addressed in the National Capability Building Framework.

The Framework is organized into 6 chapters, namely,

Chapter 1:	Introduction and Basic Principles underlying the Framework Design
Chapter 2:	Components and Logistics of the Framework
Chapter 3:	Resource Persons for Implementing the Framework
Chapter 4:	Development of Material for the Framework
Chapter 5:	Programme management, evaluation, and documentation
Chapter 6:	Estimation of Costs of implementing the Framework

The components of the training framework have been captured in brief in Table 1 of Chapter 2 (page 8 of the Framework). Thus the philosophy of the Framework has been captured into a set of courses and other initiatives that are aimed to tackle all the nuances of (a) supply side training, and (b) creating demand, which puts pressure on Panchayats to be accountable and perform. Each Chapter discusses in detail the aspects that are covered.

Regarding the costs, as per the Minister's directions, the broad estimates of implementation of the Framework have been calculated. Certain assumptions have been made, which need to be confirmed State-wise. In the case of certain aspects of the Framework, such as the costs of operating the National Panchayat Channel, I have assigned lump sum allocations that need to be broken down into detailed costing sheets.

Next Steps:

I believe that this document provides the essential logical Framework for design. However, we will need to once again discuss this in an internal peer review, where I suggest that the emphasis will be to ensure that nothing has been left out, and to make additions or deletions to the document, so as to improve it. We may circulate it among a group of peer reviewers seek their comments (in terms of actual additions or deletions suggested) and have a meeting to review the document through a common reading of the Framework.

Once approved, we can circulate this document to all States, seeking from them the actual calculations pertaining to them in the same Framework as in Chapter 6, so as to arrive at the actual costs and timeframe of implementing the Framework on a State-wise basis, after taking into account existing infrastructure available in the State.

One of the important features of the Framework is that it can be a 'plug and play' software. This is particularly true of the portion relating to sectoral training. There are several central ministries that spend money in isolated training programmes that pertain to the sectors concerned, which may or may not consider Panchayat members. Now that sectoral training has been made part of the National Framework, Ministries concerned can plug into the Framework and play their role as part of a grander design. Therefore, the Framework once finalized after peer review, can be presented to all Ministries concerned and to the Planning Commission, for their adoption.

Currently, the actual budget available with MoPR for training is only Rs. 30.5 crore, which is a pittance. However, under the BRGF, Rs. 250 crore will be provided for training per annum, which gives us a real chance of implementing the Framework and creating the seed crystal for training, around which other funding agencies can converge, at least in respect of the backward districts. I am therefore separately modifying the calculations in Chapter 6 to meet the immediate requirements of BRGF and so that the modified document version can be used as a training Framework guideline for BRGF also.

A copy of the Framework has been sent to JS(BKS) on 12-7-06, as he was preparing to send the same to the UNDP for consideration.

As discussed with SPR, the Framework is put up for information and approval of the steps proposed as above.

T.R. Raghunandan
JS(R)

SPR

Minister (PR) suggested that there should be a system for preparing a calendar for broadcast for use of PRI functionaries and office-bearers for institutions about devolved subjects like agriculture, education, health and drinking water. The calendar should be prepared by the SIRD, indicating the time schedule for each on a weekly basis. He gave the example of agriculture, which could be fixed for first Monday of every week. The District Agriculture Officer could be allotted two hours in preparing message on cultivation of recommended cultivation practices at district level at this time and the Standing Committees of the PRIs could be at District Headquarters to imbibe new technology and improve cultivation practices. The Agriculture Extension Officer at block level like-wise could disseminate this information to Members of the Standing Committees and Agriculturists at the Panchayat Samiti Level. The ISRO system should be utilized for disseminating this message through satellite system. Similarly, messages on health and hygiene, sanitation, drinking water and associated subjects should be disseminated at all levels on a similar pattern.

BIBLIOGRAPHY

Arora, R. and R. Hooja, *Administration of Rural Development*, Arihant: Jaipur, 1994.

Aslam, M., *Directory of Panchayati Raj Training Institutions in India,* New Delhi: Rajiv Gandhi Foundation, 2001.

Bandyopadhyay, D., Amitava Mukerjee and Mitali Sen Gavani, *Empowering Panchayats, Handbook for Master Trainers using Participatory Approach,* New Delhi: Concept Publishing Company, 2003.

Basu, Amrita, "Gender and Governance : Concepts and Contexts", in Martha Mussbaum *et al.* (Eds.), *Gender and Governance,* New Delhi: UNDP, 2003.

Behar, Amitabh & Kumar, Yogesh (2002), 'Decentralisation in Madhya Pradesh, India: from Panchayati Raj to Gram Swaraj (1995 to 2001)', *Working Paper 170, ODI, London,* UK.

Chambers, R. "Project Selection for Poverty Focused Rural Development", **World Development**. Vol.6, 1978.

Crook, R., and J. Manor, *Enhancing Participation and Institutional Performance Democratic Decentralization in South Asia and West Africa,* ODA Report, Delhi, November, 1994.

Curtis, D. and J.R. Watson, "Planning the Non-planers Can Do", *Journal of Rural Development,* 1987.

Das, A., "Decentralization of Development Planning Implementation", *Indian Journal of Public Administration,* 1978.

Deccan Herald (Daily), Bangalore, October 18, 2005.

Department of Panchayats and Rural Development, Government of West Bengal Annual Administrative Report, 2003-04.

Department of Personnel and Training, Government of India, Course Materials for Design of Training Course, 2000.

FAG, *Towards Improved Multi Level Planning for Agriculture and Rural Development,* FAO Economic and Social Development, Paper 52, 1985.

Gadgil, D.R., *District Development Planning,* Gokhale Institute of Politics and Economics, Poona, 1996.

Government of Tamil Nadu, *Action Taken Report on the Entrustment of Responsibilities to Three-Tier Panchayats,* Chennai: Government of Tamil Nadu, 1999.

Government of Tamil Nadu, *Action taken Report on the Entrustment of Responsibilities to Three-Tier Panchayats,* Chennai: Department of Rural Development, 1998.

Government of Tamil Nadu, *Democratic Decentralization: Powers Entrusted to Panchayat Raj Institutions,* Chennai: Rural Development Department, 1999.

Government of Tamil Nadu, *Report on Roles, Responsibilities and Powers Devolved to Panchayats,* Chennai: Government of Tamil Nadu, 1998.

Government of West Bengal, The West Bengal Panchayat Act, 1973 (as modified up to the 31st January, 2004).

Hooja, R. and B. Yerram Raju (Ed.), *Decentralised Planning in Multi-level Framework,* Jaipur: Rawat, 1993.

Hooja, Rakesh and P.C. Mathur (Ed.), *District and Decentralized Planning,* Jaipur: Rawat.

Hooja, Rakesh, "Issues in Preparing Manpower for Effective Decentralised Planning", *Political Economy Journal of India,* Vol. 3 No. 2, 1994.

Hooja, Rakesh, "Training of Panchayati Raj Functionaries. Some Basic Issues" in *Journal of Rural Development,* Vol. 16, No. 4, 1997.

Hooja, Rakesh, *Administrative Interventions in Rural Development,* Jaipur: Rawat, 1987.

Hooja, Rakesh, *Bibliography on Multi-level and District level and District Planning,* Madhya Pradesh Institute of Social Science Research, Ujjain, 1995.

Hooja, Rakesh, *District Planning: Concept, Setting and State Level Applications,* Jaipur: Aalekh, 1986.

Hooja, R. and Meenakshi Hooja, *Panchayati Rai in Raiasthan: Continuity and Change,* HCM RIPA, Jaipur, 2005.

Hooja, Rakesh, "Training for and Expectations from District Planners" in *ASTI Journal of Training and Development,* July-December, 2005.

Indira Gandhi Panchayati Raj Evam Gramin Vikas Sansthan, *Panchavati Rai Prashikshan Sandarbh Samagree. IGP,* 2005.

Issac, T.M. Thomas & Richard W. Franke (2000): *Local Democracy and Development: People's Campaign for Decentralised Planning in Kerala,* Leftword, New Delhi.

Mathew, George (ed.), *The Status of Panchayati Raj in the States of India,* New Delhi: Concept, 1994. Subsequent rewritten volume released 2000 under title *The Status of Panchayati Raj in the States and Union Territories of India,* New Delhi: Concept, 2000.

Mathew, George, *Panchayati Raj from Legislation to Movement,* New Delhi: Concept, 1994.

Mathur, Kuldeep (ed.), *Development Policy and Administration,* New Delhi : Sage, 1996.

Mathur, P.C. and Rakesh Hooja, *Projects Planning and Development Administration,* 1996.

Mishra, Shweta, *Democratic Decentralization in India,* New Delhi: Mittal, 1994.

Mukarji, Nirmal, "Decentralisation Below the State Level: Need for a New System of Governance", *Economic and Political Weekly,* Vol. 214 No. 9, 1989.

Mukherjee, Amitabh, "Decentralisation: Some Conceptual Issues" in B.N. Yugandhar and A. Mukherjee (ed), Readings in *Decentralized Planning,* New Delhi : Concept, 1991.

National Institute of Rural Development (2001), Hyderabad, India Panchayati Raj Report, Volume I.

NIRD, *"Capacity Building in Panchayati Raj"*, India Panchayati Raj Report, Four Decades of Decentralized Governance in Rural India, 2001, Ch. 9, pp. 89-103, Vol. I, NIRD, Hyderabad.

Palanithurai, G. (ed.), 2004, '*Dynamics of New Panchayati Raj System in India*', (Volume IV, Empowering Women), Concept Publishing Company, New Delhi.

Palanithurai, G., "Role of Elected Women Representatives in Evolving Alternative Governance at Grassroots", *Social Change and Development,* Vol. 3, July 2005.

Palanithurai, G., "Women in Governance for Development at Grassroots", *Indian Journal of Public Administration,* Vol. 1 No.1, January - March 2004.

Palanithurai, G., and V. Ragupathy, *Building alliance and capabilities among the Elected Women Representatives of Grassroots Institutions,* Gandhigram: Rajiv Gandhi Chair for Panchayati Raj Studies, 2003.

Palanithurai, G., *Capacity Building of Grassroots Leaders,* Gandhigram: Rajiv Gandhi Chair for Panchayati Raj Studies, 2004.

Palanithurai, G., *Empowerment of Women: Problems faced by the Elected Women Representatives in Tamil Nadu,* Gandhigram: Rajiv Gandhi Chair for Panchayati Raj Studies, 2001.

Palanithurai, G., *Role Perceptions of Legislations: A Case Study of Tamil Nadu,* New Delhi: Konarak Publishers, 1991.

Palanithurai, G., *Tamil Nadu Panchayati Government Act, Rules and Schemes (in Tamil),* Chennai: South Vision, 2002.

Planning Commission, GOI, *Report of Working Group on District Level Planning* (Chairman C.H. Hanumantha Rao), 1984.

Planning Commission, Government of India, Tenth Five Year Plan (2002-07), Volume II.

Prasad, Kamta, *Planning and its Implementation,* New Delhi: IIPA, 1984.

Rajiv Gandhi Chair, *Training Module for Panchayat Training Progress,* Gandhigram: Rajiv Gandhi Chair for Panchayati Raj Studies, 2002.

Rajiv Gandhi Foundation, *Charter of Panchayats,* New Delhi: Rajiv Gandhi Foundation, 1998.

Rao, V.M., "Decentralised Planning Priority Issues": *Economic and Political Weekly*, 1989.

Rao, V.K.R.V., "District Planning Concept" in V.S. Prakasa Rao *et al. Working Paper on District Planning Officers' Institute of Social and Economic Change,* Bangalore, 1973.

Robinson, Mark (2005): 'A Decade of Panchayati Raj Reforms: The Challenge of Democratic Decentralisation in India' in L.C. Jain (ed.), *Decentralisation and Local Governance,* Orient Longman, New Delhi.

Sisodia, Yatindra Singh (2002): 'Panchayati Raj System in Madhya Pradesh: An Appraisal' in G. Palanithurai (ed.), *Dynamics of New Panchayati Raj System in India,* Vol. II, Concept Publishing Company, New Delhi.

Social Watch India, *Citizens Report on Governance and Development,* New Delhi: Social Watch India, 2004.

State Finance Commission, *First State Finance Commission Report,* Chennai: State First Finance Commission, 1995.

State Planning Commission, *Report on Entrustment of Responsibilities to Three-Tier Panchayats,* Chennai: State Planning Commission, 1997.

Subha, K., B.S. Bhargava and Mangala Nayak, January-June 2001 "Women in Panchayati Raj Institution: Political Empowerment through Capacity Building", *SAJOSPS.*

The Hindu (2005), Capacity Building programme for panchayat members, Karnataka (news published in 27.02.2005).

The Hunger Project, *Training Module for Leadership Training for Women in Panchayat,* Gandhigram: Rajiv Gandhi Chair for Panchayati Raj Studies, 2002.

Webster, Neil (1992): 'Panchayati Raj in West Bengal: Participation for the People or the Party?', *Development and Change,* Vol. 23, No. 4.

Wieringa, S., "Women's Interests and Empowerment: Gender Planning Reconsidered", *Development and Change,* 25, 1994.